Vietnam
Rough Riders

Vietnam
Rough Riders
A Convoy
Commander's
Memoir

Frank McAdams

 University Press of Kansas

Published by the University Press of Kansas (Lawrence, Kansas
66045), which was organized by the Kansas Board of Regents
and is operated and funded by Emporia State University,
Fort Hays State University, Kansas State University, Pittsburg
State University, the University of Kansas, and Wichita State
University

Library of Congress Cataloging-in-Publication Data

McAdams, Frank, 1940–
Vietnam Rough Riders : a convoy commander's memoir /
  Frank McAdams.
    pages cm. — (Modern war studies)
  Includes index.
    ISBN 978-0-7006-1898-9 (cloth : alk. paper) 1. Vietnam War,
1961–1975–Transportation. 2. United States. Marine Corps.
Marine Division, 1st. Motor Transport Battalion, 11th–Biography.
3. United States. Marine Corps–Officers–Biography. 4. Military
convoys–United States–History–20th century. 5. Vietnam War,
1961–1975–Personal narratives. I. Title.
  DS559.8.T7M415 2013
  959.704'345–dc23
  [B]
                                        2012042381

British Library Cataloguing-in-Publication Data is available.

Printed in the United States of America

10 9 8 7 6 5 4 3 2 1

The paper used in this publication is recycled and contains
30 percent postconsumer waste. It is acid free and meets the
minimum requirements of the American National Standard for
Permanence of Paper for Printed Library Materials Z39.48–1992.

For Patty
And a registration line that fall semester

Reading the Roll of Honor, "Poor young
    chap,"
I'd say—"I use to know his father well;
Yes, we've lost heavily in this last scrap."
And when the war is done and youth stone
    dead,
I'd toddle safely home and die—in bed.

—Siegfried Sassoon (1886–1967)

Contents

A photo section follows page 124.

Glossary

AAR	after-action report; the summary of a firefight or incident
AFVN	Armed Forces (Radio) Vietnam Network
AK-47	Kalashnikov assault rifle, the standard weapon for NVA forces
AmTrac	Amphibious Tractor; the vehicle normally used for transporting troops
AOR	Area of Responsibility; the tactical area for a battalion, regiment, or division, with specifically defined boundaries
ARVN	Army of the Republic of South Vietnam
AWOL	absent without leave
BCD	bad-conduct discharge
blue line	Radio term for any river (i.e., blue on a map)
Bob-Tail	A tractor-vehicle without a trailer load
"boot"	Navy-Marine Corps term for a recruit
brig time	the time, or sentence, that a Marine or sailor has to spend in military prison
bulkhead	A wall on a ship
CAP (unit)	Combined-action platoon mixing U.S. Marines with local forces
C-4	Plastic explosive in one-pound bars, often used for cooking
Charlie Charlie	Phonetic alphabet for a convoy commander
Charlie Papa	Phonetic alphabet for a command post
chopper	Any helicopter
CIB	Combat Infantryman's Badge (U.S. Army)
CID	Criminal Investigation Division, a branch of the division legal office
Claymore mine	A command-detonated mine, throwing out ball bearings in an arc
CMC	Commandant, Marine Corps; the highest-ranking officer in USMC
COD	close-order drill
company-grade	The lower tier of officers—Second and First Lieutenants and Captain
CP	command post—the headquarters to coordinate unit operations
C-rations	Canned food designed for field consumption
CWO	Chief Warrant Officer, former enlisted, equivalent to a major
Danang (gen.)	Headquarters of First Marine Division
DCC	Division Convoy Control—the radio station controlling convoys
de-de mau	Vietnamese for leaving, running out

Defend	Radio call sign for First Marine Division Convoy Control
DMZ	Demilitarized Zone—the demarcation line between North and South Vietnam
Doofus	An inept trooper
DOR	OCS term to "drop on request"
ERB	Enlisted Record Book—the personnel file of an enlisted Marine
FAC	Forward Air Controller—the communicator to air support
field-grade	Midlevel officers—Major, Lieutenant Colonel, and Colonel
FLC	Force Logistics Command—the main supply center at Red Beach in Vietnam
foc'sle	"forecastle," the very forward compartment on a vessel
fragging	The intentional killing of an officer by a fragmentation hand grenade thrown by his own troops
fragmentary order	Also known as a *frag*—an addendum changing the original order
grid coordinates	Vertical and horizontal lines used to show map positions
grinder	A drill field
hai-ah ku	Asian slang for ASAP
hooch	A covered living space, usually with four walls and a corrugated roof
KIA	killed in action
Lima-Lima	Phonetic alphabet for a landline phone
line haul	A small convoy run
LURPs	Long Range Patrol Rations, forerunner of MREs
M-16	Standard infantry rifle for U.S. forces
M-543	Standard "wrecker"—a tow truck for Rough Rider convoys
MEB	Marine Expeditionary Brigade, a Marine air-ground task force
Med Cap	Medical Civic Action Program, the primary vehicle for providing medical aid to villages and hamlets
medevac	medical evacuation, by helicopter, of a wounded person
MP	Military Police
MPC	Military Payment Certificate, used in lieu of greenbacks
MRC-109	A radio mounted in an M-151 jeep used for convoy control
mule	A small motorized platform mainly used for transporting equipment, ammo, and supplies
mustang	An officer who is former enlisted, up from the ranks
NCO	noncommissioned officer
NSA	Naval Support Activity—a fully staffed Naval Hospital
NVA	North Vietnamese Army (the People's Army of North Vietnam or PAVN)
OC	Officer Candidate
OCS	Officer Candidate School
OOD	Officer of the Day, the unit duty officer usually on a twenty-four-hour tour

OP	Observation Post; usually set on a hill giving a wide, commanding view
OQR	Officer Qualification Record, an officer's personnel file similar to the Army 201 file
pace truck	The first vehicle in a convoy with armor underplating and a .50 caliber ring mount
PAVN	The People's Army of North Vietnam, see also NVA
piaster	A unit of currency in South Vietnam
PLC	Platoon Leaders Class; an alternative to OCS, usually in two increments
PRC-25	Personnel Radio Communication; the standard backpack radio used in combat
Psy Ops	Psychological Operations; maintained the People to People program
Quang Tri (gen.)	Headquarters, Third Marine Division, northern sector (near to the DMZ)
R&R	Rest and Recuperation (or, commonly, "Relaxation"); in the Marines, a six-day leave in a peaceful vacation spot
RF	Regional Forces; a militia force that protected a province-size area
rock and roll	An M-16 selector placed on full automatic
ROTC	Reserve Officer Training Corps—the officer program found on many college campuses
Rough Rider	A resupply convoy with infantry security, usually going through a hot area
rubber lady	A portable air mattress
sapper	An enemy soldier usually on a suicide mission
RVN	Republic of South Vietnam
S-1	Staff Personnel office, from regiment down
S-2	Staff Intelligence office, from regiment down
S-3	Staff Operations office, from regiment down
S-4	Staff Logistics office, from regiment down
S-5	Staff Psychological Operations Office, from regiment down
sit rep	A situation report; commonly called for when a unit is under fire
six-by	The standard M-54 Marine Corps truck
soft cover	A cloth military hat with a bill in front, worn with fatigues or military uniform
Spooky	A C-47 cargo plane equipped with Gatling (rotary) machine-gun capability
TBS	The Basic School—the follow-on education after OCS to study military subjects
Third MAF	Third Marine Amphibious Force, Marine Headquarters, Vietnam
trail package	The rear section of a convoy, typically including the security truck, radio jeep, and wrecker (tow truck)

VC	Viet Cong, or National Liberation Front; the guerrilla arm of North Vietnamese forces
ville	A Vietnamese village
wagon train	Slang for a Rough Rider convoy
XO	Military term for executive officer, the "number two"
X-Ray jeep	The ramrod vehicle in a Rough Rider convoy with a ring-mounted M-60 machine gun

Acknowledgments

This memoir required a lot of fact-checking and different eyes, especially from those who shared the Vietnam experience.

I am deeply indebted to Timothy J. Lomperis, professor of political science at St. Louis University and also the recipient of a Bronze Star medal for his service in Vietnam.

Likewise, I want to thank William T. Allison, professor of history at Georgia Southern University, who holds the General Harold K. Johnson Chair in Military History at the U.S. Army War College.

Both of these men gave constructive criticism, worthwhile suggestions, and support to early drafts of the manuscript.

At the University Press of Kansas I need to thank a very supportive staff, including editor Michael Briggs; Kelly Chrisman Jacques, production; and Susan Schott, marketing. Also, Jon Howard for his share in copyediting.

Fellow Marine officers Jack Carmetti and Andy Garrison went through, alongside me, much of what follows. Their help and support through the initial stages of this manuscript were invaluable, particularly validating certain important and pivotal instances. It has been great to stay in touch over the years. *Semper Fi,* guys!

Foreword

What follows is a personal account leading to two historic years in the twentieth century seen through the eyes of my wife, Patty, and me. We were half a world apart, enduring a wartime separation—Vietnam and Chicago—when the majority of these events occurred.

It should also be stated that this is a memoir, not a documentary. This initially began as my UCLA thesis screenplay, *Stagecoach Bravo*, in 1978. After several rewrites the screenplay was submitted to the Samuel Goldwyn Competition, open to all students in the University of California system. It won first place that year, 1979. Subsequently, it was optioned but never produced. I often used it as a writing sample.

In addition to *Stagecoach Bravo* the sources for this work are my files, a feature for *The Daily Bruin*, two op-ed pieces for the *Los Angeles Times*, personal letters, photos, statements, maps, and documents from the 11th Motor Transport Battalion, 1st Reconnaissance Battalion, 5th Marine Regiment, First Marine Division, Task Force Yankee, and Headquarters Marine Corps. This documentation aided me in the chronology and the events that occurred in the Vietnam sequence of this book. An additional source was the USMC website www .recordsofwar.com.usmc/vietnam, U.S. Marine Corps History Division, Vietnam War Documents Collection, in addition to letters and interviews with friends.

During the central timeframe of this memoir, 1968–1969, a series of historical events occurred. As a writer once observed, "It isn't what happened, it's *how* it happened." It began in the early 1960s and climaxed at the end of the decade with the resolution to follow.

For two people, half a world apart, this is where it began and how it happened.

For legal reasons certain character names have been changed. Also many of the pivotal scenes in this work are re-created to the best of memory. Not being verbatim, the emphasis is on the essence, especially in regard to the actual spoken words of myself, Captain J. T. Eiler, Major Aldus Ashworth, and others.

1

Down South

Upon being commissioned a United States Marine Corps second lieutenant on December 15, 1966, I knew that I was going to fight a formidable enemy. What I didn't know was that I was going to have to fight others at the same time. And I would need an anchor.

In April 1945 U.S. forces suffered 80,000 casualties in the Battle of Okinawa. By 1968 Camp Hansen, on Okinawa, had become a processing station for U.S. Marines coming from and going to Vietnam. For those of us who were under orders to Vietnam in 1968 the destination phrase on Okinawa was "Down South."

The watershed year 1968 began peacefully enough for my wife, Patty, and me. We were at Camp Lejeune, North Carolina, where I was completing the Marine Corps Motor Transport Orientation Course at nearby Montford Point. During World War II, when the services were segregated, Montford Point was known as the "black boot camp." It was now the training ground for convoy commanders. With a weekly six-pack of beer or bottle of bourbon as bribe we were able to rent a vacation cabana on Onslow Beach in between the Atlantic shore and the Inland Waterway.

By the end of January one personal incident occurred in between three historical events. On January 21 the seventy-seven–day siege of Khe Sanh began. Two days later the USS *Pueblo*, a Navy intelligence gathering ship with a crew of eighty-three, was captured by North Korean patrol boats in the Sea of Japan for allegedly violating territorial limits. Three days after that my class, at Montford Point, graduated from Motor Transport School. Five days after that the Tet Offensive erupted in Vietnam, a planned wave of attacks striking more than a hundred towns and cities. Only one month into the year and the world seemed to be reeling. I cannot recall any year that began with so much tumult. Patty would be a witness to the coming events in Chicago while I endured them in

1

Vietnam. Naturally, at that beginning, neither of us was aware that we were not only witnessing history; we were taking part in it.

While I was going through the Marine Corps processing at Camp Hansen, Patty remained at our rented apartment in Oceanside, California, next to Camp Pendleton. Previously I was warned, in the Marine Corps tradition, that wives had no place in staging battalion training prior to shipping out to a combat zone. It was a demanding four-week cycle and included many nighttime field exercises. I was assigned as the commander of a staging company with a staff of several well qualified noncommissioned officers (NCOs), some of whom were doing their second tour. Patty and I always knew our time on the front end of Vietnam would be limited. And we needed to treasure every moment. We accepted the fact that within the coming year she could be a widow, an issue discussed endlessly among family and friends. Following that reasoning, Patty accompanied me west to Camp Pendleton for the staging battalion phase. We were fortunate enough to find a nice rental on the beach in Oceanside. It was here where we watched Walter Cronkite's historical televised editorial, a reaction to the twenty-five-day siege of the Citadel in Hue City during the Tet Offensive. We didn't know it at the time, but Cronkite's address that night, February 27, 1968, would not only ripple across the nation but also shake the inside of the Oval Office, ending Lyndon Johnson's administration.

I still recall Cronkite looking straight into the camera:

> To say that we are closer to victory today is to believe, in the face of evidence, the optimists who have been wrong in the past. . . . To say that we are mired in stalemate seems the only realistic yet unsatisfactory conclusion. . . . It is increasingly clear to this reporter that the only rational way out will be to negotiate, not as victors, but as an honorable people who lived up to their pledge to defend democracy, and did the best they could.

Sleep came hard that night. I had to be up at 5 A.M., known in Marine Corps jargon as "O-Dark-Thirty." Cronkite's speech echoed in my ears while I thought, *What am I going into?*

When sleep finally came I drifted into a recurring nightmare where four Viet Cong (VC) guerrillas, AK-47s held at high port, chased me through the Jackson Park Golf Course in my Chicago neighborhood. All I had was a .45-caliber semiautomatic sidearm. And no matter where I ran or hid they knew where I was and kept coming like the Four Horsemen of the Apocalypse: Pestilence, War, Famine, and Death.

The next thing I knew Patty was shaking me. I don't remember moaning or yelling, just her shaking me. My T-shirt was drenched. This recurring nightmare began while we were at Quantico: "Post Traumatic Stress Disorder in reverse."

After a quick breakfast we got out on Interstate 5 and drove north to the Las Pulgas offramp, going into the base. When we arrived at my company headquarters it was still dark. I knew I had to keep up a façade during the intense training day in front of me. All through that day I was dragging my ass because of less than three hours of sleep, with Walter Cronkite's image mixed with the guerrilla quartet. Somehow I made it through.

With training completed our departure date was March 3, Patty's twenty-fourth birthday. We were scheduled to leave at night from the Marine Corps Air Station at El Toro. Patty would meet me at the air station and we would say our goodbyes.

Wrong!

When Patty dropped me off at Camp Pendleton that day I attended to final administration procedures, making phone calls and signing documents. As the day got longer we got a sudden alert that our flight out of El Toro had been canceled. No reason was given. What would happen was that within two hours buses would arrive to take my staging company to Los Angeles International Airport, where we would depart for Honolulu and then Okinawa. After getting confirmation, I had to make the difficult phone call to my wife that our stateside time was over. I was going out in ninety minutes. Goodbye, I love you. The last thing she said to me was, "Be safe."

When we pulled in at the backside of the Los Angeles International Airport the buses came to a stop next to a hangar. We quickly got out and formed into four platoons as the buses moved off to a Continental Airlines jetliner about 150 yards away to unload the baggage. My gunnery sergeant set the lines and called for a "left face!" He turned and nodded to me. I gave the command "forward march!" And the company began marching toward the jetliner. From the back rank someone started singing in a soft voice.

"From the Halls of Montezuma to the shores of Tripoli. . . ." The "Marine Corps Hymn" that night spread from the back ranks to the front as we continued marching to the jetliner. By the time we arrived at the ladder the entire company was singing, "We are proud to claim the title, United States Marine."

Patty's words echoed in my ears: "Be safe." Our good times and the training were behind us. She was still in Southern California and I was being processed to enter a combat zone.

The Okinawa processing took four to five days. The first thing that had to be done was to sign over a Class A uniform, which was tagged and held in a warehouse. If I was killed my body would be shipped to a Graves Registration station. What was left of me would be placed into the uniform. Then I would be shipped home.

Records and documents also had to be checked, along with signing insurance forms and submitting to a physical examination. Part of the physical included being injected with gamma globulin, a prophylactic for tropical diseases and blood thinner.

After the physical I went to an early meal at the officers mess. The movie that night was *Tender Is the Night* with Jennifer Jones, Jason Robards Jr., and Joan Fontaine. I lasted about forty minutes, sitting through this sophomoric adaptation of F. Scott Fitzgerald's novel of expatriates traipsing around Europe. I got up and went to the officers club. I entered the club, walking down the hallway. At the end of the hallway was a corkboard with various announcements. To the far end of the corkboard was the latest Vietnam casualty list from *Navy Times*. The headline stated "SEA SERVICE DEATHS." The names were in alphabetical order—last name, first name—and the Vietnam province where they were killed.

I recognized three of the names from my Basic School class at Quantico. Another name was that of a tactics instructor at Officer Candidate School (OCS). For several moments I was frozen in place staring at the names. Then I turned, walked out of the club, and went back to my room at the bachelor officers quarters. I stretched out on the bed, staring at the ceiling, recalling my recurring nightmare and now the names of fellow classmates . . . even one of my tactics instructors. *This was it*, I thought. Most likely, within three to four months, my name would be on the corkboard and Patty would be wearing widow's weeds at a military funeral. For some reason I thought of a scene in the 20th Century Fox World War II classic *Twelve O'clock High*. In the film Gregory Peck, as Brigadier General Frank Savage, has taken command of a "hard luck bomber group," the 918th, flying dangerous B-17 cross-channel missions in the dark days of the war. At a briefing Peck tells the bomber crews, "Consider yourselves already dead; it will be easier to fly those missions."

For three hours I laid on my cot staring at the stucco ceiling in those quarters at Camp Hansen. My life was essentially over because of a curious sense of adventure.

Over and over again a question kept rolling around in my head: *How did I ever get to this point?*

2

The Call

One could say that I had a "normal" boyhood in a big city. I was the second of seven children born to Frank and Irene McAdams. We were a large Irish Catholic family, Mary Irene (Molly), me, Michael, Joan, Dennis, Patricia, and Brian. Our formative years were in the South Shore neighborhood of Chicago, bordering Lake Michigan at 67th Street, where we lived in a thirteen-room house on South Shore Drive, across the street from the lakeshore.

My mother, Irene Geary McAdams, came from a politically connected Chicago family. Her father, Joseph Geary Sr., was the civil service commissioner and 4th Ward committeeman in the Hyde Park neighborhood. Both positions held the key to many city patronage jobs. Mom raised us with a three-point credo: "You get out of this life exactly what you put into it; if you start something finish it; and don't ever be called a quitter." Even in the dark reaches of night I can still hear her repeating those statements.

While in high school I had read about *Peyton Place,* Grace Metalious's scandalous novel about ugly secrets in a small New Hampshire town. And I wanted to read the novel before seeing the film. When the paperback edition came out I bought it at a local drug store. The novel had a long spell atop *The New York Times* best-seller list. I would read the book late at night. During the day, while at school, I hid it in my underwear drawer. When the film was released I happened to mention to my mother that a bunch of us were going to see it.

Mom nodded and said, "I figured you would since you read the novel."

I was caught off guard. "How did you know that?"

She smiled knowingly. "I came across it in your underwear drawer. Then I put it back."

"You did?"

She nodded. "Yes, I was glad that you were reading something."

My father, Frank J. McAdams Jr., was the captain of Notre Dame's boxing

5

team in his senior year. After graduation he enrolled in law school. By the time of Pearl Harbor he and mom were the parents of two with a third on the way. Still, my father answered the call and was soon a naval officer, the skipper of a medium landing ship. His ship, the *LSM–201*, with a fifty-five-man crew, made eleven beachheads in the Western Pacific. Then dad was wounded, in an artillery bombardment, on the second day of the Leyte invasion in the Philippine Islands. Three of the crew with him on the bridge that afternoon died instantly. Dad barely survived. When they took off his battle helmet the top part was in his hair; when they threw his kapok lifejacket over the side it sank, laden with shrapnel. The lifejacket did its job. The battle ended for dad that afternoon; but the effects of war didn't. He was treated at four naval hospitals to get the nerves in his right arm to respond. Nothing worked, not even a portable whirlpool that applied hydrotherapy after dinner each night. Finally, six years after the Leyte invasion, my father's right arm was amputated below the elbow because of dead nerves. Bluish shrapnel scars dotted the calves of both legs. In those years, after the war, he got on with his life as a practicing attorney in Chicago with an office in the LaSalle Street financial district. Dad and his partner and brother-in-law, William Kirby, were the defense team in the celebrated Preston Tucker trial.

His legal success in the postwar years was counterbalanced with two failed attempts for public office. It wouldn't be until years later when the war's true toll came in the Irish tradition of alcohol—"the creature." Tragically, it resulted in the bittersweet end of a law career that didn't reach its full potential.

Despite the missing arm, he could tie a tie faster than most men. I used to marvel at how fast he could tie his shoelaces with one hand. He would put his shoe up on a chair and move the fingers of his left hand so fast that I couldn't keep track of the laces.

My parents often hosted backyard summer barbecues. One summer I brought a girl I was dating to the barbecue. As soon as we entered the backyard I introduced her to my father. He immediately offered her his left hand. Later, driving her home, she was silent. I sensed that something was irritating her. I asked what it was. "Frank, why didn't you tell me that your father has only one arm? I felt so embarrassed when I went to shake hands."

I thought for a moment. Then I said, "We don't consider dad to be handicapped. He can do more things with one arm than I can with two, which he often tells me."

In my senior year at Mt. Carmel High School, at the urging of my father, my brother Mike and I joined the Naval Reserve, a six-year obligation that included monthly weekend drills with the moniker of being a "weekend warrior." The center phase of this enlistment included two years on active duty either at a naval station or on a ship-of-the-line. I started with the accelerated boot camp at the Glenview Naval Air Station outside Chicago during that summer. Upon graduation we were given the month and year of going on active duty, pending a school deferment. I was told that my active duty date would be October 1960. Right away I began inquiring into the process of getting a college deferment. I could continue with college as long as I was deferred from active duty.

During this time I applied to three universities. My high school academic standing had me in the "mumbling middle." But I did fare better on the college board exams. Today they are called the SATs. My applications went to St. Ambrose College in Davenport, Iowa; Tulane University in New Orleans; and the University of New Mexico in Albuquerque. I chose the latter because it was the farthest from Chicago, a new environment. I attended Naval Reserve drills in Albuquerque in a building out near the airport dubbed the "dry-land battleship." It was here where I decided to strike for the rate of a hospital corpsman. I found the classes interesting and challenging.

I was a dormitory student at New Mexico. And I quickly made new friends by organizing a flag football team from our wing in the dorm. It wasn't just a college intramural league. This was a gateway to a new social life and beer busts up in the Sandia Mountains and out in the mesas. It was my time as a "party boy." And I took full advantage of the opportunities.

Also, I managed to alienate the personnel staff at the Naval Reserve Headquarters. I had heard nothing from my application for a one-year college deferment from October 1960 to October 1961. The personnel office, headed by a senior chief petty officer who was a World War II and Korean War veteran, treated me like the "boot" that I was. At the conclusion of each drill weekend I would inquire about my deferment request. The answer was always the same: "It's in the system." As time rolled on I wasn't just concerned—I was very concerned.

When winter turned to spring I made the decision to use my father's connection to Senator Paul Douglas's office in Washington, D.C. This became known as a "C.I.," a congressional inquiry, a thorn in the side of any military organization. I was dealing with a ticking clock to get that one-year deferment. It was more than possible that my college years would be interrupted by orders to active duty. At the next drill that chief petty officer called me in for a royal butt-chewing, emphasizing the unnecessary paperwork I had caused. He ended the meeting by saying, "You haven't heard the last of this, McAdams!"

The first time I heard the expression "draft dodger" was from my father. Often, during election time in Chicago, when a candidate's résumé was being scrutinized, dad would check the candidate's profile to see if any time was spent in uniform. He often explained how some candidates glamorize their service, even fictionalizing a combat record. Several times, while reading a profile, I would see him pause. He would then mutter, "What a fake."

Once, at a political breakfast, after Senator John Kennedy had announced his presidential candidacy, the subject came around to the senator's controversial wartime experience in the Solomon Islands, where his torpedo boat was rammed in a nighttime patrol. Kennedy and his crew were missing, presumed dead, for days. After they were found, Kennedy was awarded the Navy–Marine Corps Medal for heroism. It was later recounted in *The New Yorker* magazine, a book, and then a movie, *PT–109*, starring Cliff Robertson and Robert Culp.

One of the men at the table, a successful businessman, questioned Kennedy's Ivy League and silver-spoon background along with his leadership potential. "What kind of an officer would allow his boat to get that close to a Japanese destroyer and get it cut in half?" The man snickered.

Dad stared at him for a beat. I knew the look. The gentleman was so unprepared. *Oh my God*, I thought. *Now it's coming.*

And it did.

Dad softly put down his fork. Then he swung his right stub up on the table so everyone could see that there was no arm in the sleeve. "We're about the same age, wouldn't you say?" The man nodded. "Matter of fact, Senator Kennedy is younger than you and me." The man nodded again. "I'd say that the difference is that Kennedy went. As a matter of fact, Kennedy pulled strings to get a combat command." Dad took a stage pause to ensure that the entire table was listening.

The table was listening.

Dad continued. "Let me ask, what did *you* do in the great World War II?"

I don't think I've ever seen anyone caught so off guard in a social situation. The man paused, noticing everyone looking at him, suddenly realizing what he had walked into. Beads of perspiration were forming on his forehead. "Well, I, uh, had a business to run. But I did contribute to the war effort."

"You mean back here in the states?" asked dad.

"Uh, yes, you see I had a family."

"So did a lot of *us*," said dad, emphasizing the word *us*. "Yet you can criticize someone who wore a uniform and put his life on the line." Dad paused again and looked around the table. "I think we should realize how fortunate some of us are, to be able to survive a world war." He took another pause, going in for the kill. "Where some of us went. And others, who are now critics, didn't."

A strange silence came over the table. Dad's steely eyes were boring a hole through the man, as the silence continued. And then dad picked up his fork and continued eating as if nothing had happened.

The successful businessman quickly finished his meal. At the first opportunity, he got up and left the table. It was at that breakfast table where it dawned on me how a wartime combat situation stayed with my father, the ultimate lifetime experience. It not only affected him but those around him.

My time at the University of New Mexico came to an abrupt end. I spent that summer in Chicago taking political science and history courses at Loyola University, intending to transfer the credits to Albuquerque. When I returned to Albuquerque I started classes, staying in the same dormitory. Two weeks into the semester I got a phone call from a yeoman at the Naval Reserve Center. He was calling on the phone in the alcove at the end of the hall. *What now*, I wondered, as I walked to the alcove. He asked me if I had received a response from my deferment request. I didn't think anything of it. I simply answered, "Not yet."

In a calm voice he said, "Then you're on orders to active duty."

My stomach turned. "But I'm enrolled for the fall semester here. That's why I applied for a deferment."

"Sorry, McAdams, these orders came from the Bureau of Naval Personnel. You're to report here for the drill weekend and be processed to the Naval Receiving Station in San Diego."

I hung up the phone and stood there in the alcove, my head spinning. Then I recalled what the chief petty officer said months before, "You haven't heard the last of this, McAdams!" I felt like I had been pole-axed. I immediately called my father in Chicago. It was shocking news to him. And there was nothing either of us could do at this stage. I headed back to my room and ceremoniously closed my books and got out my uniforms.

During the drill weekend I had to control seething anger, sensing a gloating feeling from the chief petty officer. I went out of the chain of command. And I paid the price. Each time he saw me in the hall that weekend I noticed his slight grin. But it wouldn't be the last time I went out of the chain of command. By Monday morning I was in uniform on the train from Albuquerque, facing two years of sea duty.

After six days at the 32nd Street Receiving Station in San Diego I was assigned to the Medical Department aboard the USS *Ticonderoga*, an Essex-class attack aircraft carrier that saw considerable action in the Western Pacific during World War II and Korea. I went aboard as a hospitalman apprentice. Within four months, without attending Hospital Corps School, I passed the exam for hospitalman. By January I was working on the sick-call crew. It was at sick call one morning where I happened to meet a disbursing clerk (payroll) named Lester Marineau. I recall that he was complaining of flu symptoms. I didn't know it at the time, but we would meet again under tragic circumstances.

In the second week of May 1961 we departed San Diego for a Western Pacific (WesPac) cruise. The ship made ports at Pearl Harbor in Hawaii, Yokosuka, Sasebo, and Iwakuni in Japan. Even though this was the "peacetime Navy" we lost pilots and aircraft in flight operations. The first was a pilot in a flameout where his jet engine quit right after the catapult launch; the ship ran over his plane. We never found him. He was married with two children. The next afternoon a memorial service was held on the hangar deck. About three weeks later another pilot was lost at night because of a sudden fire in his cockpit. He was married with three children. Once again, a memorial service was held on the hangar deck.

One month later another plane from squadron VF-51 hit the ramp during recovery operations, skidded 200 feet along the flight deck, and careened over the port side. After searching for six hours the only thing recovered was his flying helmet. He was married with two children and a third on the way. It always seemed to be the married pilots.

We made port in Hong Kong twice. During this time my sister Molly was married back in Chicago. In the Philippines we anchored off Manila and had several in-port periods at the Subic Bay Naval Base.

On the surface the Philippines gave off an "animalistic magnetism." Its mirror image was an ugly underbelly. Many of the bars, watering holes for sailors and Marines, had bands that played popular U.S. rock music. Three of the most popular clubs were Club Oro, The U&I, and Club Tropicana. Two of the smaller clubs were Club Taurus and 1622.

During another Subic Bay in-port period I ran into Marineau again. This time his complaint was a dog bite. He ended up being treated for rabies because the dog couldn't be located. What I didn't know at the time was why Marineau was bitten by the dog.

It seemed that on a previous tour Marineau was stationed at the base. During this time he met a young bargirl and began a relationship. Within a short period this girlfriend became pregnant by him. Marineau was able to support her on his small salary. They shared a house off the main drag in Olongapo. At the time it was an idyllic situation. They were a family—that is, until he got orders for sea duty on the *Ticonderoga*. By the time he reported to the ship in San Diego he was a third-class petty officer. His motivation was to return to

Olongapo and begin the process to marry his girlfriend and have her and the child sent to his hometown, somewhere in Georgia.

At the start of the Subic Bay in-port periods Marineau began looking for his girlfriend and child. She was no longer working at any of the bars. It was during this time when he received the dog bite. Then one night Marineau returned to the house they once shared. By this time the dwelling was converted to a "Benny Boy House." This was Filipino slang for a gay brothel. On this night business was booming—until the Shore Patrol showed up—with Marineau being apprehended. They hauled all military personnel into a patrol wagon, pulled their ID cards, and took them back to the base.

Marineau was escorted aboard ship by a Shore Patrol sailor and turned over to the officer of the deck at the gangway. Upon returning to the ship Marineau went down to the disbursing office, where a night crew was working on payroll records. It was a hot August night, and no one in the office paid any attention as Marineau entered the office and opened the pistol rack where the .45 semiautomatics were stored. As the clerks continued typing, Marineau placed a loaded clip in the handle of a pistol and pulled the slide back, chambering a round. He then placed the pistol next to his right ear and squeezed the trigger.

Click—it was a misfire. The clerks went right on working, not even looking up.

Marineau then pulled back on the hammer and squeezed the trigger again. His head jerked and he went down, dropping the pistol. Everyone in the office was suddenly shaken with the blast.

That night I was on duty in the treatment room writing a letter to a friend in Chicago. The back hatch to the sick bay suddenly opened and I heard running footsteps. A disbursing clerk, face white with shock, looked at me, "We need a corpsman in the disbursing office. A guy shot himself!"

My throat went dry as I stood. "How bad?"

"In the head!" He turned and ran back out.

I immediately ran to a bulkhead (wall) and grabbed a ready first-aid bag. At that moment one of the senior corpsmen, Ernie Elliott, was in the passageway holding a coffee cup. I told him I was heading to disbursing, that someone had shot himself.

Elliott followed me down the passageway. By this time there was a crowd at the hatchway. I remember yelling, "Corpsman here! Make a hole!" Inside the office I was looking down at Marineau. A pool of thick brain blood and matter was under his head; his eyelids were half open. I bent down and felt for a pulse. It was a small beat, a sign that his body was shutting down. There was little that I could do with a head wound like that.

Elliott immediately picked up the .45, which was on the deck under Marineau's right knee. He ejected the clip from the handle and pulled back on the slide. This ejected the next round. Two more corpsmen entered the office with a stokes stretcher. Marineau was placed in the stretcher and carried to sick bay. Elliott set the pistol down on a desk, turned to me, and shook his head. I nodded to him. I never opened my first-aid bag.

The office clerks were visibly shaken. Several were sitting at their desks staring into space, realizing that one of their own had taken his life right in front of them as they were working. The ship's chief master of arms entered and looked around. Then he asked, "Who's going to clean up this mess?" I stared at him, astonished at his callousness.

By the time I got back to the treatment room several corpsmen and one of the ship's doctors, Lieutenant Kent, had Marineau on the treatment table. Dr. Kent took off his stethoscope and stared at Marineau. He shook his head, "He's gone."

We spent the next hour preparing Marineau's body for transfer to the base hospital morgue. As I helped wash him down I noticed the scratches on his fingers from the earlier dog bite. Then I realized that his eyes were still half open. I reached over, with my right thumb and forefinger, and gently closed them. It wouldn't be the last time I did this. One of the office corpsmen pulled Marineau's medical record to accompany the body. That's when we saw that he was from Georgia.

In the end, the episode was ruled a suicide. Marineau's girlfriend and child were never located.

During the long periods at sea I began intense reading, anything that I could get my hands on—novels, poetry, and current nonfiction from the ship's library. I reread J. D. Salinger's *The Catcher in the Rye* and F. Scott Fitzgerald's *The Great Gatsby*, coming away with a new understanding of both novels. I remember devouring William L. Shirer's Pulitzer Prize–winning *The Rise and Fall of the Third Reich*. I came away from that read astonished at how the European community and certain American quarters did nothing while Adolf Hitler carried through his program of rearming Germany, ignoring the Treaty of Versailles. Consequently, this inaction set the stage for World War II. George Santayana was right: "Those who cannot remember the past are condemned to repeat it."

During the in-port periods in the Philippines the Marine Detachment scheduled forced marches with rifles, helmets, and field packs. They also needed a corpsman who could stand the pace. While at Subic Bay, during an in-port period, the scheduled corpsman came down with a fever. I volunteered as his replacement. It was approved by our chief petty officer in the Medical Department and I was told to report to the Marine Detachment for an orientation.

At the Marine Detachment I met the gunnery sergeant, a stocky Navajo Indian and Korean War veteran. I recall sitting across from him in an office while a mean-looking buck sergeant stood nearby. The gunnery sergeant explained the distance of the forced march, up and down hills at a fast pace. He then asked what kind of physical shape I was in.

"Good," I said. "I wrestled and played football in high school."

The buck sergeant snickered. The gunnery sergeant shook his head. "I didn't ask what the fuck you did in high school. I want to know what kind of shape you're in now."

I looked straight at him: "Good, I'll keep up."

"Well, sailor-boy, we'll find out tomorrow," said the gunnery sergeant. The meeting ended, but the phrase "sailor-boy" spoke volumes. He was asking, "Do you pack the gear?"

The next morning I was on the quay wall waiting as the Marine Detachment came down the gangway, carrying field packs, rifles, and helmets, under the sweltering rays of a tropical sun.

It looked like one of those World War II films with the Marines disembarking onto a foreign shore. I was waiting in my Navy-issue dungarees, with a corpsman's first-aid bag, as they lined up in two files. Instead of the Dixie Cup hat, I was wearing a helmet. The detachment commander, Captain Harry Mills, took his place in front, gave a forward signal, and we were off, a guidon flag fluttering in the slight breeze at the front.

As anticipated, the forced march was punishing. They positioned me at the end of the two files to pick up stragglers or heat cases. Somehow they commandeered a personnel carrier to follow us in case of a serious incident. I remember a Marine falling out to get rid of his breakfast, which he did in short order. After a quick check he jogged back in line.

At times an accordion effect developed where the rear end had to run faster to keep up with the rest of the column. During a water break I dispensed salt tablets. I could tell that some of these guys were hurting more than me. The gunnery sergeant approached and asked how I was doing.

"No problem," I answered. "How are you doing?" He gave me a wondering look, turned, and walked back to the front.

Two Marines fell out on the back leg of the march. Both were heat cases. I gave them a quick water wash on their faces and offered each another salt pill. They were placed in the personnel carrier to be classified as "sick, lame, or lazy." Then I ran to catch up. When we returned to the quay wall my shirt was drenched, but I had held my own, running faster than the others because of being at the tail.

Standing in front of the detachment next to the guidon carrier, Captain Mills said some words about keeping fit. He then singled me out for volunteering, then added something about the Navy corpsmen being the saviors of Marines in combat. Several of the Marines in the ranks turned and looked at me. I had crossed a line.

After the detachment was dismissed the gunnery sergeant and the buck sergeant from the interview approached me. The gunnery sergeant said, "Doc, you did good." The buck sergeant gave me a wondering look, staying silent. No compliments from this guy. Then the two turned and walked toward the gangway. I knew that their initial opinion of me had changed.

When I returned to sick bay one of the senior corpsmen, First Class Petty Officer Nyman Harris, noticed my drenched shirt and smiled. "Out for a morning walk with the jarheads, I see."

From that morning I was drawn to the Marine Corps camaraderie. They requested me for another forced march. And I became friends with several of them. We even pulled a few liberty nights together in other ports. I saw how the Marines had a deep respect for Navy corpsmen built from World War II and Korea. It was the start of something.

The married guys on the ship were looking forward to coming home for Christmas. But the international situation in Laos boiled over. It appeared that a communist takeover was possible unless the United States and Soviet Union came to an agreement. For weeks the situation remained fluid. The Pentagon, on orders from the Kennedy White House, extended several ships to be on station in the Western Pacific. The *Ticonderoga* was one of them. The married guys took the news bitterly. It was a tense situation, and an American aircraft carrier was needed on station. A six-month WesPac cruise turned into eight months as we patrolled the South China Sea.

On the morning of January 14, 1962, we approached Point Loma off San Diego. I went up to a weather deck to observe the squadrons as they were launched off the forward catapults. Once airborne they were to rendezvous at a certain altitude and head to their various bases. It was on this morning where I witnessed the midair collision of two attack planes. One veered off and came back to land on the flight deck. The second plane hit the water. We watched as the helicopter rescue team got to the pilot. But it was too late; he was dead. It was the last hour of our Far East cruise, and we had lost another pilot. His wife was waiting for him at Moffett Field near San Francisco.

We tied up at the North Island Naval Air Station and prepared for a six-month refitting at the Puget Sound Naval Shipyard in Bremerton, Washington. I took a leave to Chicago and made an application to resume college classes at Loyola University. During this time my brother Mike was called to active duty as a radarman. Coincidentally he was also assigned to an aircraft carrier, the USS *Forrestal* out of Norfolk, Virginia.

Five weeks after I was released from active duty the Cuban Missile Crisis began, freezing retirements and discharges in the U.S. Navy and Marine Corps. I had just made it out during the days that the CIA and naval intelligence discovered that the Soviet Union had nuclear missiles in Cuba. I returned to Chicago and enrolled in night classes at Loyola University, working full-time during the day at a downtown insurance office. It was a demanding schedule. I gave up on having a social life. It was all work and studying: English literature, constitutional law, and political science. It was in the English literature class where the professor, Dr. Spencer, produced a transistor radio, and the class listened to President Kennedy's Missile Crisis speech announcing the blockade of Cuba. I recall Dr. Spencer taking out his draft card, staring at it as Kennedy's words spread across the classroom. In the succeeding days the nation watched as we drifted closer to nuclear war. Finally the Soviets backed down and withdrew the missiles.

I thought that being a Navy corpsman on a ship in Seventh Fleet forced me to learn time management. Now I was learning what college time management demanded, heightened by working full-time. If I didn't get my reading and writing assignments done by Monday morning I was toast for the week.

Two things happened at this point. My parents separated, and I had to confront a reaction of being confined to working full-time and carrying the added load of three demanding nighttime college classes.

In a short period I realized that the call was coming back. This time it wasn't the U.S. Navy; it was going "before the mast." I had picked up a copy of *The New Yorker* during a break in the library. After reading several articles I noticed a small box advertisement for Windjammer Cruises, Inc., operating out of Miami Beach. I wasn't thinking of being a cruise passenger; I wanted to know where they got their crewmembers. My sense of adventure was at work again.

By the late spring of 1963 I was in the Miami office of Windjammer Cruises, Inc. During the interview I heard how many young men my age applied at Windjammer looking for Caribbean adventure. And after a short time at sea they quit because of the work schedule: twenty-four hours—eight on, four off—at $75 per month. I was given a choice. I could join the crew that did ten-day cruises in the western Caribbean, or I could go for a bigger one, a three-month exploration cruise to the Galapagos Islands that needed one more crewmember.

I chose the latter and agreed to report to Pier Three in Miami the next morning to board a tourist boat to Bimini, where the *Brigantine Yankee*, a two-masted ninety-six-foot brig, was anchored. The *Yankee*, the center vessel in the Windjammer fleet, was a famous ship in its own right. Once owned by the noted Captain Irving Johnson, it had made five round-the-world cruises with amateur crews. I was told that I would be the junior of an eight-member crew, including a stewardess, captained by Laurence Jordan, an Australian and certified navigator. Coming with me on the tourist boat was a cute, blue-eyed blonde named Caroline Benson from Orlando, Florida. She thought spending the summer on a Windjammer as a stewardess was going to be "life in the raw." We spent some time walking around the casino on the boat, watching passengers lose money to slot machines and at the roulette and craps tables. Caroline also spoke of her parents' second home in Connecticut. Several times she mentioned looking forward to the summer at sea, being on her own. After four hours we anchored in Bimini and caught sight of a sleek two-masted schooner with a clean white hull. Later, a launch pulled alongside with two grungy-looking men. They yelled something about "*Brigantine Yankee*." I gave them a wave. Within minutes Caroline and I were going down the gangway, carrying our gear, and got into the launch. But we didn't head for the sleek schooner. We were headed to the brig behind it. This was the *Yankee*. And it looked as old as its years, circa 1914. The steel hull had streaks of rust. The furled sails looked old and worn. Caroline and I exchanged concerned looks.

In Captain Jordan's cabin I had to sign British Sea Articles, as we were sailing under the Union Jack, the ship being registered in Nassau. I recall one of the clauses stated that if I participated in any mutinous attempts I could be subject to the maximum penalty under the common laws of the realm, or words to that effect. For the moment I felt that I was putting my signature to a historical document . . . or a death warrant.

The crew was a cross-section of human nature. First mate was Aaron Hanson, who grew up in the hills of Tennessee, worked on several farms, and finally went before the mast. Next was the cook, D. J. Johnson, a black Korean War veteran who could scramble together a gourmet's delight of a sauce from scraps. Les Bannister, one of the grungy men, was an ex-con from Fort Pierce, Florida. Gruff and blunt at first, he took some time before liking you, a holdover trait from his prison experience for armed robbery. Phil Braxton, who did time as a day sailor, was from Miami and had just been released from a mental ward, the survivor of a complete breakdown, now on the mend. Then there was Halo, the second of the grungy men. Halo was a stocky, well-built Hawaiian guy my age. He carried a guitar and a good voice, partial to the current trend of hootenanny. And he had done a lot of sailing around the Hawaiian Islands.

When I came up on deck I was told that Caroline was returning to Miami. After sizing up the crew she decided against seeing life in the raw and being independent. Captain Jordan then asked me, "Are you staying or going?"

A silence fell over us on the quarterdeck as they waited for my answer. I looked at the crew, then over to Captain Jordan. "I signed so I'll be staying."

Les and Halo helped Caroline back into the launch. I stood at the railing, watching the launch head back to the tourist boat. *Good luck, Caroline*, I thought. Actually she should have been wishing me good luck. I never saw her again. The initial crew of eight was now down to seven.

When Halo came back from the ferry he showed me to my bunk in the forward foc'sle (forecastle). As I began unpacking he wondered what sort of Windjammer sailor I would turn into. "It's one thing to be a sailor on a big ship. It's different here, going aloft in a driving rainstorm. You think you can handle that?"

Quickly I thought of the Marine gunnery sergeant. I looked at Halo and nodded. I knew captain and crew would be watching my every move on deck.

From Bimini we spent one night in Nassau, then headed out, around the Windward Passage of Cuba, where we hit a series of squalls and got buzzed by a U.S. Navy intelligence plane snapping some quick reconnaissance photos in the middle of the night. The Navy kept a close watch with a patrol boat for the next day as we headed to the Panama Canal. At Colon, on the Atlantic side of the canal, we spent two days packing stores for the voyage. Then we took on twenty-six members of the Los Angeles Geographic Society as passengers. From there we cast off and made the canal transit. The next morning we set sail for more than twenty anchorages in the Galapagos, the noted archipelago of volcanic islands, 650 miles off the coast of Ecuador.

Two nights later we hit another squall. This one was worse than the ones in the Windward Passage. At about 2 A.M. I got rousted from my bunk with a command: "All hands on deck!"

Captain Jordan gave the order to take in the foresail, the main square sail on the forward mast, then reef the mainsail for storm running. Reefing the main was easy compared to taking in the foresail. We had to climb up the shrouds, hand by foot, in the dark with windy rain pelting our faces. Then we had to straddle the yardarm, haul in the sheet, and tie it off. I had seen this done in movies but never gave a thought that one day—or night—I would be doing it. It was not only difficult; it was downright dangerous. One slip and I would go crashing to the deck. Or if we were on a broad reach, which we were, I'd go nautical. Over and out.

The foresail was pulled in and the mainsail was tied off at the reef points, giving off a short sail to ride through the foul weather. That done, Captain Jordan secured those not on watch. Within minutes I was back in my bunk with the anchor clanging against the hull next to my head. I was so exhausted that I slept soundly as the ship rolled and tossed through the night—that is, until first light. By then we had passed through the squall line. And Captain Jordan wanted to make up for lost time. It was all hands on deck again. Out of the bunk and up in the shrouds once more to reverse the process. When we finished it was time for morning chow—hot coffee, Canadian bacon, and scrambled eggs—from D. J. the cook.

It was hard, being a Windjammer deckhand. There was never a full sleep; eight on and four off. We were divided among the passengers who took part in our wheel watches. During this time I read Irving Stone's biography of Jack London, *Sailor on Horseback*.

At different times during the day, Captain Jordan would come out of the wheelhouse and "shoot the sun" with a sextant and stopwatch, confirming our position. The crew had to keep the ship on course, making notes in the watch log. And we had to record oil pressure numbers periodically to make sure that both engines were running properly. We flew the flag of Ecuador from our foremast during the anchorages in the Galapagos. These were the islands where the HMS *Beagle* anchored in 1835, allowing a young naturalist named Charles Darwin to do research for a published work that became known as *On the Origin of Species*. I was surprised to learn that each island had two and sometimes three names. At one of the anchorages we saw the names of various yachts and ships painted on a block of rocks. Captain Jordan noted one of the names, *Zaca*, Errol Flynn's yacht. Our last anchorage was the heavily forested Cocos Island off Costa Rica. Before we anchored in the bay the Ecuadorian flag was replaced with the flag of Costa Rica on the foremast. After departing Cocos Island we headed to the port of Puntarenas, Costa Rica, where the passengers left the ship and took a train to nearby San Juan, where they caught a plane back to Los Angeles. We stayed anchored in Puntarenas for several days doing ship's maintenance. Then we weighed anchor and set a southeastern course around Azuero Peninsula and into the Gulf of Panama. Closer to Panama, Captain Jordan pulled out a small American flag from the pennant locker. As we did in previous anchorages the *Brigantine Yankee* flew the flag of the port we were entering from the foremast. Because the United States controlled the isthmus, Panama was considered an American territory. Captain Jordan gave me the flag. "It's your turn to flag the foremast," he said.

For some obscure reason going up in the shrouds of the foremast made me think of the Marines who raised the flag on Iwo Jima in February 1945. It was a ceremonial nautical custom, but it still did something to me, climbing up to the line where the clips were, hooking the flag, and then raising it to the peak of the foremast. After I tied off the line I looked down. The entire crew was on the quarterdeck looking at me. That doesn't go away; it was one of those moments.

By this time I was a hot Windjammer sailor. My plans were to take the ship back to Nassau and sign on for a round-the-world cruise commencing the following January. I felt that it was the dream of a lifetime, going around the world and getting paid for it. My hopes were dashed with one phone call home to Chicago. My parents had reconciled but were no longer in the big house on South Shore Drive. They were now in a large apartment on Crandon Avenue. And my father, in his wisdom, explained that if I signed on for that cruise I would never finish my degree. "I never saw you as a college dropout," he said. "You give this serious thought."

"Dad, this is the chance of a lifetime," I countered. "How many people my age get the chance to go around the world and get paid for it?"

"And too often I meet people in their forties who tearfully regret never finishing college when they had the chance." He took a pause. "And you have the chance . . . now!"

I realized that he was echoing one of mom's three doctrines: *If you start something finish it.* But the call of the sea, and adventure, was so very tempting.

My father and I struck a deal. I would return to Chicago and get a part-time job to pay for expenses and books, and he would foot half my tuition at Loyola. I remember pausing for about thirty seconds. Then I softly said, "Okay."

So much for the adventure of a round-the-world cruise. I said goodbye to Captain Jordan and the crew, leaving the *Brigantine Yankee* in mid-September 1963. Later, I learned that the round-the-world cruise caused the end of the great windjammer. It got hung up on a reef off Rarotonga, in the Cook Islands, on July 23, 1964, about halfway through the cruise. Crew and passengers abandoned ship, leaving it to die. The *Brigantine Yankee* rests on that reef to this day.

I returned to Chicago and picked up where I left off at Loyola. Later that fall, like the rest of the nation and world, I was stunned at the news that President Kennedy had been assassinated in Dallas. I was enrolled in a philosophy class, Theory of Logic. I remember trudging to class, shaken like the other students. Someone produced a transistor radio. Thirteen months prior, in Dr. Spencer's English literature class, we listened to another transistor radio as a very serious President Kennedy gave his Missile Crisis speech. And now he was gone. We listened to the updates; a suspect with a rifle was in the custody of the Dallas police. And that the president's body was in flight back to Washington.

The professor entered the room appearing drawn and haggard. I remember him looking around and then raising his hand. "No class today. Go on home." Then he turned and walked out.

A few of us went down to the student union, where a television was set up in the lobby. Air Force One had returned to Andrews Air Force Base. The casket was being lowered to a waiting vehicle. The cameras closed in on Jacqueline Kennedy, still in shock, standing there in her blood-stained pink suit. I looked around noting the serious looks from students and faculty. Chins were quivering, eyes watering, man and woman alike. I went to a phone and called my mother. She was in the kitchen listening to the radio. I remember telling her it was like a bad dream. Then I returned to the television and watched Lyndon Johnson give his first speech as president. I remember him reading from a prepared statement saying that he was going to do his best to complete what President Kennedy had started. Naturally I had no idea of how the long-term effects of that statement would affect me. That weekend I spent with brothers and sisters doing school assignments and playing Password. We also had the television turned on, looking at the president's casket lying in state in the Capitol Rotunda. By chance, late at night, we saw our brother Mike, in his Navy uniform, approach the flag-draped casket and snap a salute. He had hitchhiked all the way up to Washington from Norfolk and waited hours in the line.

By the following spring, 1964, I was still attending classes. And I put a down payment on a used Honda motorcycle, as I couldn't afford a car. It provided good transportation, and gas was cheap. I was getting along on a shoestring budget, loading trucks on the docks off the Stevenson Expressway for United Parcel Service. That summer I got a better-paying job with Country Delight, loading ice-cream trucks. My clock was turned around with this job. I had to work nights loading ice cream from a freezer onto refrigerator trucks waiting at a dock. We had to wear heavy freezer suits with hoods and gloves. And we had to take fifteen-minute breaks every two hours, a union rule. It was back-breaking work, but the pay was good. It covered expenses, tuition, and payments on the motorcycle. And I was putting money away for emergencies and future tuition bills. But still, no social life.

After a night shift I would jump on the motorcycle and hit the expressway. Within forty minutes I would be in Father Mentag's American history class. Everyone was fresh-faced, whereas I had a windblown look, wearing a rumpled sweatshirt. When class ended I was back on the motorcycle to get home for a stretch of daytime sleep. By 6 P.M. I was up and ready for a ride back to Maywood and another shift. I studied during the breaks and on weekends, again knowing that if I didn't I'd be toast at exam time. Father Mentag's class was a turning point. I became fascinated with historical events mixed with the mistakes and blunders made by powerful leaders that led to other scenarios. I recalled being impressed with Shirer's *The Rise and Fall of the Third Reich.* And now I was fascinated by the events surrounding Abraham Lincoln's assassination and the corruption of the Ulysses Grant and Warren Harding administrations. I decided to declare history as a major.

During one of the truck-loading breaks I picked up the back-picture page of the *Chicago Tribune.* It carried a wire photo of a North Vietnamese PT boat that was part of a force that had attacked two U.S. destroyers. I remember staring at the photo wondering what this incident in the Gulf of Tonkin would turn into. I was surprised to see that the carrier-based aircraft, from Fighter Squadron VF–51, were launched from the *Ticonderoga.* I was still staring at the picture when the shift foreman came in. "Back to the freezer," he said. I took one last look at the wire photo. On my ride to Loyola later that morning I couldn't get the photo out of my head. I wondered what all of it meant. Two days later, August 7, 1964, Congress passed the Gulf of Tonkin Resolution giving President Johnson a blank check to repel any armed attack made against the forces of the United States. In the meantime planes from the *Ticonderoga* and USS *Constellation* continued to launch air strikes against North Vietnam.

As I began my junior year at Loyola I met Patty Rafferty, a blonde, blue-eyed education major who had just returned from a semester studying in Rome. Patty's parents were separated at the time, and she lived with her mother, Joan, in South Shore.

Patty and my sister Joan were in a registration line, changing a class, as the fall semester of 1964 began. Joan introduced me. By the end of the day, Patty later told me, she knew that I was going to ask her out. Like many things, she knew more than I did.

Both of us were seeing other people. I was now working at The Red Garter, a nearby banjo bar in the Rush Street nightclub district. Despite working and going to school I managed to finally have a social life, dating here and there. Patty was also doing the same thing. But after several dates with Patty, I changed things. And so did she.

We began seeing each other exclusively. It wasn't long before I got hit with the thunderbolt. My mother once told me in a conversation during high school, "You'll know when it happens."

It happened.

Patty and I often met at the library to study together. I was carrying a full load as a history major plus working four nights a week at The Red Garter, two as a bartender and two as a waiter. The latter provided more tips for expenses and books.

In February 1965 two historic incidents occurred. Malcolm X was gunned down in front of 400 people in the Audubon Ballroom in New York City. I remember some Loyola students breathing a sigh, "Thank God it wasn't some white guys who killed him." The second incident was a news report that U.S. Army advisers in a compound in the Central Highlands of Vietnam came under a full-scale mortar and ground attack. Nine U.S. soldiers were killed and 128 wounded. The compound was near the village of Pleiku. I had never heard of it. During the next two weeks the Pleiku mortar attack was the number-one topic in the student union, especially among young men. Every guy was becoming concerned about his draft status and the process to acquire a student deferment. I was already classified in the inactive reserves, having done two years on active duty. Still, I knew that what happened at Pleiku had the potential to go hot. I had a sample of it in the Laos crisis when the *Ticonderoga* got extended in the South China Sea.

One month after the Pleiku attack, in March 1965, two battalion landing teams from the 9th Marine Expeditionary Brigade (MEB) landed at a beach northeast of Danang to provide security for the air base. I had no idea how prophetic that would be. The beach was later christened Red Beach (where our convoys would later stage). The base security would be threatened much later when a North Vietnamese regiment crossed Song Cau Do River to hit the Danang air base coming over the bridge at Cam Le, beginning the summer offensive of 1968.

As 1965 continued I began writing feature articles for the campus newspaper, *The Loyola News*. And there were daily discussions in the student union about the Vietnam War. It was during this time when I began to observe a student contradiction toward the war. Naturally there were students on both sides of this charged issue. An antiwar faction was already forming, getting the nickname "Doves." Likewise, the prowar side, the "Hawks," was making its voice heard.

I found myself in the middle. But it wasn't hard to notice the concern and fear coming from my peers. Some of the Hawks, amazingly, were discussing ways to avoid the draft. The easiest path was to get into graduate school and apply for a student deferment. My father observed during that time, "If the selective service act was repealed the graduate schools would empty out overnight."

In the student union one of the Hawk students told me about the "handball method" for taking the draft physical. Approaching the blood-pressure station, at the Van Buren Street Armed Forces Examining Station, he surreptitiously slipped a handball into his left arm pit. The Army medic, seeing him as another in a long line of young men, wrapped the cuff around his bicep and began pumping, unaware that the blood flow had been altered by the handball. The medic took two readings and then marked his form in red: "low B.P." Before the medic left for his meal break he indicated that another reading would be required at a later date. If that reading was the same he would be a candidate for a medical deferment. I heard later that he got the deferment. And he continued with his hawkish views on Vietnam, right toward graduation.

My father was also surprised at some of his peers in the law profession. They supported President Johnson's continued escalation of the war. But they didn't want their sons going. It was common back then, in Chicago, how a phone call to a high-level officeholder could change a young man's draft status while family members supported the president.

Dad even recommended the son of one of his friends to Senator Paul Douglas for an appointment to West Point. The son qualified after the difficult application process. Just before the son was to report for his plebe summer he formally withdrew his application. I remember dad expressing frustration for recommending the young man. "He saw nothing wrong with wearing an officer's uniform during peacetime. But now the possibility of leading a jungle patrol suddenly changed his outlook." That same month a student named John called me at home wanting to know if I was interested in accompanying a group of Loyola students down to Alabama, where a fifty-four-mile march was planned from Selma to the state capital in Montgomery, led by civil rights activists John Lewis and Hosea Williams. I had three midsemester exams on the horizon and knew what that trip would do to my preparation. I declined to go, something I still regret.

At the Edmund Pettus Bridge, on the outskirts of Selma, the marchers were brutally assaulted by heavily armed state troopers and police deputies. Tear gas was thrown at the marchers as they retreated across the bridge to downtown Selma. More than a hundred troopers and deputies pursued the marchers where they attacked stragglers in a frenzy.

That night, as I was watching *Judgment at Nuremberg* with my sister Joan and brother Dennis, the film was interrupted with footage of the full-scale police riot. The first thing I thought of was John and the other students who went down there. Two days after the Pettus Bridge riot Dr. Martin Luther King Jr. led another march to the bridge and held a prayer vigil.

When the students returned to Chicago a presentation was held in the law school building, where each one gave his or her personal account of what they saw that afternoon. One of the presentations came from a nun who said it was the most frightening experience of her life, the viciousness and hatred that she witnessed. A student related that he knew they were in trouble when he noticed a button on the shirt of a state trooper. The button had one word on it—Never! Those were chilling testimonies. As Joan, Patty, and I sat in the audience we knew that this would lead to further racial violence.

On Fridays Mister Jones's, one of the nearby bars, was a student gathering place. The jukebox had a variety of songs such as Herb Alpert's "The Lonely Bull," Al Martino singing "Spanish Eyes," Frank and Nancy Sinatra's "Something Stupid," and Barry McGuire's "Eve of Destruction." Two of Staff Sergeant Barry Sadler's ballads were also played: "The A Team" and "The Ballad of the Green Berets." The latter had some of the guys providing a background chorus, pumped up by a collegiate amount of beer muscles with echoes of joining the Green Berets after graduation. In the end it was a lot of hot air despite the popularity of the ballad.

The civil rights struggle and the war continued, as did classes. Many of us were becoming aware that we were living in difficult but historic times. Despite what the politicians claimed, the split in the country was growing as segments of the younger generation refused to accept the philosophy of the older. And I was heading toward a decision.

Patty and I continued dating. We both knew that our feelings were growing toward each other. But in my heart I was having a major conflict. The Navy was solely about me; the Windjammer cruise was likewise about me. But this was different. It was a decision that carried the ultimate risk and would affect other people.

In November 1965 the world learned of the Battle of Ia Drang Valley (the basis for the Paramount Pictures adaptation of *We Were Soldiers Once . . . and Young*). This was the first time U.S. forces engaged a unit from the regular North Vietnamese Army (PAVN).

Before going to bed in those days my brothers and sisters and I would watch the CBS Evening News with the latest reports from Vietnam. I kept my feelings close, not revealing how I truly felt. As the war progressed through 1965 and early 1966 I felt that it was going to be the biggest issue for our generation. There were two avenues open to me: ignore it, I had already served; or get into it, cold and simple. The former was easy, the path of many. The latter was much harder. And it could result in my death.

My brother Dennis and I, naturally, had absolutely no indication that we would take different paths but still end up in Vietnam at the same time.

After classes one day, without telling anyone, I popped into the Marine

Corps Officer Selection Office on Van Buren Street. I was directed to the desk of Captain Robert Thrasher. I still remember his name. Captain Thrasher briefly summarized the procedure for officer selection: ten weeks of a grueling physical program at the Quantico Marine Corps Base in Virginia. After being commissioned a second lieutenant this would be followed by twenty-six weeks at The Basic School (TBS), which emphasized leadership, tactics, map-reading, administration, communications, artillery, and military legal procedures. I remember asking, "What's the attrition rate at OCS?"

Captain Thrasher gave me a serious look. "Between thirty and forty percent. You need to be in shape." He paused and added, "Or else you'll wash out." He made me think of the Windjammer applicants who were looking for adventure and later quit.

The officer selection process started with a written exam. I sat for the exam that afternoon. I was never told the exact score I got. I was only told that I passed. Several days later I reported for the physical exam. At the blood-pressure station I thought of the hawkish student who took the handball offramp. Samuel Johnson had a point with one of his quotes: "Patriotism is the last refuge of a scoundrel."

Next was a sit-down with Patty. I remember calling her one afternoon saying that I had something important to discuss. I parked my motorcycle in front of her apartment building, realizing the importance of the next hour. We had talked about a life together in general. I explained that I was not going to take the normal path, obtaining a degree, getting married, and hiring on with a good company with an impressive starting salary leading to a suburban home. Now she would know where I was headed—not just back to the military but into combat. She listened and took a pause. Then she put her hand on mine and said, "Okay." I still remember being astonished. And I realized that I loved her even more for saying it.

The final academic requirement at Loyola at that time was to pass both the History Department Comprehensive Exam (Comp) and the Graduate Record Exam (GRE). I always felt that the latter was unnecessary. Most of us history majors had no intention of applying for graduate work. Still, it was a way for Loyola University to maintain its high academic rating.

It was now time to let my parents know of the Marine Corps decision. My mother gave it serious thought while my father asked, "You're sure about this?"

"Yes," I said.

"They're using real bullets over there."

I nodded. "So are we."

He gave me his left hand and said, "I'm proud of you."

My mother came from a different angle. She had survived World War II with a seriously wounded husband. His wounds, physical and psychological, would be ongoing. Now it was the next generation and her oldest son—who didn't have to go.

"I remember the afternoon your father came home and said that he applied for the Naval Officers Program. The first thing I told him was that he didn't have to go." She paused, looking at me. "And now I'm saying the same thing to you."

I sat for a GRE preparation exam at Northwestern University in the late winter. I felt loose that Saturday, wanting to get a feel for the exam and the pacing. I had to get a certain score to satisfy the Loyola requirement. I received the results in the mail and I made the cut, high enough for Loyola's graduation. All I had to do now was sit for the exam weekend, the Departmental Comprehensive on Saturday and the Loyola GRE on Sunday.

In the meantime I had second thoughts about Patty and me. The opinions of family and friends contributed to it. My immediate family—parents and brothers and sisters—supported it because it was my decision. Outside of that I got skepticism mixed with wondering looks. Many of my high-school friends were already in graduate school with a deferment. They wanted nothing to do with Vietnam; several of them said so.

Others had a skeptical reaction: "I dunno, Frank. That's a tough program at Quantico. This war is not like World War II or Korea." And then I would change the subject.

As the spring semester began I made another pivotal decision. I told Patty that it was best if I went to the Marine Corps alone. This was my call. And it was hard on both of us. I kept my time in the student union between classes to a minimum. We went for almost two weeks without any contact.

And then one day a letter came. I immediately recognized the clear Palmer Method Catholic handwriting. I opened it.

Dear Frank,
So often it seems that I am unable to say
What I feel at the moment I am asked. This
Is true for often it is a feeling which
has not demanded the words to express
it. Now I feel it necessary to bring this
feeling into words. It is difficult to find the words emoting

the completeness for this feeling; I only hope
you find it possible to understand what I am
inadequately attempting to express.
I too know that our life in marriage may be
cut too short to fulfill all the joys we desire to
give one another. How wonderful to live each
day not slipping into the sedentary life of
routine and complacency found in the philosophy,
"There's always tomorrow." Frank, I don't want a
9 to 5 husband, the white picket fence and the same
four walls of suburban air.

I remember putting the letter aside at this point. I went to my bedroom, laid down, and slipped into deep thought. I couldn't believe what I was reading. If anything had changed my outlook on the future it was this letter. I got up and went back to it.

Our position would lead to a more thoughtful relationship, for every moment would
   be of greatest importance. Unable to hold back the
the possibility of the completion all too soon, I
would thank God for the days of ultimate happiness
spent with you.
I hope these words find understanding and
acceptance, for more than anything I desire to
be your wife—the wife of a serviceman.
XO

When I finished the letter I went to the phone. She had convinced me to take the risk, that whatever the future held we would face it together.

The following weekend was the Comp and GRE exam on the Lake Shore Campus. After the Comp I felt good. Several of the essay questions I had prepared for were there. I outlined each answer and then began the essay. The next day at the GRE sitting I found myself mentally exhausted. It was because of the previous day's sitting. Still, I had to stay with it.

It was after a busy Saturday night at The Red Garter when we were clearing the tables, placing beer mugs and pitchers on the bar for cleaning. Then we had to put the chairs on tables to clear the floor for the early-morning cleaning crew. At that moment another waiter, Tom O'Brien, and I both saw it—a crisp twenty-dollar bill lying under a nearby table. We both jumped at the same time. But I was closer and scooped it up. Tom simply looked at me and then smiled. I was twenty dollars richer than the minute before. What was I going to do with it?

A thought suddenly hit me: Use this and some other funds to put a down payment on an engagement ring.

I gave Patty the ring on a cold April Saturday night at the Michigan Avenue Bridge next to the Chicago River. The next morning Patty's family gave her an impromptu champagne breakfast.

A week later I got a letter from the dean's office notifying me that my score on the GRE exam fell below Loyola's acceptance level. I had failed. I sat down in a chair, holding the letter, stunned beyond belief. Hundreds of thoughts raced through my head. After the spring semester I had one elective to take, which would be during the summer semester. And then I would be done. But now, with the low GRE score, graduation wasn't going to happen. And my application to OCS would be placed on hold; I wasn't going anywhere.

It took me a week to crawl out of the dumps while going to class. Everybody in the student union knew who had passed the Comp and GRE. And everyone knew who didn't. I remember that a few students, who also failed, dropped out of school. It was that devastating. I still recall one student who approached me with a slight smirk. "Frank, better luck next time." I held my feelings in, realizing that he enjoyed my dilemma; it was somebody else's misfortune. I gave no response, turning and walking away.

That semester I was in Dr. Paul Lietz's class, History of Mexico. Dr. Lietz was also chairman of the History Department. I scheduled a meeting in his office. At the meeting he explained that I'd have to wait another semester to sit again for the GRE. There were other history majors in the same situation. I told him how surprised I was with the low score. Then I added that I sat for a preparation GRE at Northwestern.

He stared at me for a moment. Then he leaned forward. "What was your score?"

I told him, remembering the number from the notification.

"You're sure about that number?" he asked.

I nodded. "Yes, why?"

"If it can be verified you can substitute the score," explained Dr. Lietz. "That's a passing score in this department."

"What do I need to do?" I asked. It was a heart-pounding moment.

"Contact the Educational Testing Service in Princeton, New Jersey. Give them the date of the exam and the venue and have them forward the score to this department. You'll probably have to pay a small fee," he explained. I ran out of his office and into the bookstore in the student union. I gave the cashier a five-dollar bill and asked for three dollars in quarters, the rest in singles. Then I went to a payphone and called Princeton information. Several minutes later it was done. They would send me an invoice for the transfer fee. If the score matched. the verification I would be cleared for graduation after the summer semester.

Within a short period my GRE score was successfully substituted and verified by Loyola's History Department. And the word quickly got around that I would be graduating after the summer semester. A day or two later that same smirking student approached me, quite surprised at the outcome. "I heard you pulled an end-run around the History Department."

I shook my head. "It was more like a final-minute desperation pass. I took a practice GRE at Northwestern and substituted the score. I did better the first time." I gave him a quick smile, picked up my notebook, and walked off. I never spoke to him again.

That summer my sister Joan married Robert Klaus, a graduate history student she had met at Loyola. It was an enjoyable wedding with many friends from the South Side and Loyola.

My brother Dennis had been attending junior college after his graduation from Mt. Carmel High School. However, he dropped a summer-school course for a well-paying job at one of the steel mills in the South Chicago district. Dropping out of college in those days was risky. And it came back on Dennis. Later that summer he got his greetings: report for a draft physical.

The rest of the summer passed quickly. My orders from Headquarters Marine Corps arrived. I finished my last class at Loyola, History of 20th Century Politics. And I began a physical regimen that grew out of my initial conversation with Captain Thrasher at the Officer Selection Office. A boyhood friend, Leo Tierney, had gone through OCS and TBS at Quantico the year before. He told me what to expect from the program and to report in the best possible physical shape. I set up a daily schedule of side-straddle hops, pushups, situps, and squat thrusts capped with a three-mile run along Lake Michigan. To this day I remain thankful to Leo. It was time well spent.

On October 9, 1966, Patty and I enjoyed a night downtown knowing it would be my last as a civilian. In the morning my mother drove me to Midway Airport. On the way she told me about driving my father to the LaSalle Street Station, in early 1942, where he boarded a train to Princeton, New Jersey, for the Naval Officer's Indoctrination Program set up on the campus. My father roomed with four other midshipmen. Later he found out that he was the only one to survive the war. I kissed my mother goodbye, got out of the car, and headed to the Marine Corps.

3

Quantico

By the time the plane landed at National Airport in Washington, D.C., on October 10, 1966, I met three other officer candidates: Bob Sikma and Rich Watson from Nebraska and Jim Grosshans from Iowa. Because we would be locked in for the next several weeks we decided to see Capitol Hill before reporting to Quantico. After a quick tour of the Capitol we grabbed a late lunch—our last civilian meal.

Gathered at Union Station that fall afternoon was a generation of young men brought up on the idealism and hope of John F. Kennedy to the reality and call of Lyndon B. Johnson. In their hearts they knew that this journey into the Marines, then to the jungle, would be the most dramatic in their lives. Nothing, from this moment on, would come close to comparison. For those who would not survive there would always be the lingering and tragic question of what they could have done with their lives.

We got off at the Quantico station and were told to "stand by." This was the beginning of a military procedure known as "stand by to stand by." Ninety minutes later we were still standing by. We had grown to twice the original size since another train from Washington brought in more candidates. The twilight shadows were gathering. Then we heard a rumbling sound as several buses pulled up to quick stops, airbrakes hissing in the early darkness. We boarded the buses in silence, carrying our OCS orders and small grips. The light-hearted conversations of the train were replaced by a fear of the unknown as we headed down the highway to a remote area known as Camp Upshur.

The buses pulled into a flood-lighted parking lot and stopped. Silence for the next thirty seconds. Then the door opened and a staff sergeant, with a chest full of ribbons wearing a "Smokey Bear" hat, came aboard. In a booming voice he announced, "You candidates have arrived at Camp Upshur. Grab your gear and GET THE FUCK OFF THIS BUS NOW. MOVE! MOVE! MOVE!"

There was a sudden, frenetic logjam at the door. We poured out of the bus into the glare of the lights; a few even stumbled and fell. They quickly lined up my group in three files and dressed us down, each file being a squad. We were then ordered to refer to ourselves in the third person; there would be no personal reference. In order to ask a question one had to request to speak. There was no normal talking from the drill instructors (DIs). It was all yelling at us "maggot civilians and country club shit-assed college boys." We were now a candidate unit, 4th platoon, Golf Company. Then we were marched to a warehouse-type building where various personnel stations were set up. During this process I noticed a guy with golf clubs. Some of the DIs were already making remarks about what was waiting for him, sending the frat boy home to mom. Nearby was another candidate with hair down to his shoulders. This guy got some likewise remarks and mean looks. They checked our orders and medical forms. We were then shuffled to a nearby supply warehouse where we were issued a sea bag, three utility uniforms, soft covers, combat boots, shoeshine gear, thermal underwear, and sweat clothes. Then it was back out in formation, punctuated by more yelling. From there we filed into a barber shop where six civilian barbers were waiting. Each barber had a clippers—no comb or scissors. We quickly rotated in and out of the barber chairs; each haircut lasted about forty seconds. Four or five zips with the clippers and we were all shorn, Marine Corps–style. Then it was back outside.

One candidate stepped forward and made a request to call home. The DI quickly turned and shot a snarling look at him. "Call home, where you from candidate?"

"Sir, the candidate is from Minnesota, sir!"

The DI walked closer to him. "Minnesota? That's northwest of here, correct?"

"Sir, that is correct, sir!"

The DI then ordered the candidate to climb up the side of the nearest Quonset hut and position his maggot self on the roof. He was then ordered to face in a northwesterly direction maintaining his balance, placing hand to mouth and, in a loud voice, call "Home! Home!" He got to call home.

We were then marched to a Quonset hut where we piled in and picked out a locker and bunk. They ordered us to place our dopp kits on the bunks and to stand at attention. The platoon DI and sergeant instructor started at opposite ends of the hut checking our dopp kits for any kind of contraband, which included prescription drugs. Suddenly the sergeant instructor, the lanky Buck Sergeant John Harkrader, pulled two golden second-lieutenant bars out of a dopp kit. He stared at them for a moment and turned to the candidate with an angry look, "We'll just see if you get to pin these on, candidate!" When the dopp kit inspection was completed we had less than five minutes to make up our bunks—two sheets, one pillow case, and a Marine Corps blanket. It was here where I met my bunkmate, Ed Howsam, from Cincinnati.

The first thing he said after introductions was "bunkies gotta stick together." We were then ordered to strip down to our underwear, now known as skivvies, and climb into the bunks. Reveille would be at 5 A.M. No one was permitted outside of the hut unless making a "head call" in the nearby latrine. I will never forget that Quantico introduction. To this day I recall whimpers and soft crying from that night. We all pretty much felt the same way as we drifted into sleep: *What have we gotten into?*

The next day began loud, "O-Dark Thirty." At 4:55 A.M. Sergeant Harkrader lifted the lid off a garbage can and began banging it repeatedly. This was the OCS alarm clock. Within seconds we jumped to the deck and were standing tall in front of our bunks. It seemed like seconds since we went to sleep. We were ordered into utility trousers, physical training (PT) shirt, and soft cover, then out into formation and marched to a field near the mess hall. The PT exercises were exactly as Leo Tierney outlined to me months earlier: side-straddle hops, pushups, situps, squat thrusts. Then we were led to a nearby isometric area and quickly went through those exercises. That phase completed, we marched back to the Quonset hut where we were given ten minutes to "shit, shower, and shave." Anyone not back in formation in ten minutes would be written up and get demerits.

We were then marched to the mess hall for morning chow. Going through the food line I swear that I saw a buck sergeant who looked familiar. And he was, because he was a lance corporal with the *Ticonderoga* Marine Detachment back in the Philippines. It brought back a quick memory, but I never saw him again. If we didn't eat everything on our food trays we got sent to a nearby table to finish eating with a warning, "What you take you'll eat candidate!"

Back in the Quonset hut squad bay we had a quick orientation on how to wear the Marine Corps utility uniform and the blousing of boots. We also had to pin silver OC devices onto our collar lapels. We weren't cadets or midshipmen; we were lowly candidates. After stenciling our names on the backs of the utility blouse we were issued M-14 rifles, which we had to carry just about everywhere.

At the end of the first day we heard about a meltdown in one of the other platoons. A candidate collapsed in front of his bunk, curling up in a sobbing mass, pleading, "Please! Please, let me go!"

A team of corpsmen appeared and helped him into a waiting ambulance. He was never seen again. Two of the platoon candidates were ordered to inventory his gear and send it to sick bay. The attrition process had begun.

The days passed quickly. There was never enough time, even for letter-writing. My favorite military hour was 2200 (10 P.M.). It was lights out and sleep. Then we were up at reveille and into sweats for morning PT, an interval run followed by exercises that carried more brutal repartitions. The Golf Company commander, Major Vincent Vernay, patrolled the ranks with the DIs, making mental notes as to who was having a tough time. Then it was back to the hut with ten minutes to shit, shower, and shave.

This was followed by a two hour close-order drill session (COD) on the grinder where we began to march as a platoon. Some of these drill sessions called for rifles, others without. And then, at random selections, different candidates were called out to command the unit, often with comedic results. If the selected candidate didn't have a commanding voice he was quickly yelled at, ridiculed, and sent back to ranks. Another candidate would be called out. Our platoon commander, First Lieutenant John Rowe, a graduate of Texas A&M University, and Staff Sergeant Lee Parrott, the DI, were studying each of us for command presence. Like Sergeant Harkrader, Lieutenant Rowe and Staff Sergeant Parrott were Vietnam veterans, the latter two with Purple Hearts.

We marched everywhere. The afternoons were spent in class, being oriented into the Marine Corps world. We learned how to break down the M–14 rifle followed by the .45 semiautomatic pistol. And then came the hikes, starting with an initial three-mile trek with field pack, helmet, and rifle. I could have mentioned to the guys that it wasn't my first Marine Corps hike, but I kept my mouth shut, thankful that I spent the summer getting into shape while other candidates who didn't were now paying a painful price. It was during the hikes where the true OCS test came. Each hike was longer than the preceding one. And the unprepared candidates literally began falling by the wayside.

For the first five weeks we were isolated at Camp Upshur. Some of us knew of the Marine Corps training mantra: tear the man down and then build him into a Marine. There was time off on the weekends for attending to our gear, shining boots, cleaning rifles, organizing a field pack, letter-writing, and getting together at a nearby "slop shute"—a beer bar near the grinder.

My first time in the Camp Upshur slop shute I noticed framed photos with nameplates of lieutenants from both world wars and Korea. In my second visit to the slop shute I was informed that the photos were of lieutenants who were recipients of the Congressional Medal of Honor, many of them posthumously. Then I learned that the streets at Camp Upshur were named for lieutenants who were killed in action in past wars. Already I could see who the candidates were that were having a tough time adjusting.

The beer sessions helped us to get to know each other. It was here where I met Tom Dineen, from Philadelphia; Fred Williams, Sutter's Mill, California; and Rex Garvin, Waco, Texas. Jay Boswell, from Chantilly, Virginia, had done one year at the United States Naval Academy. After he left, Boswell went into the Marine Corps as enlisted. Along with several others, he qualified for Enlisted Commissioning Program (ECP). At one of the slop-shute sessions a candidate happened to mention that this was the worst experience of his life. If he had been warned about the DIs and the brutal schedule he would have joined the Air Force. Another candidate shook his head and smiled, "Hey, this is the Marine Corps. In case you haven't heard there's a war out there."

The other candidate stared at his beer mug. "I didn't expect this." And then he added, "I don't like being yelled at all the time. This place is crazy."

I remember exchanging looks with Howsam and the other candidates. I knew this unprepared candidate had the infamous two chances of making it through: slim and none. Several days later he did a "DOR"—drop on request. When one requested a DOR he went to the platoon commander's office, banged on the doorjamb, and yelled, "Sir, Candidate Smith requests permission to enter!" After entering the office the candidate would brace himself at attention and ask to DOR. Within a short period he would clean out his locker, change to civilian clothes, and wait for transportation main side, no questions asked. His medical and personnel files would be forwarded to the OCS personnel office. Then he would be taken to the train station. I often wondered what those young men who requested a DOR said to family members upon arriving home. Today their reactions would probably cover the entire spectrum.

The training continued while the ranks thinned.

There were two attrition boards: the first at the fifth week, the second at the ninth. I can still recall the reaction of those candidates who were informed that they were being called to the fifth-week board. The standard was mainly physical, being able to do the PT exercises and not falling out on the hikes. There was also grading on the written exams that came from the classes. Some of those questionable got through the fifth-week board; others didn't and were sent packing.

The first Saturday in November we said goodbye to the grinder and remote hills of Camp Upshur (now referred to as "Camp Upchuck") and were bused to main-side Quantico. They put my platoon on the second floor of a brick dormitory building next to another slop shute. Over the stairway entrance on the first floor hung a sign with the Marine Corps symbol at the top: "Gentlemen, in a military community where one is the senior and the other a junior the former should never have to remind the latter; and the latter should never forget it."

We were to retain the same bunkmates. Looking out of the squad bay window I could see the lawn sloping down to the Potomac River. On the other side were the railroad tracks. At 10 P.M. we would be in our bunks listening to "Taps" from the loud speaker system. About forty-five minutes later a train would rumble by, either heading to or coming from D.C.

We were becoming an OCS platoon, handling the schedule much better. This included marching to a better gait, keeping up on the hikes, mastering the manual of arms with rifles, and studying late at night. Knowing my difficulty with multiple-choice exams I forced myself to study harder.

At the ninth week the questionable candidates were notified who would be called in front of the final board. Several were the ones who had passed the fifth-week board. One was an ECP candidate who had received negative peer evaluations. The results came back the day before graduation. When the names were announced a few of them merely sat down on their footlockers and stared into space. One broke down in tears, his heart and dreams shattered. The ECP candidate who got negative evaluations didn't make it. But these men would remain in the Marine Corps with the enlisted rank of a lance corporal or corporal.

The second Saturday of November 1966 I found an available two-and-a-half room apartment in nearby Triangle for Patty and me while I attended TBS. I put down first month's rent and security deposit. As I was signing the papers I thought, *My God, our first apartment.* That week Jay Boswell informed me that he had seen a recent award list for the Laos crisis. On it was the Armed Forces Expeditionary Medal. Those who qualified to wear it included the officers and crew of the USS *Ticonderoga.* A quick check at the company level, where I had to produce my Defense Department form DD 214 Navy discharge, showed that I qualified for the medal.

On the morning of December 15, 1966, the 42nd Officer Candidate Class raised their hands in the main-side theater and took the oath of a Marine Corps second lieutenant. Jay Boswell was named 4th Platoon honor man. John Esslinger, a Yale graduate, was named Golf Company honor man. Again, like flagging the foremast on the *Brigantine Yankee,* it was one of those moments. Now, forty-odd years later, I still recall that moment. Outside, in the lobby, Lieutenant Rowe shook my hand. In keeping with Marine Corps tradition, I took my first salute from Staff Sergeant Parrott and handed him the traditional silver dollar, as did the other lieutenants. That morning always stayed with me. It's probably the reason why second lieutenant was my favorite officer's rank.

That afternoon we checked into Camp Barrett, Headquarters of TBS. We were no longer the 42nd Officer Candidate Class. We were now Basic Class 4–67, split into three companies: Golf, Hotel, and India. I was assigned to Hotel Company, 3rd Platoon. The next day I caught a ride with two other lieutenants, leaving Quantico for Chicago, Christmas break, and marriage.

Patty and I were married on a snow-covered Tuesday at St. Philip Neri Church on December 27, 1966, at 2 P.M. My best man and ushers were my three brothers, respectively, Mike, Dennis, and Brian. I wore the Marine Corps dress-blue uniform with the National Defense Service Medal and the Armed Forces Expeditionary Medal (Laos). Patty wore my sister Joan's wedding dress—two for the price of one. The reception was held nearby at the home of Patty's aunt and uncle, Modween and Bob Conners. We were having such a good time at the reception that we were literally "kicked out" because a second and third booze run was called for.

That night we entered a suite of rooms at the Drake Hotel overlooking Lake Shore Drive and Lake Michigan. After a short honeymoon we drove east to Triangle, Virginia, and our first apartment. Arriving on New Year's Eve I had to feel my way to the back of the complex in the dark to get the power running. Happy New Year! There was no postal delivery; we picked up our mail at the local post office. That first morning we were awakened by roosters at first light.

We toured Washington, D.C., that weekend. It was Patty's first time in the capital. She laughed upon seeing the street sign Democracy Boulevard. The following Monday classes began at TBS. It was the start of twenty-six weeks of Marine Corps officer subjects—classes mixed with field problems. The curriculum was divided into three sections: squad, platoon, and company tactics. Being a newly married second lieutenant I had a locker in a dormitory room in O'Bannon Hall with bachelor second lieutenants Dick Pipe and Carl Pock.

On one of the first Saturday nights, Patty and I accompanied Ed Howsam and his wife, Nancy, along with Kent McCargar and his wife, Linda, to dinner at the main-side Officers Club, Waller Hall. Near the office I saw another familiar face, Harry Mills, former commander of the *Ticonderoga* Marine Detachment. I approached him, now Major Mills, and related who I was and how I accompanied his detachment on the hikes in the Philippines in 1961. Major Mills shook my hand and smiled. "So you decided to become a jarhead." I nodded and he added, "Take care of your men and keep your butt down."

Before the Vietnam War intensified, the normal TBS week was five days. My class had to do a five-and-a-half-day week, including Saturday mornings. Patty and I made the most of our thirty-six-hour weekends knowing what was ahead.

It was during this time when my brother Dennis's Army training at Fort Campbell, Kentucky, was completed. His replacement detachment reported to Travis Air Force Base outside San Francisco en route to Vietnam.

The curriculum at TBS was more academic than OCS, elaborating on the military subjects of infantry tactics, leadership, land navigation, communications, and support. Some have referred to TBS as the "Marine Officer's finishing school." The days were long and so were the field exercises, many of which were at night. When those ended we had to be ready for morning formation at 7:30 A.M. The instructors were mostly decorated veterans, from captain to full colonel. That first week the commanding officer of TBS, Colonel Bevan Cass, held an orientation for the wives. He explained what their husbands would be enduring, adding that his staff was comprised of instructors and company and platoon commanders, while adjunct support would come from the wives. Colonel Cass emphasized that all elements were necessary to carry out the mission. Patty adapted very well. On the other side there were wives who had trouble adapting. This was complicated by the long hours and the fact that the husbands wore the uniform. The wives did not, even though many mixed social functions were scheduled. For example, a memo went out to the wives before one of the mixed social functions about what to wear: "hats and white gloves are appropriate." Upon reading this Patty simply smiled and "shrugged it off." Other wives took umbrage at being told what to wear. It soon became apparent as to which lieutenants were having trouble at home. One of the wives had had enough about halfway through and decamped for home. Patty looked at it philosophically, that we were at TBS for the curriculum. Then we'd be on orders to Vietnam.

Once, Patty filled in a void for the platoon wives when we had a nighttime field problem. It was scheduled for March 17, 1967. While we were in the field the wives got together at our apartment for a St. Patrick's Day party. It came off well and helped some of the wives get to know each other better.

One of the instruction packages was Technique of Military Instruction, which prepared officers to present classes and briefings in a military format. We were split into sections. I chose Tank-Infantry Coordination because of the teamwork element. It took some research, and Patty drew, freehand, a poster of a tank with a bikini-clad beauty sitting on the turret. It quickly got everyone's attention.

One of the presentations was in military history, a capsule biography of Confederate General Robert E. Lee. The lieutenant, who hailed from Alabama as I recall, had several teaching aids, a photo of Lee in his uniform, and several lithographs of the general on his horse, Traveller, with his staff at various battle sites where he defeated a succession of Union generals. The lieutenant mentioned that Lee was the first choice of the Federal War Department to command the Union Army but chose to remain loyal to Virginia. He also peppered his presentation with quotes from the noted historian Douglas Southall Freeman, adding that, "Lee was a proven tactical genius." I remember that my head kinked to one side upon hearing the genius observation. Upon conclusion the lieutenant fielded questions. After the third or fourth question I jumped in. "You stated that Lee was a 'proven tactical genius.'"

The lieutenant nodded. "That's pretty well documented when you put his record up against the Union generals."

I paused and said, "He was a great leader and very decisive but I don't think he qualifies as a tactical genius."

The lieutenant shook his head, "We part company there."

"We're talking about the man who went against General Longstreet's advice and ordered Pickett's charge into the center of Cemetery Ridge at Gettysburg," I explained. "Some historians contend that this is what lost the battle . . . along with the heart of the Confederacy."

I expected him to counter me. Instead he growled, "I've had it with you Yankees, slamming this great man!"

The captain instructor quickly jumped in. "We haven't got the time for a Civil War debate here. Thank you, lieutenant." The lieutenant gathered his teaching aids and moved to his seat, but not before he gave me a parting glare. That afternoon was a lesson for me—of how some men my age were brought up in the South, reflecting thoughts from a bygone era that had not totally gone by. What surprised me was that he used the word "Yankee" instead of "northerner."

It was during this period when I first began to experience my VC nightmare, the four guerrillas with AK-47s at high port chasing me through the Jackson Park Golf Course. It was always the same. No matter where I ran or hid they knew where I was and kept coming. Each time Patty would wake me after my moans got louder. And then I would have to change T-shirts. This was something that I would have to live with.

The leadership aspect of the curriculum included a weeklong legal course emphasizing military investigations and the three levels of courts-martial: summary, special, and general. As I took notes during the law classes I never envisioned that I would one day be prosecuting special court-martial cases on the battalion level even though I was not a law school graduate.

We were oriented to the drug problem in Vietnam, particularly with Marines on patrol and convoy duty. Several of the instructors used personal anecdotes, giving stark realism to ongoing leadership problems that they faced. I found myself wondering what sort of leadership problems I would have. Naturally I assumed that they would stem from the Marines under my command. I had no idea that when the time came the biggest leadership problem would be coming from my company commander.

One day Patty returned from the Triangle post office with a letter from my mother. Mom had a proposal for me. My uncle, Michael Howlett, who was currently the auditor for the State of Illinois (State Controller), was friends with a Marine Corps lieutenant colonel. The lieutenant colonel happened to be the commander of the Naval ROTC unit at the University of Mississippi in Oxford. The commander's assistant, a lieutenant, had received orders overseas. A replacement was needed. According to mom, my Uncle Mike could have the colonel request me after I completed TBS. This carried the safeguard that I would spend a good portion of my Marine Corps tour as an instructor in an ROTC unit. Mom had a point. She already had a son in Vietnam. Would there be two? I recalled the five Sullivan brothers from Waterloo, Iowa, who were lost on the USS *Juneau* during the Guadalcanal campaign in World War II. After the loss of the Sullivan brothers the War Department adopted the Sole Survivor Policy. However, this did not pertain to our family because there were two other sons, Mike and Brian.

I gave my Uncle Mike's offer much thought, particularly in light of the recurring nightmare. And I also thought of the hawkish Loyola student who took the handball offramp. Would I use a political connection to avoid going into a combat zone?

I set her letter aside for a day or two, thinking about the proposal. Patty and I talked about it that night and the next afternoon. Then I sat down and wrote mom a reply:

> . . . *I can understand how you feel about having two sons*
> *overseas, especially in Vietnam. It is a nice advantage*
> *having someone in a high place who can reach down and help*
> *you. About 98% of the guys in my class don't have that advantage. They have to go*
>   *where the Marine*
> *Corps orders them. And for almost all of us, it will*
> *eventually be Vietnam. Last week, we had to fill out*
> *forms as to where we would want to be stationed. They*
> *only give you three choices: overseas, east coast & west*
> *coast. So it really doesn't make much difference what*
> *you put down.*

Mom, I could tell you to go ahead & let this colonel,
whatever-his-name-is, request me, but I really doubt
if I would like it. The true test of a Marine officer is
whether or not he can efficiently command a unit in
combat . . . [John F.] Kennedy once said that only a
selected portion of every other generation is granted
the role of defending freedom in its maximum hour of
danger . . . I picked this life knowing all consequences
involved. Patty is well aware of this also. It just wouldn't
be right—to take the easy way out at this time. That war
won't last forever.
. . . Please don't be upset. Just try to look at it from what I
said and how I feel. I could get a nice comfortable duty
assignment, maybe even leave the Marine Corps after my
3 year tour is up, get a safe and secure job with a big
company, spend the rest of my life going downtown to the
office—and never really knowing for sure what it would
have been like and how I would have conducted myself.
When it comes time for me to pass on, the question would
still remain unanswered.
Write and tell me how you feel now. I'll tell you something
—I am a little scared of what is in the future—but I feel I would
be running away. You wouldn't want me to do that, would you?

I gave the letter another read. Then I sent it off. I had no idea that my mother would keep it, with other letters, the rest of her life.

The bulletin board at O'Bannon Hall was constantly pinned with letters from lieutenants in Vietnam describing a small-unit war mixed with battalion-size sweep-and-clear operations—patrolling through villages and hamlets—as well as the marijuana problem. These missives also included sad notes on lieutenants who had been wounded or killed. They carried the daily, grim reminders not only of where we were going but also what we would be facing.

Living for the moment, Patty and I scheduled every other weekend for a mini-vacation at the many historic and tourist venues. Among these were Williamsburg, the Luray Caverns, and several Civil War battlefields. As we walked across the field at Fredericksburg, toward the wall at Mayre's Heights, I wondered what it must have been like for Union officers to receive orders from General Ambrose Burnside's headquarters during those December days in 1862. The Union regiments made a series of assaults on the Confederate entrenchments at the heights. Each time they were repulsed with more casualties. Yet Burnside continued ordering the attacks until he finally realized the futility. After the battle General Robert E. Lee wrote, "It is well that war is so terrible—otherwise we would grow too fond of it."

One of the more difficult field exercises was the amphibious landing at Little Creek, Virginia. From Quantico we were bused, with field packs, helmets, and rifles, to the Naval Amphibious Base, where our company lined up on the quay wall and boarded the USS *Chilton*, a troop transport that saw service during World War II and later the Bay of Pigs and Cuban Missile Crisis. The accommodations were lean, which is why it was dubbed the "Chilton Hilton." The bunks in the living spaces were stacked four high. We had to hang our packs, helmets, and rifles on the chains alongside the bunks. The mess hall was lined with counters because we had to eat standing up. One look and I longed for the *Ticonderoga* and we hadn't even put out to sea.

It's true that the Marine Corps established itself as an amphibious force. And it's also true that many of them don't like the rolling sea. By the next morning the stench from the vomit drifted in from the heads. By now we were issued kapok lifejackets. I studied mine, thinking how this piece of equipment saved my father's life during the Leyte invasion.

As we were checking our equipment a warning came over the ship's 1MC (the main loudspeaker), "Now hear this, now hear this, landing force stand by!" This gave us time to get our packs on and turn our backs so that the other guy could take care of any needed adjustment. And then it was reversed.

The 1MC squawked again. "Now hear this, landing force report to debarkation stations, landing force report to debarkation stations."

We headed out in files, into the passageway and up the ladder to the weather deck. Once topside we went to the assigned debarkation station. Hitting the sea air we got strong whiffs of diesel fumes coming from the Higgins boats below. The cargo nets had already been dropped over the side. Here we were ordered to unbuckle the chinstraps on our helmets, a safety precaution. Another announcement came, "Landing force, stand by to go over the side."

As we were waiting one of the guys turned and remarked, "Did John Wayne actually do something like this?"

"Only in the movies," quipped someone else.

"Now hear this, landing force man the cargo nets!"

Then some wise guy quipped, "Now hear this, there will be no movies tonight!"

Four and five at a time, laden with packs, rifles, and the bulky kapok lifejackets, we stepped up to the railing on blocks, threw a right leg over the side, got a footing on the first rung of the cargo net, and came back with the left leg. We went downward, rung by rung, to a waiting Higgins boat (or Landing Craft Vehicle Personnel) that was bobbing up and down. I remember pausing, waiting for the boat to rise back up. Then I let go of the cargo net and dropped into the well deck. As soon as the Higgins boat was filled the coxswain signaled someone on the ship and we headed out to the ready circles. The ready circles were where Mother Nature came to bear another curse—the combined rolling and bobbing mixed with diesel fumes. We couldn't see out over the side to view what was going on. The Higgins boats, back alongside the ship, were still filling up.

In our Higgins boat we started emptying our stomachs. I remember a guy near me moving aside, bending over, and letting his breakfast go. And that's all that was needed. The bobbing and weaving mixed with the fuel stench spread faster than a quick wind. A second, third, and fourth were bent over as the well deck received more than one regurgitated breakfast.

Al Loane, standing next to me, said, "Mac, help me up over the side. I'm gonna lose it." Two of us got under Al and boosted him up over the gunwale. He was able to get his head over the top before everything came up. When we got him back into the well deck I noticed several other guys doing the same thing. We all felt the same way: *Get us to the Goddamn beach and drop the fucking ramp!*

It was almost another half-hour before the coxswain got the signal to break from our ready circle and approach the departure line. All this time we remained herded in that well deck with the platoon's vomit sloshing back and forth over our boots. I found myself thanking Divine Providence for my time on the *Ticonderoga* and the *Yankee*.

The coxswain then yelled, "Approaching departure line!" The departure line is a designated mark in the water anywhere between 500 and 1,000 yards offshore. It is where the landing force crosses friendly waters into those of the enemy.

The coxswain then called out, "Line of departure crossed!" The diesel engine revved up as we made our run to the beach.

Our platoon commander, Captain Michael Downey, ordered, "Load and lock!"

"One minute to the beach!" yelled the coxswain.

We all pulled back on the bolts of our M–14s and rammed them home, causing a loud series of clicks. Then we got into a crouch position for a start once the ramp went down. "Thirty seconds!" yelled the coxswain.

The boat came to a halt. Then came a lurch as it went forward. The engine revved up higher and the sound of a cable passed our ears. Then the ramp went down. We all rose at the same time, moving forward down the ramp and into the water. I remember skidding down the ramp and jumping into the water. I thought it would be ankle-deep; it went up to my knees. Like the guys next to me I sloshed through the water onto the sand and up to a berm line. Here, I got rid of the kapok lifejacket. I looked up and down the beach watching more Higgins boats unload. I thought of the World War II film *The Longest Day*, where American forces stormed out of the Higgins boats onto the beaches of Omaha and Utah. And I read later that those extras, U.S. Marines all, were just as seasick.

As TBS graduation neared, Patty and I came to treasure those short weekends. And after the Military Occupation Specialty Schools we would be going over, first to Okinawa and then down south.

During the convoy-tactics phase of the Motor Transport Orientation Course at Montford Point, North Carolina, I waited for Patty to turn in one night. Then I sat down and wrote a longhand letter to her, outlining what to do in the event of my death and to allow the Marine Corps to handle the arrangements. I sealed the letter and later gave it to her mother, Joan. To Joan, I added that if I survived to destroy the letter.

4

Danang, RVN

March 1968. When I awoke the next morning at Camp Hansen I was in a different frame of mind after reliving what brought me to this point. Seeing those names on the corkboard at the Officers Club caused an epiphany. What helped me get over the shocking realization was accepting the fact that death was now part of the contract. Looking back I feel that nothing can prepare one for the reality of this. I was embarking on the most dramatic experience of my life. I had to accept that it was my doing from the start, my curious sense of adventure.

The flight from Okinawa to Danang was much like the bus ride to Camp Upshur—a strange silence with each Marine in his own thoughts. Most of the passengers on the Continental Airlines 707 were enlisted men and company-grade officers, captains, and lieutenants. I did notice a lieutenant colonel sitting forward. He was like the rest of us, in his own thoughts right up to when we went into the landing pattern at the 15th Aerial Port, the name for the air base at Danang.

While the plane was doing a taxi to the debarkation point the pilot keyed the intercom. "We have arrived safely in Danang. And we hope you have enjoyed the flight." There was a pause as I looked at the sergeant next to me. And then the pilot added, "Good luck and godspeed." It was March 9, 1968; the Tet Offensive's aftermath was still in play.

The sergeant said, "This is my second tour and it's the first time anyone hoped that I enjoyed the flight." When the door opened we were hit with a strong wash of tropical humidity. The cabin's air-conditioning system suddenly shut down.

Welcome to the jungle, I thought.

Slowly we filed out of the plane through the forward door. A flight attendant, we were told, dashed into one of the lavatories and locked herself inside.

The flight attendants were volunteers and received extra pay for being on the Vietnam run. This was her first flight; I had something in common with her.

When we got down the steps there was a nearby group of Marines. Each one had that jungle look, the tanned, weatherbeaten face, the bush hats, some men with curled gunfighter mustaches, others with sunglasses, worn and faded utilities and boots. They had survived and were waiting to take our 707 "back to the world."

Then some bright agent in this group raised a bugle to his lips. He began blowing a variation of Chopin's Funeral March, "*dum dum de dum dum de dum dum de dum . . . .*" He then went into a reprise. We stood there as notes came forth. When that ended several of them chanted, "You'll be sorrrry!" Welcome to the war.

I followed the rest of my group to the baggage area where we waited for our sea bags. At the waiting area I saw one of the lieutenants from my Montford Point Motor Transport class, Tom Igoe. He was sitting on a bench furiously writing a letter. I approached him and said hello. He nodded and kept writing. "I'm headed to First Marine Division Headquarters," I said. "How about you?"

He stopped writing for a moment and looked up. I could see white fear in his eyes. "I've been attached to the Twenty-Sixth Marines up in Khe Sanh. I'm waiting for a C–123 right now. Got to get a letter off."

We were both aware that, the day before, a C–130 transport crashed coming into the Khe Sanh airstrip, killing almost everyone onboard. "Good luck, guy," I said.

From the 15th Aerial Port several of us lieutenants and the lieutenant colonel were transported to the First Marine Division Headquarters, a series of huts with corrugated tin roofs built by Seabees (the Navy's construction battalion). The headquarters complex was set into a hillside overlooking an expanse of rice paddies. In front of the headquarters was a helipad. Next to the helipad was the headquarters of the 1st Force Reconnaissance Battalion, the so-called eyes and ears of the division.

The commander of the First Marine Division at this time was Major General Donn J. Robertson, a Navy Cross recipient from Iwo Jima. Within a short period we were in an air-conditioned conference room listening to General Robertson's chief of staff give an orientation. He explained that our tours would be thirteen months, one month more than in the Army. The lieutenant colonel was going to a staff position at the headquarters. Two of the lieutenants would be going to infantry battalions, one to an engineer battalion; I was the only one assigned to a motor transport battalion. The chief of staff added that the recent Battle of Hue City brought out how important motor transport support had become, that the "Rough Rider" resupply convoys were the lifeblood of the division. He concluded, explaining that somewhere in our tour we would be granted a six-day Rest and Recuperation (R&R) period, something that was unheard of in Korea and World War II. The chief of staff wished us good luck. The meeting ended. Back outside I was approached by a Lieutenant Mike Robinson from the 11th Motor Transport Battalion. He had a jeep waiting. On the short ride north to 11th Motors he explained that the battalion was in a fairly safe area but occasionally a rocket and mortar attack put everyone on full alert. He looked at me with a smile, "The pucker factor time comes with the convoys, particularly the ones through the Hai Van Pass. It's the only road north to Phu Bai and Hue."

"I remember seeing it on a map," I recalled.

"As we were taught in tactics classes, terrain dictates," he said. "Some people feel that Tet isn't over. They ambush us, we plow through, and they break contact. Until the next ambush." He paused and added, "It gets hairy." We rode the rest of the way in silence.

We took a left off the division road and headed west through the village of Khon Son. A line of villagers carrying bundles of wood, hanging from poles balanced on their shoulders, was coming from the mountains back to the village. After passing through the village we made a quick right turn into the battalion compound that would be my new home. At the gate of the battalion was a wooden red shield. Across the top was 11TH MOTOR TRANSPORT BATTALION. Curved around the bottom of the shield was THE ROLLING 11TH. In the middle was a pair of dice that showed six on the first, five on the second. (The dice represented the number of the battalion while the word "Rolling" was a metaphor for the convoys.)

I reported in to the battalion adjutant, First Lieutenant Harry Grunwald, a former gunnery sergeant a "mustang" up from the ranks. Grunwald took my orders and gave my officer's qualification record (OQR) a quick read, noting that I had done two years' active duty aboard the *Ticonderoga*. When Grunwald took me into the S-3 operations hooch I was suddenly forced to stand aside. A Rough Rider convoy, returning from Phu Bai through the Hai Van Pass, was reporting a KIA—someone killed in action. First reports indicated that a truck went into a hairpin turn too fast and careened off the road and down a steep incline. Listening to the radio transmissions I heard that the casualty was from Transport Company.

It took about twenty minutes for things to calm down. Next was meeting the battalion commander. His office hooch was two down from the S-1 personnel office. This was Lieutenant Colonel Sherman Arnold, a Korean War veteran, in his early forties and a tad overweight for a Marine field-grade officer. After introductions Colonel Arnold offered me a chair and began giving my OQR a quick scan. "So, you graduated from Loyola University." I nodded. "Do you go to church?"

"I was raised Catholic," I said.

"No doubt, but my question is do you go to church?"

"Yes, I do colonel," I answered.

"That's fine, lieutenant. I distrust people who don't go to church." Colonel Arnold then explained how the battalion psychological operations section was building a school in Khon Son. He shook his head. "I don't know what will come of these people. They were here before us and will be here after we're gone. Still, I think they're the most childish people I've ever seen."

"I'm sorry, colonel," I said. "Childish?"

"Yes, they have little regard for human life. I couldn't figure it out at first. Then I realized that they're just different from us."

"Maybe, colonel, that they feel the same about us." I was surprised at my offhanded remark.

"Possibly." He thumbed through more pages in the OQR. "So you were a Navy corpsman."

"Yes, sir, two years on the *Ticonderoga*, with a cruise in the South China Sea," I added.

He nodded, then closed the OQR. "You're going to Transport Company as a platoon commander. It's a heavy truck company. The other companies, Alpha, Bravo, and Charlie, are tasked with the smaller six-bys. We rotate the convoys as the orders come down from division." I nodded, listening intently. "During Tet our convoys went through a series of ambushes getting cargo and supplies through the Hai Van Pass. Often when we request air or artillery support we don't get it right away because the infantry has priority."

"The chief of staff mentioned that the Rough Rider convoys are the life-blood of the division," I said.

Lieutenant Colonel Arnold nodded. "There's a price to that. Last month we lost a lieutenant and his radio jeep driver."

"What happened?" I asked.

"They drove over a box mine on the way down to Hoi An. The only things left were feet in the boots," said Lieutenant Colonel Arnold with a grim expression. "The week before the lieutenant's wife gave birth to twins." He shook his head.

"How soon will I be going on convoys?" I asked.

"That's up to your company commander," replied Lieutenant Colonel Arnold. "Rest assured it will be soon. We work seven days a week. Fifteen- and sixteen-hour days are normal." He stood, signifying the end of the meeting.

At Transport Company I met First Sergeant Roy Duncan, known as "Top," who supervised the office clerks. I gave him a copy of my orders. A short while later I was introduced to the company commander, First Lieutenant Bob Gordon. His number-two, the executive officer (XO), was First Lieutenant John Parker. I sat down with both of them in the company commander's office cubicle. "You'll take a day or two to orient yourself then you'll go on a convoy as an observer in the back of my command jeep. Then we'll start you as a trail officer, keeping the tail end in shape." Gordon paused looking at Parker. "With a couple of convoys under your belt, you'll be given a convoy command."

"Is it just north to Phu Bai and Hue?" I asked.

Parker shook his head. "We go where division sends us, out in the valley, south to Hoi An and Chu Lai. The order usually comes down in the afternoon for the next day's convoy. It gives us time for a convoy briefing that night."

"What about convoy security?" I asked, recalling classes in convoy tactics back at Quantico and Montford Point.

"Usually a platoon of infantry," replied Parker. "They spread out the squads at pace, command, and trail." (A platoon has three squads. The first squad would be placed one or two vehicles behind the pace. The second squad would be placed about halfway back. The third squad would be on one of the rear trucks, in front of the trail jeep.)

"We're a lot like the Eighth Air Force in England during World War II," explained Gordon. "We have a nice compound here compared to the infantry battalions, a staff-officers club, a theater for movies, and USO shows. But when we go on the road we're bare-assed and rolling." Gordon paused looking at Parker. "You'll see your share here. Tet's not over yet."

"I've already heard that," I said.

"So far it's been a quiet month," observed Parker.

"John, don't say that!" snapped Gordon. In a combat zone one tends to get superstitious.

Later, I was assigned a cubicle in a hooch with several other lieutenants. Captains and above had their individual hooches nearby. Our hooches were constructed by Marine combat engineers and Navy Seabees. They were built several feet off the ground with step-ups. This was a common technique, countering the seasonal monsoonal rain that would wash the angled earth downhill. The hooches came with wooden floors and corrugated tin on the sides and the pitched roofs. The lighting was tropical primitive: a cord running down the center with light bulbs set at various points. Many of the bunks came with mosquito netting. For the junior officers—second and first lieutenants—there were four and five to a hooch. Each lieutenant had a locker with a light bulb to ward off the humidity. The latrines were standard wooden "four-holers" that emptied into cut-down 55-gallon drums filled with diesel fuel that got burned off every other day. For straight urination the field expedient here was a cut-down artillery shell that emptied into a hole that contained rocks and crushed beer cans, better known as a "piss tube."

I turned in my medical record at sick bay, the battalion aid station. It was here where I met "Doc" Poppell, a Navy third-class corpsman. The first thing he told me was how to take the malaria pill. Poppell explained not to take this horse pill all at once, to cut it into quarters and take it over a four-day period. "Why is that?" I asked.

Poppell grinned. "If you take it all at once it'll play havoc with your insides. You'll get the dribbly shits." It was a good piece of jungle advice.

I returned to my hooch and quickly dashed off two letters, one to Patty back in Oceanside and the other to my parents in Chicago. The following morning I met my platoon sergeant, John Woodard, who gave off a likeable first impression. Then I received my first assignment as a platoon commander: inventory the personal effects of Sergeant Edward Krasny, who was killed during the previous day's convoy. It was a strange morning, itemizing the personal effects of a man I never met who was alive the previous morning. Lieutenant Parker returned from Graves Registration over at the Naval Support Activity (NSA) facility, where he had to identify the body. When Sergeant John Woodard and I were finishing the inventory Lieutenant Gordon came in. "We have a convoy to Phu Bai tomorrow."

Sergeant Woodard stood. "How many vehicles, skipper?"

"Anywhere between forty to sixty," said Gordon. "Get down to the motor pool and make sure that the X-Ray jeep has new tires."

Sergeant Woodard left, and I closed out Sergeant Krasny's inventory. Then I asked Gordon, "What's an X-Ray jeep?"

"An M-38 jeep with a flattened windshield and a specially mounted M-60 machine gun. The X-Ray is the ramrod of the convoy, keeping the vehicles in line and closing the gaps," explained Gordon. "Without an X-Ray jeep the convoy would be a clusterfuck. You'll meet Sergeant Thomas, the X-Ray driver. He marched out of the Chosin Reservoir with Chesty Puller's regiment, an old Gyrene salt."

In the motor pool that afternoon I met the ramrod, Staff Sergeant Donald Thomas, who had a slight frame and a weathered face. Sergeant Thomas and Sergeant Woodard then coordinated the preparation for the next day's convoy.

The first vehicle was a sandbagged six-by truck with heavy armor plating along the undercarriage, a protection against road mines. The truck also had a ring mount for a .50-caliber machine gun allowing it to swing 360 degrees to any target. Next came the security trucks that would carry the infantry platoon.

That night Gordon gave a convoy briefing in the staff conference room to the drivers and infantry security. Gordon went through the convoy commander's checklist, which included current area intelligence, the route, air cover, convoy speed, and checkpoints. This convoy would be approximately forty-four vehicles from various units. Parker would be riding in the trail jeep. I would be in Gordon's command jeep as an observer. That night at the staff-officers club Gordon advised me to listen to the radio traffic as the checkpoints were called into division convoy control (DCC). There were also pre-set artillery targets along the road in areas where there was reported enemy activity. These targets changed frequently depending upon the G–2 intelligence reports.

Gordon, Parker, and I met in the mess hall the next morning. It was here where I noticed another jungle field expedient: rice sprinkled in the tops of the saltshakers, another humidity prevention. Afterward I was issued helmet, flak jacket, and a .45-caliber sidearm.

The infantry platoon was already down in the motor pool getting their truck assignments. After breakfast I went with Gordon to Lieutenant Colonel Arnold's office to check the latest intelligence reports. These reports, classified as secret, were carbon copies issued to the support battalions. On this morning enemy activity in the Hai Van Pass and along the road to Phu Bai was negative. "It means that recon didn't see anything yesterday or last night," said Gordon, thumbing through the copies. "I read reports like this on a convoy last month. When we got through the pass all hell opened up on us."

"How bad was it?" I asked.

"The helicopter pilot, Cowpoke, told me that I had about forty people moving along a ridge line above the Bowling Alley [an old rail line; see below]. He made a gun run parallel to us." Gordon replaced the clipboard. "Saved our butts." Now I knew what he meant by being bare-assed and rolling.

In the motor pool Gordon began the commander's preconvoy routine, checking out the pace truck and the ring-mounted .50-caliber machine gun. Then he had the pace and trail people go through radio checks with Defend—the call sign for DCC. He then coordinated with the infantry commander, a lieutenant, whose platoon was providing security. The infantry squads were strategically placed at intervals. I was told that the infantry liked convoy duty; it gave them a break from humping through valleys and rice paddies—that is, until they found themselves in a road ambush.

In short order we left the battalion compound under the throttling noise of jeep and truck engines. Lieutenant Colonel Arnold and Major Claude Brauer, the executive/operations officer, were observing the column as it passed through the gate. That first convoy reminded me of one of John Ford's cavalry films in which the troops ride out of the fort to a rousing chorus. No such pomp and circumstance here: All we had were loud engines and caustic diesel fumes belching from the exhausts into the tropical morning air.

In the jeep I noticed that Gordon had his rifle wrapped in a white cloth tied with a string. He took the weapon out, and I was looking at a Kalashnikov AK-47 with a banana clip. "What are you carrying that for?" I asked.

Gordon smiled. "It's a better weapon than the M-16. Only problem is when I fire it guys turn their heads at the sound thinking that the NVA [North Vietnamese Army] is behind them. It can get hairy."

When we arrived at Red Beach we pulled over to the shoulder. This was the same beach where, in 1965, I watched on television as units from the 9th MEB came ashore. And now it was a staging area for Rough Rider convoys. Here the convoy picked up the added vehicles and a few Seabee trucks that would join us for protection on the fifty-nine-mile trek. We had to wait for a green light while the combat engineers swept the road to see if any mines, or other explosive devices, were planted during the night. I followed Gordon around as he made last-minute checks. And then several Regional Force (RF) vehicles suddenly appeared as add-ons. The Regional Forces were local militia units organized to defend certain regions against VC cadres with castoff World War II weapons.

Gordon quickly conferred with Parker to have the RF jeeps and trucks placed at the very end. "Just make sure that they stay at the end, all the way to Phu Bai." Parker nodded and we headed back to the command jeep.

"Why do you want them at the end?" I asked.

"Because if we step into some shit they'll jump out of their vehicles and . . . *de-de mau*," said Gordon. (*De-de mau* is Vietnamese slang for leaving or running out.) "I've had them jump out, leaving the engines running, blocking the road."

"Then why even place them in the convoy line?" I asked.

"Because we're allies and if we don't they'll raise hell with division." He smiled. "Welcome to the war."

As we waited for the engineers to clear the road Vietnamese vendors began hawking their wares up and down the convoy line. They were selling everything from makeshift Confederate flags to black-market Coca-Colas. Several of the troops mocked the Confederate flags that had six-pointed stars instead of the original five-pointed symbols. Occasionally a trooper would buy something, using either military payment certificates (MPCs) or Vietnamese piasters. The convoy line had become a marketplace.

About an hour later DCC was notified that the road sweep was complete; we had a green light to checkpoint three-eight: Phu Bai. Gordon keyed his radio handset, "Pace, this is Transport six. We have a green light. Let's go north." After the pace truck acknowledged, the engines up and down the line fired up. Slowly the front vehicles of the convoy began to leave the shoulder of the road, get into line, and move out, heading up into the Hai Van Pass. It was at this point when the infantry security troops began inserting magazines into their M–16s and pulling back on the bolts to chamber the first round. I was on my first Rough Rider convoy through the most dangerous mountain passage in Vietnam.

The word "dangerous" was first applied to the Hai Van Pass by a Vietnamese poet, Nguyen Phuc Chu, in the eighteenth century. Like most poets, he knew about what he was writing. I later learned that the pass was part of the Annamite Mountain Range that divided two ancient kingdoms.

It was written long ago that "in beauty there is treachery." As we headed toward the peak of the pass I could see where nature gave a willing nod to that observation. The unpaved road twisted with treacherous hairpin turns and switchbacks going one direction then abruptly reversing to another. As we climbed higher the inclines got steeper. It was easy to envision the tractor-trailer that Sergeant Krasny was driving, going off the road and plummeting hundreds of feet to rest in a tangled and twisted mess. Officially the speed through the pass was listed at 10 miles per hour. But this often changed when a gap occurred in the convoy line. And no driver wanted to be caught in a gap, especially in the Hai Van Pass. As I studied the terrain on both sides it was apparent that a small guerrilla squad, less than ten soldiers, could spring a devastating ambush with only small arms, bringing a convoy our size to a destructive halt. It's the old maxim: terrain dictates.

Just before we reached the top of the pass I looked off to my right. I found myself looking down on one of the most beautiful beaches that I ever saw or have seen since. It was a white crescent of sand set into a natural cove looking out on the Bay of Danang, which went into the South China Sea. Suddenly I was realizing that Vietnam was a naturally beautiful country. And in the middle of that natural beauty a vicious jungle war was being fought, death coming daily to both sides. *After all this is done,* I thought, *there's probably going to be a Hilton or Marriott beach resort down on that crescent-shaped beach.* An abandoned rail line ran north out of Danang, snaking along the coast through a tunnel, underneath the pass, and out again, heading north by way of a straight line called the "Bowling Alley" to Phu Bai and Hue.

At the top of the pass, checkpoint two-seven, several brick structures stood guard, two and three stories high. These were built by the French forces during the Viet Minh days. There was a Combined Action Platoon (CAP) and a Marine communications relay team here. A CAP consisted of U.S. Marines and troops of the Army of the Republic of South Vietnam (ARVN). Near the old French fort was a vendor shack that offered various items plus "33"-brand local beer and barbecued dog meat on wooden skewers. A Vespa motor scooter was sitting in front of the vendor shack. The top of the pass also served as a province divider, much like U.S. state lines, going from Quang Nam to Thua Thien.

On the north side of the pass there was a hairpin turn followed by another switchback. Coming down on the north side revealed a commanding view of the picturesque seaside villages of Loc Hai and Lang Co. It reminded me of something out of the World War II musical *South Pacific*. Sergeant Thomas's X-Ray jeep moved up and back getting vehicles to close gaps, moving through the thick road dust.

I monitored the radio traffic that Gordon conducted within the convoy vehicles and back with DCC in Danang. Once the convoy cleared the top of the pass the relay station, Defend Alpha, handled the radio traffic going into Phu Bai. The remainder of the trip was uneventful, with Gordon calling in the checkpoints. The convoy terminated at the end of the Phu Bai airstrip. Here the vehicles were cut loose. But the convoy control vehicles, the pace, the trail, the wrecker (tow truck), and infantry security, circled together, staging for the return the next morning.

That night, as we dined on C-rations, Sergeant Thomas pulled up in his X-Ray jeep with a case of beer. I found out later that Gordon slipped him some MPCs to make a quick run to the nearby 1st Medical Battalion Staff/Officers club. As night fell we sat around drinking, talking about the convoy and what to expect in the morning. Parker pointed out slit trenches near the end of the airstrip in case of a rocket or mortar attack.

Later I blew up a "rubber lady" air mattress and stretched out under a truck. My sleep was interspersed with air traffic coming in and leaving the airstrip. In the distance I could hear small-arms fire. I went into sleep thinking of the panoramic views from the Hai Van Pass. It was an hour or two later when it came in.

WHUMP! WHUMP! WHUMP! And then someone yelled, "Incoming! Incoming!"

I was off the rubber lady in an instant, awkwardly trying to get into my boots as people ran past. I grabbed what I could—boots, flak jacket, and helmet—and ran in my stocking feet to the slit trench as the bombardment increased. A siren wailed from somewhere. In the slit trench I got into my flak jacket and quickly put on my boots. The sound of the explosions got louder as the ground shook. *Blam! Blam! Blam!* Someone up the line said that they were trying to hit the airstrip with rockets.

And then came the dreaded call, "Corpsman! Corpsman!"

It ended as quickly as it began. But we stayed in the slit trenches until the all-clear siren. As I walked back to my rubber lady, Gordon and Parker appeared, making a check. The wounded Marine was not from among our people. He got hit in the legs and arms with shrapnel while running to the slit trench.

"You look okay," commented Gordon. He smiled. "You've been baptized."

"Not bad, not bad," I said, realizing it was my first time. And, like any first time, I would always remember it. I would also remember not to take off my boots in a situation like this. "Get used to it. Happens a lot up here. I'm a short-timer and I still can't take this shit. Goddamn rockets!" Gordon shook his head and walked off.

I went back to the rubber lady and slid under the truck. About an hour later rain came in, light at first and then with a slashing force. I tolerated it the best I could, until my rubber lady—with me aboard—floated out from under the truck. Again, welcome to the war. Not much sleep after that.

The next morning I found out from where the nighttime small-arms fire came. Intelligence reported that a bridge security team from a CAP unit came under fire near Phu Loc just before we got hit. It was an NVA unit making an attempt to rush the bridge and blow it with satchel charges. They were beaten back before they got to the bridge, taking many casualties.

For the return convoy I rode in the pace truck. As we headed south the convoy approached the bridge that came under attack the night before. It was here where I saw my first enemy body. But it wasn't an NVA soldier. It was a Chinese adviser who was with the NVA unit. His body was now a trophy, hung up by the ankles, wearing sky blue pajamas dotted with blood, arms dangling at his side. He looked well over six feet tall with a good portion of the right temporal region of his head blown away. It reminded me of the press photos of what the Italian partisans did to Mussolini's body after he was executed in 1945.

At 11th Motors we were greeted with the news from Armed Forces (Radio) Vietnam Network (AFVN) that Senator Eugene McCarthy of Minnesota won 42 percent of the votes in New Hampshire's Democratic primary. The next day I was named to lead an observation-post (OP) patrol overnight on Hill 364 behind our compound. Hill 364 commanded a wide, unobstructed view of the valley below. Periodically, at night, enemy movements would be detected and called in to the battalion. Battalion would then report the movement to division, emphasizing size, direction, weapons, and time of the sighting. Nothing more was required from an OP. Hence, it was an expendable position. I was assigned a fire team and a radioman (five Marines) with a PRC–25 radio. We each took a box of C-rations for the night's meal. Just before twilight we assembled near the communications hooch, where I introduced myself and explained the mission. A corporal from the personnel office, who had been on previous OPs, would be the guide.

According to the corporal it was a nice break from his daily routine. He added that "it's boring up there, nothing happens." I didn't like hearing that. My combat superstitious syndrome had already taken hold from the Phu Bai mortar attack. We adjusted our gear and headed out with the corporal walking point. I had the radioman give a test transmission and told him to stay right behind me. Often, on patrols, a sniper will stalk a patrol and wait for the unit to halt either for a map check or to call in a checkpoint. When the patrol leader takes the handset the sniper then knows who is in command and takes his shot accordingly. The next shot is at the radioman; sometimes it's vice versa.

The footpath up the hill had been carved out with machetes. It was thick undergrowth, which I was glad to see. It meant a terrain obstacle for any enemy coming up the hill. The climb up the incline was challenging. I was glad that I was in shape. And, as the officer in charge, I had to show that I could keep up. The footpath twisted back and forth as we continued trudging uphill with gear on our backs and M-16s slung on the shoulders.

Finally, as evening shadows set in, we broke through the brush and emerged at the topographical crest of Hill 364. It was a spectacular sunset view. There was a heavily sandbagged bunker nearby. The radioman and I climbed to the roof of the bunker and I called in our arrival. I put the fire team on 50 percent alert. Each fighting hole commanded a field of fire to cover our front facing the slope and valley floor. A band of concertina barbed wire was stretched across the front, approximately forty yards, just out of hand-grenade range. There were beer cans hung at strategic points on the barbed wire. Inside the cans were stones. If anyone made an attempt to cut through the wire the cans would give off a noise similar to a baby's rattle. It was a time-tested field expedient.

With the fire team set in the radioman and I returned to the bunker roof. I pulled the rubber lady from my pack and settled in as darkness fell. My orders were to call in every thirty minutes for routine checks. If movement was spotted below, or sounds heard, those demanded an immediate call to battalion. I took off my flak jacket and began opening the C-ration cans for the evening meal. I opted for beans and franks. There would be no fires.

It started out to be a clear night with a full moon. There was no relief from the heat. I took off my utility blouse. This time I only unlaced my boots, settling in for a "recon nap." I awoke later and called in a report, "All secure on the Oscar Papa," phonetic alphabet for "observation post." Then I walked the line, where it seemed to be quiet enough. In each hole one Marine was on guard while the second got some sleep. Then I returned to the bunker roof and stretched out for another nap. I told the radioman to wake me in twenty-five minutes. This again made me realize how fortunate I was to be able to fall asleep for quick naps.

Minutes later I was jostled awake. "Lieutenant, we got a probe in the wire."

I shook my head and stood. "Where?" I asked.

The Marine pointed off to the right. "In that sector."

I reached for the flak jacket and helmet and strapped on my .45 sidearm. Then I heard it: the rattling of beer cans. By now the moon had drifted behind heavy cloud cover. My first thought was to use a hand flare. I had five in my pack. However, even though a flare would expose whoever was down there it would likewise throw out an umbrella of light exposing our position.

Another rattling sound came up from the wire. "Lieutenant, there's someone out there."

I nodded, looking in the direction of the sound. "Pass the word to hold fire." I went to the radio and called in a situation report (sit rep). I reported that we were getting a probe "on the Romeo side of our pos," that is, the right side of our position. Battalion replied to keep them informed.

Several minutes went by in silence. The stifling nighttime air seemed to thicken, complementing the tightness in our throats. While we sat there I reached down and picked up a hand grenade, waiting for the next rattling sound. I didn't have to wait long. The sound seemed closer now, down to the right of the bunker. I remembered the timeworn phrase "close only counts in horseshoes, dancing, and hand grenades." I marked a spot in the darkness, straightened the cotter wires on the grenade, and pulled the pin, keeping a firm grip on the spoon. Then I threw a football pass down to the area. The spoon flew off, arming the grenade as it landed with a soft thud. I counted the seconds, "One potato, two potato, three potato . . ."

And then came the blast. This was followed by a cloud carrying the acrid TNT smell as it drifted back uphill.

Standing on the roof of the bunker with unlaced boots, helmet, and flak jacket I took out my .45 and waited. There was nothing for several moments. And then we heard a soft moan. And then another one, "Ahh . . . ahh!"

Here I was, less than ten days in-country, standing on the roof of a sand-bagged bunker on Hill 364, and I just killed someone. I gave another order to hold fire. We settled in for a long wait that was punctuated by several more moans. I had the radioman call in the incident, adding that we were now on 100 percent alert, standing by, no shots fired. "Roger, keep us informed," came the reply. If this was a probe, there had to be more than one. Where were the others?

There were several more moans. I laced my boots and stayed awake for the rest of the night, wondering who was down there and if there would be more rattling sounds from the beer cans. Periodically I finished off the rest of my C-rations.

When first light appeared I raised my binoculars and scanned the area. I picked up a form lying below a small mound. But I couldn't make out what it was. Setting the binoculars aside I selected two Marines for a quick look-see. We slowly went down the slope in a triangular formation, with me hanging back in the center. We went past the small mound and stopped. And then I saw what I had done.

Lying below my feet, on his back, was a rock ape with a slight grin.

By the time we returned to the compound I learned that Lieutenant Colonel Arnold was reading the radio log. He called me into his office and asked a few questions, adding that the monkeys that occupied the mountains around us usually threw rocks at the outposts, hence the moniker "rock ape." When I came out of the mess hall later that morning I was met by several of the Marines from the patrol. They presented me with a hastily configured aluminum medal on the end of a ribbon. I was now initiated into "The Order of the Monkey."

My next convoy was a short one, what was called a "line haul" (a small convoy run). It consisted of several trucks, with Staff Sergeant Thomas in the X-Ray jeep. Lance Corporal Wilson was on the M-60 while Sergeant Thomas kept a .45-caliber "grease gun" within arm's reach. We were to take a package of several trucks including a low-boy tractor-trailer carrying a bulldozer out to a compound near Marble Mountain. At S-3 operations, Major Brauer gave me the order simply to get out there, unload the trucks and the bulldozer, and return. I was to call in checkpoints along the route. In the motor pool Sergeant Thomas showed me the Marble Mountain route on a map marked with the checkpoints.

Leaving the compound I called in "departing Charlie Papa" (command post). We swung around Danang Harbor and headed toward the peninsula. On the way I called in several checkpoints to battalion. Sergeant Thomas explained that the road approaching Marble Mountain was hairy, with snipers and landmines. As we made a turn I noticed an engineer crew sweeping the road. We were waved through and kept going to the appointed compound. Sergeant Thomas slowed the X-Ray jeep to less than 10 miles per hour, standing up over the flattened windshield looking for anything suspicious in the road. Several minutes later we pulled into the compound. As they were off loading the bulldozer a sergeant approached us and asked, "Did you guys just come in with that low-boy?"

I nodded to him. "Yes, is there a problem?"

He smiled, "Well, not now." I gave him a puzzled look. "What your convoy did was sweep the road for us."

Sergeant Thomas and I exchanged shocked looks. "What? An engineer crew back there waved us on," I said.

"They shouldn't have because that section of the road hadn't been swept. There was some activity out here last night." He paused. "If your jeep triggered a mine back there the only thing left would be your boots. You guys live right." He made me think of the lieutenant who had left this world not even seeing his newborn twins.

Before we departed the compound Sergeant Thomas advised me not to say anything about the incident. "If you mention this it will cause more paperwork. And they'll come down on you for being a green second lieutenant, a newbie. It's over. Let's keep this between our ears." I deferred to Sergeant Thomas's suggestion. He was in the Marine Corps when I was in grammar school. And he had been at the Chosin Reservoir, "the frozen Chosin," with Chesty Puller's regiment. Upon return to 11th Motors I reported back to operations hoping that the other compound didn't say anything. And they didn't. The incident never went any further.

Two days later Parker informed me that I would be the trail officer on a 117-vehicle convoy to Phu Bai. Gordon had received orders to Camp Lejeune and was notified that he was "off the road." It was battalion policy that officers and NCOs under orders to depart stateside within ten days would have no convoy duty. I was told that it stemmed from a convoy ambush where a sergeant, who had less than five days left in country, was killed.

At the briefing that night Parker identified me as the trail officer. It would be a large convoy, one of the bigger ones in recent weeks. The next morning after breakfast we headed to Lieutenant Colonel Arnold's office to look at the intelligence reports. Enemy movement was reported on the north side of the Hai Van Pass and along the Bowling Alley ridgeline at checkpoint five-five. Parker kept staring at the report, "I don't like this."

"What does it look like?" I asked.

"Two different enemy sightings, both on the north side of the pass." He hung up the clipboard. "We're going to be walking into it."

I had some time, so I went to the company armory shed and selected a 12-gauge shotgun and a bandolier of ammunition. Then I headed down to the motor pool with my convoy bag.

We met with our drivers, Sergeant Thomas, and the infantry platoon commander from 3rd Battalion, 7th Marine Regiment. Parker explained to keep it tight coming through the pass, to close the gaps. He turned to me and said, "Let me know if there are any gaps on your end. The NVA likes to take advantage of gaps in the convoy line." I nodded and we went to our vehicles and moved out to Red Beach, where the convoy would stage.

As I began lining up the trail package I noticed Lieutenant Colonel Arnold approaching in a jeep driven by a corporal. I figured that headquarters had seen the overnight G–2 intelligence reports and wanted to ensure that the convoy got off properly. By the time I approached Parker, Lieutenant Colonel Arnold was conducting an interrogation—how many add-ons, where will the security trucks be placed, have the radio checks been done, etcetera. Parker answered each question calmly. But I could sense that he was clearly irritated with the implication that he didn't know how to stage a Rough Rider convoy.

When we were alerted that the road sweep was almost completed Lieutenant Colonel Arnold returned to his jeep and departed. Parker made some quick notes and turned to me: "I think I've been on fifty or sixty Rough Riders. I've seen my share of road mines and ambushes." He paused, putting away his notebook. "Take a guess at how many convoys Colonel Arnold has been on."

"I wouldn't know," I replied.

"Not even one." Parker shook his head, turned, and walked back to his jeep. Several minutes later we got the green light to move out. Being at the trail, my radio driver and I had a passing conversation while waiting for the vehicles to head out. And then our section got in line and we moved with the trail package heading up into the pass. The road dust was just as thick as the previous convoy. It gathered on your face like heavy makeup. I could hear Parker talking to the pace, telling him to slow down. Sergeant Thomas was going up and back keeping the gaps closed in midtrain. I snuck a quick glance down at the crescent-shaped beach, knowing that I probably would never get a chance to walk on that beautiful, white sand.

We got to checkpoint two-seven, the French fort at the top of the pass, and headed downhill through the switchbacks. As we came out of the pass the convoy's speed picked up. I called in a checkpoint to Parker at the Lang Co Bridge. About one minute later I heard it.

There was one loud explosion, then a pause followed by three more in quick succession. And then small-arms fire erupted, with the security troops firing back. Sergeant Thomas came on the radio: "Transport five, this is X-Ray, the middle security pony has been hit, looks like Claymores." The small-arms fire was now in stereo—over the radio and just up the road.

"Roger X-Ray, advise me of the situation," said Parker.

"Transport five, we have some casualties back here," said Sergeant Thomas. "The wagon train has halted."

Parker then called me: "Trail, advise me of your situation."

As the back end of the convoy was stopped I jumped out, holding the shotgun. I could see the trucks up the road. There was a black cloud drifting skyward. I figured it was TNT from the Claymore mines. The small-arms fire continued. I got back in the jeep, grabbed the handset, and keyed it. "Transport five, this is trail. My package is okay. Up ahead I can see black smoke and hear small arms."

Parker gave me a "roger" and began talking to X-Ray: "Give me grid coordinates, X-Ray."

Sergeant Thomas gave the map coordinates, which were copied by our Forward Air Controller (FAC). Hopefully we would get some air support. Then I realized that with the excitement I forgot to load the shotgun. I pulled out some shells and loaded them into the magazine. Some of the security troops closest to me suddenly opened up with their M-16s. As soon as one started more chimed in. Then their sergeant ordered them to cease fire. I had no idea what they were firing at. Whatever it was it appeared to be from the ridgeline side of the road. I got out of the jeep holding the shotgun at high port, all the time listening to the radio traffic. Then I ran to the rear security truck and told the sergeant to keep his troops on the truck, that we would be moving shortly. He nodded to me, looking around. "How long will it be, lieutenant? Our asses are hanging out here." He rubbed some sweat off his cheeks.

I held up a hand, sensing his nervousness. "Just hang in there. They have casualties up the road." I turned and jogged back to my radio jeep, feeling the sergeant's concern that we were sitting ducks out there. No wonder this stretch of the road was dubbed "Ambush Alley."

The convoy finally moved forward. As we rounded a curve I noticed Sergeant Thomas's X-Ray jeep parked on the shoulder. The troops from the security truck were in a defensive perimeter in the clearing. They were waiting for a medevac helicopter coming in to take out three wounded. Sergeant Thomas explained that there was one KIA. The Claymore mines were strategically placed alongside the road and detonated by remote control, shooting a pattern of steel balls into the air in a 60-degree arc like a shotgun. As the medevac helicopter approached everyone kept a sharp eye, knowing that the enemy was still in the area.

When my trail jeep pulled into the end of the airstrip at Phu Bai, Parker approached me and wanted a handwritten after-action report (AAR) based on what I saw. Everyone was on edge that night, expecting another rocket and mortar attack. But nothing happened. The return convoy was uneventful. I felt that we had gone through enough for one convoy. It turned out to be an assumption.

When we returned to 11th Motors we learned that Dr. Martin Luther King Jr. had been assassinated in Memphis. A suspected white man was at large. Rioting had broken out in many U.S. cities. Less than a week before, President Johnson had announced that he would not be running for reelection. And now the leader of the civil rights movement had been gunned down, in a southern city no less.

That afternoon rioting broke out in the Danang brig. Farther south, at Long Binh, there was more rioting at the Army stockade known as Long Binh Jail— "the LBJ." Walking through the motor pool during those tense days one could sense the loss and anger among the black Marines. I reflected back to John's phone call, during my campus days, wanting me to accompany a student group to Alabama to what became known as the Pettus Bridge Riot. It went without saying that Dr. King's assassination would add to our leadership challenges, making some sense of the argument that with all the racial unrest in the United States Black Marines in Vietnam were fighting the white man's war.

5

A Memorial

Chicago, May 7, 1968

Hi Frank,

We're back in the big city safe and sound. Mom flew out to San Diego and we took the southern route back to Chicago, through Arizona and the Grand Canyon. I always thought the Grand Canyon pictures in shades of purple were fake but those incredible mauve and lavender shades are real. Truly breathtaking.

When we stopped for lunch I couldn't believe my ears when a man in the booth behind us said, "When you've seen one hole in the ground you've seen them all." The Grand Canyon! Mom and I almost wet our pants laughing.

Thank God you sent that money order. I used it to buy a new set of tires. The original tires on the VW would have never made it to Chicago. It was perfect timing.

Something else, we got pulled over by a State Policeman in New Mexico. He said that we were going fifteen to twenty miles over the speed limit. I didn't know what to say at first. Then I said, "That's impossible, this is a VW. It can't go that fast." I could tell that he had never seen a VW up close. He walked around it and studied the fenders. After this he walked back and gave us a warning to keep the speed down. When we got back on the road he stood there watching our "bug" move down the highway. I watched the speed the rest of the way. Before Mom came out, Sandy Reed and I drove over to the historic Mission San Luis Rey for the eleven o'clock memorial mass for Dr. Martin Luther King. We got there early because we knew it would be standing room only. And it was. The sermon was a testimony not only to him but to the Civil Rights struggle. It was pointed out that his work, far from finished, began with the end of the Civil War. As we know, there are elements in the South and the rest of the country that just won't accept change in these times.

Before the memorial ended the choir started with Amazing Grace. We thought that was going to end it. Then they went into The Impossible Dream from Man of La Mancha. There wasn't a dry eye around us.

62

Sandy and I didn't say much on the drive back to Oceanside. It was a beautiful day but we were in our own thoughts. So much has happened this year in such a short time. First it was the Tet fighting in Vietnam. Then President Johnson announces that he won't run for re-election. Then Senator Eugene McCarthy wins the New Hampshire primary. And now Bobby Kennedy is in the race. Student anti-war demonstrations back here are gearing up. The S.D.S. seized five buildings at Columbia University in New York. Maybe you read about that.

Mayor Daley's office is already making sounds to back Vice President Humphrey for the Democratic nomination. I guess the showdown will be here in August at the convention. Some of the girls and I are thinking of doing volunteer work when the convention starts. Great time to be in Chicago! Wish you were here.

In the meantime I'm going down to the Operation Head Start headquarters to see what they have to offer. I've got my degree in education and I'm certified with the Chicago School Board. So I'm sure there's a place for me. Wish me luck.

I know you're in danger over there, particularly when you're on a convoy. So it goes without saying that you need to keep that boney butt of yours down. I love you and want you home to pick up where we left off. Remember how you left so abruptly? I'll never forget that phone call. You were supposed to be home for a last dinner. Then you called to say you were staging to leave for Vietnam. So much for long good byes. I still can't believe that it happened on my birthday. Love the Marines but not sure that they love the wives.

Love you and miss you!

XO

6

The Captain

I went on several more Rough Rider convoys as trail officer, becoming familiar with the procedure, the terrain, and the twisting road in the Hai Van Pass. There were more sniper incidents near checkpoint five-eight in the middle of the Bowling Alley. It seemed to be a favorite area of the NVA because of the nearby ridgeline and winding rivers that snaked out to the Gulf of Tonkin. My weapon of choice on those convoys was the 12-gauge shotgun. And I didn't have to be reminded to load it once the convoy moved out. My rationale for choosing this weapon was simple. The pace and security trucks had mounted .50-caliber guns. Plus the security troops had M-16s along with M-79 grenade launchers. I wasn't that worried about getting pinned down on the road. But if close quarters came I wanted something that would shoot out like an umbrella.

New people came in as the older ones rotated out. One night we said goodbye to Gordon. I even helped him store his AK-47 into the door of his small refrigerator. He intended to take it home as a trophy. As an automatic weapon it wouldn't be allowed into the States. But he became attached to it. I assume it passed through the inspections and today rests on his mantle somewhere.

One afternoon I was called to Lieutenant Colonel Arnold's office. Being called to the battalion commanding officer's (CO) office was akin to being summoned to the principal's office in high school—a bad sign.

Lieutenant Colonel Arnold had me stand at attention and read a promotion order from Headquarters Marine Corps. The order was dated 1 February 1968. It had just caught up with me: I was now a first lieutenant. Colonel Arnold took off my gold bars and pinned silver bars on my collars. I was told that promotions come faster during wartime. Now I was seeing it: Word quickly spread that I was now a "silver bar." That night I took $25 in MPCs and put them on the bar in the Staff/Officers club. I still swear that in less than forty-five minutes the guys in the club drank up my promotion money.

That same week two things happened. Parker's orders to Camp Lejeune came in, taking him off the road. And we got two new second lieutenants, Jack Carmetti from Massachusetts and Andy Garrison from Washington State. Not only would Jack be in Transport Company; he would occupy the same hooch with me, as would Andy Garrison, who was assigned to Alpha Company. Before Parker left we got another second lieutenant, Rich Cobb from New Jersey, who also settled into our hooch. And we got a new truck master, Gunnery Sergeant Robinson Rayhorn, a six-foot-tall bear of a man.

Major Brauer also rotated stateside. He was replaced by another major, a slow-talking Texan named Brent Bradley. In such a short time the battalion was full of changing faces. Bravo Company got a new commander, Captain Aldus Ashworth, who was easily six-feet-four, with a Marine Corps "high and tight" haircut to fit his rigid personality. We were told that Captain Ashworth was in the promotion zone for major.

We also got an intelligence report that "five enemy, two carrying weapons, were sighted on the east slope of Hill 364." That was on our side. An ambush patrol was sent in that night, but there were no further sightings. When I heard of the report it made me think of my first "kill"—the rock ape at the top of the hill.

The battalion was now tasked with moving the 26th Marine Regiment from the 15th Aerial Port to various cantonments. The 26th was the initial Marine regiment defending Khe Sanh. They were airlifted down to Danang. As one of the units came off the C–123 cargo plane I searched for Tom Igoe but couldn't find him. There were also more convoys to Phu Bai, supporting operations Mameluke Thrust and Allen Brook, the latter sweeping through Happy Valley. It was during this time when I commanded my first Rough Rider convoy. Jack Carmetti was my trail officer. The middle of the convoy developed a gap coming out of the Hai Van Pass, and there was sniper fire reported just after we passed through Lang Co on the south end of the Bowling Alley.

After John Parker rotated stateside I was the interim company commander. This required my presence at the late-afternoon company commander's meetings held in the conference room behind Lieutenant Colonel Arnold's headquarters. Because I was an interim, I didn't bother settling into the company commander's cubicle. But I did use the desk for signing reports and making up training schedules. First Sergeant Duncan ran the office and ensured that all reports to battalion were handed in on time. I was also informed that we would be getting a new commander shortly, a captain on his second tour. That seemed appropriate, I thought.

One afternoon a package arrived from Patty. It was a green shamrock flag against a white field with a green border. And it had three string attachments. In her letter she mentioned that she made the flag herself.

On the next Rough Rider convoy, at the Red Beach staging area, I attached the shamrock flag to my radio antenna. And soon several of the troops nodded and smiled. We were still waiting for the engineers to complete the road sweep when Major Ashworth pulled up in a jeep. His promotion order had come through and he was now in S–3 operations. The first thing he did was approach me, pointing to the flag. "Lieutenant McAdams, that flag is not regulation."

"I know major. My wife sent it to me. I thought it would add a little color to my jeep."

He shook his head. "Still, it's not a regulation flag. Take it down." I couldn't believe what I was hearing. "Now," he added. "Take it down."

I took the flag down and placed it in the backseat of the jeep. Soon we got the green light to head out. The convoy moved north up into the Hai Van Pass. When we reached the old French fort I had my radioman-driver pull over. I got out of the jeep and put the shamrock flag back on the antenna. Then we got back into the convoy line. Within minutes I got a "thumbs up" from Staff Sergeant Thomas.

It was several days later when I entered the conference room for the company commander's meeting I noticed a captain sitting across the table from me. He was about my size (5′9″) with a moon face. I sensed that this was the new Transport Company commander. Major Bradley conducted the meeting in Colonel Arnold's absence. The first thing he did was introduce Captain J. T. Eiler, "who will take command of Transport Company." Major Bradley pointed to me: "Lieutenant McAdams has been holding down the fort for you."

I nodded to Captain Eiler. He gave me an indifferent glance, then looked at his notebook. When the meeting ended Captain Eiler approached me and wanted to see the company office and then take a tour of our sector at the battalion perimeter. At the office I gathered the clerks and First Sergeant Duncan and introduced Captain Eiler. He said he would meet them individually later. Then he said, "Lieutenant McAdams, show me our sector of the perimeter."

We walked down to the command bunker, the center of the Transport Company sector. On our left we tied in with Charlie Company. On the right our area went all the way to the road that paralleled the compound and went into the village of Khon Son. There were about 250 yards of rice paddy directly in front. I pointed out Khon Son. Then I gestured with my hand to the village on the other side of the rice paddy, "Over there is Bong Mui."

"What's it like at night here?" he asked.

"Pretty quiet since I've been here. It gets hairy when we go out on the road," I said.

"How many convoys have you been on?"

I thought for a moment. "About fifteen. I say a prayer each time I go out."

He gave me a wondering look. "Any ambushes?"

I nodded. "On the other side of the Hai Van Pass."

"The Hai Van Pass." He gave off a chuckle. "On my first tour we used to ride Vespa motor scooters through that pass to Phu Bai. It was a lark."

I shook my head. "It's not like that now, captain. That pass is known as the most dangerous ride in the I Corps area." He looked away as my words sunk in.

"What's the convoy security like?" he asked, studying the rice paddy.

"Usually a platoon of infantry with the three squads placed strategically down the line." I paused, remembering the Claymore-mine ambush north of Lang Co. "They like to hit with Claymores and small arms. And then they're gone."

"What about air and artillery?" he asked.

"If we're lucky we get a Huey [helicopter gunship] on station. Infantry has priority," I explained.

He nodded and walked over to the command bunker. Then he looked at the front facing the perimeter wire, slowly walking around the side, looking at the M-60 machine-gun tower on top. "Who put this bunker here?"

"It was here when I reported in, captain," I said.

He replied, "It should be in the middle of our sector. It's too far over to the left."

I looked at the gun tower and the sector out to the wire. "The gun will still be able to cover it."

"No, it's giving up a field of fire," he said.

"Captain, we have two men to a fighting hole all along this sector. And the gun covers the area all the way to the road."

He shook his head. "No, I'm going to change it."

"It worked well for Lieutenant Gordon and the company CO before him," I said.

He gave me a stern look. "I'm not Lieutenant Gordon. And this is my company."

Before the guard detail was set that afternoon, Captain Eiler ordered me to call a formation outside the company office. I waited until the ranks were formed, called them to attention, and had the lines dressed down while Captain Eiler stood off to the side. With everyone set I nodded to Captain Eiler and did an about-face. He approached me and I saluted. Then I took my place with the other officers and NCOs at the rear.

Captain Eiler looked up and down at the men. Then he ordered, "Parade rest!"

The troops went to parade rest. "Men, I'm Captain J. T. Eiler. I'm on my second tour. I did my first tour when most of you were in high school."

In the rear, Sergeant Thomas shook his head and softly said, "Not me."

"Just as Tet caused a change there is likewise going to be a change here. I am going to make that change. We are fighting a heathen enemy. And we will defeat him. Our convoys will help in that defeat." Captain Eiler paused, looking up and down the ranks. "I am a book man. I take no prisoners and I have an instinct for the jugular. Remember this: I am going to make you a better company." He took another pause and called the company to attention. Then he looked at me in the rear. "Lieutenant McAdams."

I moved from the rear of the formation to the front, approaching him. I saluted and he gave the formation back to me. Captain Eiler then went inside the company office. I waited for the screen door to close then dismissed the company.

Then I walked over to Jack Carmetti, Rich Cobb, and Staff Sergeant Thomas. "We definitely have a new company commander," said Jack.

"Sergeant Thomas, you've knocked around this man's Corps. What do you think?" I asked.

Sergeant Thomas shook his head. "Too early to tell. But I did pick up one thing."

"What's that?" I asked.

"That last statement. He used the word *I* five times."

The next day the company got an order, a Rough Rider convoy to Phu Bai. Captain Eiler told me that he would go as an observer. When I reported to Major Bradley (who now had the nickname "Major B. B.") at operations he explained that it would be approximately seventy-five vehicles, mixed U.S. Army and Seabees. He added to be especially aware of the Vietnamese vendors at the Red Beach staging area. "We can't do anything about them walking up and down the road. But keep them away from the trucks. There have been reports of sabotage on other convoys."

That night I gave my convoy briefing in the conference room. At my opening

I saw Captain Eiler enter and stand in the back. Halfway through the briefing I noticed him taking notes. At the end of the brief I asked if there were any questions. Several people asked about the security through the Hai Van Pass and the ambush rate along the Bowling Alley. I emphasized how gaps have a tendency to play to the ambushes, that I will slow the convoy speed when necessary to close gaps in the train. I concluded by stating, "If we step into anything tomorrow, have your drivers downshift and get out of the area."

The next morning, after breakfast, I went to Colonel Arnold's office to read the overnight intelligence messages. An NVA unit was observed on the north side of the pass. It was estimated to be a reinforced company. In the motor pool I met with Staff Sergeant Thomas, Jack Carmetti, and the infantry platoon commander. As I spread a map on Sergeant Thomas's X-Ray jeep Captain Eiler approached. I told them about the enemy sighting and pointed to the coordinates.

Captain Eiler studied the map. "How sure are you of this?"

"Each morning the division G-2 reports are updated in Colonel Arnold's office," I explained. "Recon probably spotted that movement either yesterday or last night."

"Make sure you position the command jeep behind the second security truck," he said.

"I usually set in about one-third of the way back, captain. The second security truck is halfway back."

Captain Eiler shook his head. "Then put us halfway back."

Everyone was suddenly looking at me. "Captain, convoy doctrine says that the command vehicle should be one-third back in line."

"It's the convoy commander's choice to place his vehicle where he chooses." He paused looking at the map. "Halfway back behind the second security truck." He turned and walked away.

Sergeant Thomas looked at me. "Lieutenant, you're right. The command jeep should be one-third back."

I nodded, folding the map. "But he's our company commander."

"I'll be back at trail, saying a prayer," said Carmetti.

Before we left the battalion compound Captain Eiler settled in the back of the jeep with his own map. We staged at Red Beach for about forty-five minutes until the road sweep ended. Then I got the green light. On orders from Captain Eiler I had to position my command jeep directly behind the second security truck. As soon as we moved out he took out his small notebook and began writing. After clearing the top of the pass we headed down the north side. Captain Eiler kept checking his map, looking out at the terrain and making notes. Coming out of the pass I could see a gap up ahead—and it was getting longer. I was learning that this was normal going through Lang Co and entering the Bowling Alley.

As I keyed the handset Captain Eiler said, "You've got a big gap up there."

"Yes, sir, I can see it," I said. Then I called the pace truck and told him to bring the speed down to 10 miles per hour.

The convoy straightened out after passing the village of Lang Co. I turned to Captain Eiler and said, "This straightaway is the most dangerous stretch." I pointed out checkpoint five-eight, which was an overturned railcar.

The rest of the convoy was uneventful. After we pulled into the airstrip at Phu Bai I called in our arrival and checked out of the net. Captain Eiler then had Sergeant Thomas drive him to the operations building at the north side of the airstrip, where he could catch a helicopter back to Danang. That night there was another rocket and mortar attack that caused us to hit the slit trenches again. It was a short attack with no casualties.

As soon as the convoy returned to 11th Motors I was summoned to Captain Eiler's office, where he gave me a critique. There was nothing positive. I was criticized for faulty radio procedure and allowing gaps in the convoy line on the north side of the pass. It seemed futile to give a counterargument, so I kept quiet. He then showed me a diagram of the new position for the command bunker. "I want you and Sergeant Woodard to get a four-man working party and start digging a foundation twenty yards to the right of the present command bunker."

That afternoon Sergeant Woodard and I assembled the working party and marked off twenty yards to the right of the bunker. After a half-hour of digging the working party halted. They couldn't dig any deeper because of a buried boulder next to an old tree trunk. Sergeant Woodard explained that our choices were to go more than twenty yards or less, that the boulder and the tree trunk were set too far into the ground. So I had them start on a new foundation two and a half yards to the left. I gave the working party a meal break, left a note on Captain Eiler's desk, and headed to the mess hall.

After lunch I was called into Captain Eiler's office again. He was clearly irritated. "When I give an order I expect it to be carried out exactly as stated."

"Captain, I can explain about—"

He interrupted. "That foundation is seventeen and one-half yards to the right. I told you it has to be situated twenty yards to the right. Is that so difficult to comprehend?"

"Captain, at the twenty-yard interval we found a buried boulder and an old tree trunk," I explained. "So I had them start the new foundation at seventeen and one-half yards."

"I don't care how you do it, lieutenant, but get that boulder and tree trunk out of there."

"They're wedged in too deep, captain. Sergeant Woodard says that it would take a package of dynamite or C–4 to clear it," I said. "It's easier to set the foundation at seventeen and one-half yards."

Captain Eiler shook his head. "That's unsat! [Lingo for "unsatisfactory."] Halt the work at seventeen and one-half yards. I'll request an engineering team to set in a C–4 explosive package and we'll blow those obstacles." He gave me a studied look: "When I say twenty yards it will be twenty yards."

A company memo was sent to operations that afternoon requesting a demolition team from the 7th Engineer Battalion to eliminate the obstacles with C–4 plastic explosive. The reply came back denied after the company commander's meeting. According to Colonel Arnold and Major Bradley there would be no engineering team blowing away anything. The next morning Captain Eiler informed me to have the working party resume digging the new foundation at seventeen and one-half yards.

"Seventeen and one-half yards will still work, captain," I said. "I knew that the C–4 request would be denied."

"That's not a discussion item. Get down there and get the job done," he said.

It took several days, and the command bunker was moved. Captain Eiler said nothing more about the two-and-a-half yards difference.

During this time I received an order appointing me as battalion prosecutor/ trial counsel. I was stunned for the simple reason that I was not a lawyer. With order in hand I went to the battalion adjutant, Lieutenant Grunwald. "This means I'll be prosecuting court-martial cases."

Grunwald nodded: "We rotate the battalion prosecuting and defense counsels. You drew the short straw for the prosecution."

"That would be fine if I was a law school graduate," I said.

Grunwald shook his head. "This has come up before. The attorneys at division legal are overwhelmed with murder and rape cases for general court-martial. Those have a priority. Division has ordered that the lesser cases, the special and summary courts-martial, will be handled by captains and lieutenants at the battalion level."

I shook my head. "This isn't right."

"Right or not, it's a division order, Frank," said Grunwald. "You're the new battalion prosecutor."

Walking back to the company office several scenarios came into my head. *I'm going to be in front of a court-martial board. I'm going to have to give a legal argument to prosecute some young Marine and I'm not qualified to do it. Yet I've been told that it is division policy and that I will do it.* It made me think of a World War II expression: "Eat the apple and fuck the Corps." There was nothing I could do about it. I would eat the apple.

That night in the Staff/Officers club I learned that the appointed battalion defense counsel was Jack Carmetti. If a court-martial came up we'd be going against each other, both from the same company living in the same hooch. We were joking about it when a loud burst came from the other end of the bar. Captain Eiler was in a discussion about the Democratic nomination. I heard the names of Senator Eugene McCarthy and Bobby Kennedy.

Captain Eiler doubled his fist and slammed it on the bar. "It can't be Kennedy, he'll take us all to hell. He's a Goddamn disgrace and a communist!" Captain Eiler shook his head. "Something has to be done to keep him from that nomination."

Jack and I were about twenty feet away from Captain Eiler. We exchanged looks. "That's our company commander down there," said Jack.

I looked down the bar, remembering how steadfast Captain Eiler was over the two and one-half yards for moving the command bunker. Those two and one-half yards seemed to be a challenge for him. And he was denied. Beyond that, his criticism of my convoy decisions seemed picky in light that he had just arrived. I did detect that he seemed nervous during our passage through the Bowling Alley. Also, I had assumed that he would be with us on the return convoy. Instead, he took a helicopter back to Danang. That night in our Staff/Officers club something told me that I was getting into a leadership problem, not with an enlisted man or an NCO but with my company commander.

About two days later I was down in the motor pool checking tires with Sergeant Woodard. It was a hot morning, and a group of us gathered at a leather canteen that held several gallons of water. A shelter half over our heads provided a welcome umbrella from the intense sunrays. A few moments later a lance corporal, Gary Watson, came walking across the motor pool. I saw the look on his face. He seemed upset as he approached us. "Watson, what's wrong with you?" asked Sergeant Woodard.

Watson gestured with his thumb back in the direction of the company office. "It just came over AFVN. Somebody shot Senator Kennedy."

"Watson, is this some kind of a bad joke?" I asked.

Watson shook his head. "I wish, lieutenant. It happened in a hotel in Los Angeles. He's being operated on right now."

I began the walk from the motor pool up to the company office. By the time

I arrived only one clerk, Corporal Steve Adair, was on duty because the other clerks, along with Captain Eiler and First Sergeant Duncan, were at the mess hall. Corporal Adair was sitting at the clerk's bench staring at a typewriter. A radio, tuned to AFVN, was on a shelf above his head. I stood at the front counter as a news report continued. Corporal Adair turned and looked at me. Then he softly said, "He's dead."

"Senator Kennedy?" I asked.

Corporal Adair nodded. "Died in the operating room."

I walked around the counter, closer to the radio. Corporal Adair stood and turned the volume down. "Hold it," I said. "I want to hear."

Corporal Adair turned the volume down lower. "You need to hear what Captain Eiler did when the first report came in."

I asked, "What are you talking about?"

"Captain Eiler, lieutenant," said Adair. "He got up from his desk and did a little dance in his cubicle. Then he said that it was time somebody shot that Commie son-of-a-bitch." I took a deep breath and tried to hide my disgust. "You're lucky, lieutenant. You're down in the motor pool or on the road. We have to work with him."

I shook my head and walked out. I wondered, *Is this going to get worse?*

It didn't take long for the word to get out about Captain Eiler's "Kennedy remark." I was surprised at how many of the Marines in our company were following the primary elections back in the world along with the Paris peace talks. For the next few days all anyone talked about was the "Kennedy curse."

That Friday afternoon the officers and NCOs were required to attend a marijuana orientation class given by a gunnery sergeant from the division legal office. The marijuana problem in our battalion and in the First Marine Division was growing, showing up more in court-martial cases. At the end of the presentation the sergeant brought in a metal bucket and lit some marijuana leaves, letting the sweet smell waft throughout the conference room. "So if you get a whiff of this on your perimeter one night you'll know that one of your troops is smoking dope." He paused. "Or maybe they're passing the joint around, a pot party."

Captain Eiler then asked a question. "What's the maximum sentence for smoking and possession of marijuana?"

"According to the *Manual for Courts-Martial* repeat offenders could be sentenced to ten years in a military prison," replied the sergeant. "First offense is usually a bust of one or two pay grades and the loss of two-thirds of base pay for six months. Second offense is harsher with a sentence in the Danang brig."

After the class Captain Eiler called a company meeting with First Sergeant Duncan and all officers. We sat on map stools in his cubicle as he began the meeting. "We're going to deal with this problem head-on," said Captain Eiler. "Marijuana is part of the reason we're in Vietnam. It's part of the International Communist Conspiracy, corrupting our minds with dope. And the student antiwar movement back in the States is a classic example of how it's working. Those stupid, long-hair hippie pukes have no realization that they're dupes of the Communist Party." Jack Carmetti and I exchanged looks as Captain Eiler continued. "Here the method is being employed by both the Viet Cong and the NVA."

Lieutenant Cobb then broke in. "Does that make it a joint effort?"

Jack and I broke into laughter as Cobb enjoyed his one-liner. Captain Eiler glared at Cobb. "I don't appreciate joking about a gravely serious issue, lieutenant."

Cobb said, "Sorry, captain, I thought it might make a humorous point."

"Well your point tonight will be the observation post up on Hill 364. Report to operations at 1800 hours," said Captain Eiler.

The meeting ended. Outside of the company office Cobb said, "Serves me right for cracking a joke. Now I get to go to the mountain, just like Dr. King."

As the XO I got the bright idea for a Sunday beach party. The troops had been working long, hard hours. They were upset not only with the Bobby Kennedy assassination but also Captain Eiler's ugly remark in the office. I figured a company party at China Beach with hamburgers and beer would be the right recipe to cool things off.

It was easy enough to plan. I got two cases of frozen hamburgers and a tub of baked beans from the mess hall, as well as a couple of cases of beer from the Staff/Officers club which Jack, Cobb, and I chipped in on. Transportation posed no problem. Staff Sergeant Thomas and Gunnery Sergeant Rayhorn lined up three six-by trucks. I was surprised that Captain Eiler approved it. But he did, adding that he would remain behind. We even got a corpsman from sick bay, Doc Poppell, to provide medical aid. Poppell willingly offered his services in return for an afternoon at the beach with hamburgers and beer. "War is hell," said the man.

It turned out to be a great afternoon. While the burgers were cooking we had a touch football game in the sand. The game ended in a tie and we headed to the water. China Beach was a scenic piece of sand, something out of a Southern California surfing movie, stretched out on a little lip going into Danang

Harbor. For those few hours, war seemed to be a world away. It was a perfect morale-builder. Coming back on the trucks the troops were singing and laughing, their bellies full of hamburgers and beer.

When we got back First Sergeant Duncan said that Captain Eiler was down at operations getting a convoy order and our presence was requested. Major Ashworth was now the S–3 operations officer after Major Bradley went to G–4 (DCC). At operations Major Ashworth gave Eiler the order for a 140-truck convoy scheduled to depart Red Beach the next morning. The enemy activity for the month of June had increased, especially through the Hai Van Pass. This convoy was one of the biggest, compared to the previous sixty days, with such cargo as bunker beams and 105-millimeter ammunition for artillery batteries. There wouldn't be just one platoon of security; this one called for two, in squads spaced out accordingly.

When Sergeant Thomas, Jack, and I arrived at the operations hooch Major Ashworth was sitting at his desk in front of a laminated I Corps map dotted with red markings and colored pushpins. Captain Eiler was sitting nearby, with a grim look, writing in his notebook. We sat down in front of Major Ashworth's desk and took out our notebooks. Indeed, this one had the potential to be the godfather of all Rough Rider convoys. Sergeant Thomas kept eye balling the map behind Major Ashworth. At the end of the order Captain Eiler turned to Jack and me. "Lieutenant McAdams will be on the pace truck. Lieutenant Carmetti will be at trail. Lieutenant Cobb will remain back here with Gunnery Sergeant Rayhorn."

Several items rushed through my mind. First, I had never been on a Rough Rider convoy that was so big it had to have a pace officer. Second, if we did get hit most likely it would be at the front. I was more than glad now that I had picked the afternoon for a beach party. While Captain Eiler and Major Ashworth were discussing a point Jack turned and mouthed something to me. I didn't get it at first. Then I realized what he was saying, "He doesn't want to go." I cringed.

As we left the operations hooch, vehicles were already entering the compound and lining up in the motor pool. We had everything: U.S. Army, Seabees, civilian contractors, even several Air Force trucks. When we arrived at the company office Sergeant Thomas said that he needed to have a meeting. Captain Eiler nodded and we assembled in his cubicle. Sergeant Thomas spread his map out on Captain Eiler's desk.

"As we know this is one big convoy, captain."

Captain Eiler nodded. "Tell me something I don't know, sergeant."

"It's telling the NVA to 'come and get us,'" replied Sergeant Thomas. "I'll lay a dollar to a donut that we're going to be hit with that many vehicles coming out of the pass. We're asking for it."

"Where do you think out of the pass?" asked Captain Eiler.

Sergeant Thomas leaned over the map, grabbed a pencil, and pointed to three places: "Number one, right after Lang Co Bridge on the northern end of the finger; number two, just before the overturned railroad car in the Bowling Alley where that river winds around; or just before the bend at Phu Gia Pass where the convoy has to slow down." Sergeant Thomas paused, staring at the map with the rest of us. Then he looked at Captain Eiler: "It's their pick as I see it."

There was silence in the cubicle. The only sounds heard were vehicles getting positioned in the motor pool. Then Captain Eiler said, "Well, we'll see how it plays out." I could taste the brassy fear in my throat; I could also see it in Captain Eiler's eyes.

"There is another way," said Sergeant Thomas.

"And what's that?" asked Captain Eiler.

"Break up the convoy into three serials. Run them over a three-day period, approximately forty-five vehicles per," suggested Sergeant Thomas. "The odds of getting hit would be diminished."

"It would need to be approved by operations," I said. "The request would have to be made right now."

"That's negative," said Captain Eiler. "That artillery ammo has to be in Phu Bai by tomorrow. Besides, we'd have to provide logistics for those troops and trucks for that time." There was more silence in the cubicle as we studied Sergeant Thomas's three ambush points. "Fuck it, we're going with the entire package," said Eiler.

The meeting broke up. Jack and I went back to our hooch and began preparing our gear. After getting a meal in the mess hall we went to the conference room for Captain Eiler's briefing. It was standing-room-only with people stacked outside listening in. I was certain that not everyone could hear what he was saying. A horrible feeling swirled into my stomach. I had a creeping sense that Captain Eiler had no idea what was waiting for us. After the briefing ended I went to the armory and drew the 12-gauge shotgun with a bandolier. Then I returned to my hooch and wrote two quick letters, one to Patty and the other to my parents. I stayed away from mentioning what I suspected of the coming convoy. I wanted to get the letters off just in case something did happen. Then I made an attempt to get some sleep. A lot of things ran through my head that night. Finally, sleep came. As I was washing up in the morning I realized something: I had been in country exactly three months, and I had yet to have the recurring nightmare. It was a bright omen on a dark morning.

After breakfast I went to Lieutenant Colonel Arnold's office and checked the overnight G–2 intelligence reports. The reports went back three days with enemy sightings on each day, all on the north side of the pass. I wrote down the coordinates and replaced the clipboard. I remember staring at the clipboard for several moments. *They're out there waiting for us*, I thought.

Captain Eiler was in the motor pool with Staff Sergeant Thomas, Jack Carmetti, and the infantry platoon commanders. They were studying a map spread out on the hood of Captain Eiler's command jeep. As I approached, Captain Eiler was explaining the radio relay procedure on the north side of the pass.

Captain Eiler turned and glared at me. "Nice that you can join us, Frank."

"I was at Colonel Arnold's office, checking the overnight intelligence messages."

"We're almost ready to head out to Red Beach. You should have been down here earlier," snapped Eiler. I looked at Sergeant Thomas and Jack then back to Eiler. "Captain, the overnight intelligence reports need to be checked. Usually it's the convoy commander's responsibility."

I got another glare. "Don't tell me how to run a convoy. I was doing this when you were partying with co-eds."

I drew a deep breath. "Still, you should know that there were three enemy sightings on the north side of the pass, all within the past three days. I wrote down the coordinates." I was astonished that Captain Eiler never bothered to check the intelligence messages.

"Show us," said Sergeant Thomas. "I need to know where they were seen."

I pulled out my notebook and read off the coordinates. Sergeant Thomas traced each one with a finger. He nodded several times as I exchanged concerned looks with Jack. "Uh-huh, between Lang Co and Phu Gia, still hanging around out there."

Captain Eiler was looking at the map when battalion called on his radio giving us the go-ahead to Red Beach. We quickly scrambled to our vehicles. I went to the pace truck and tossed my gear aboard. The .50-caliber gunner was already positioned on the ring mount. I nodded to the driver, Lance Corporal "Davy" Crockett. Then I did a radio check. Captain Eiler called in and told us to move out. Once again the cavalry was riding out of the fort into Indian country.

Lance Corporal Crockett pulled the pace truck up at the edge of the road along Red Beach. The rest of the convoy followed and we began the wait for the completion of the road sweep. About ten minutes later the command jeep pulled up and Captain Eiler got out. He came up to the pace truck and wanted to know the coordinates of the enemy sightings. I pulled out my notebook and read them to him. He wrote them down, turned, and walked back to his jeep. I expected him to say something about admonishing me in front of the others, that I was only helping out and that he, as convoy commander, should have checked the clipboard. I expected too much.

While waiting I monitored the radio traffic between division and the engineers doing the road sweep. My father told me that one of the agonizing aspects of any war is the waiting. It causes head games, always thinking of the worst scenario. I kept wondering, *Where would I be at the end of the day?* It was a lot like a locker room before a football game where everyone is in his own thoughts while the tension mounts.

Finally we got the green light from Defend DCC. Crockett started the engine. The next transmission was Captain Eiler, "Transport Pace, this is Six, move out."

I gave the sign for Lance Corporal Crockett to head out slowly. Then I called back to Captain Eiler that we were moving out. I put on my flak jacket and began inserting shells into the shotgun magazine as we headed up into the pass. I remember Crockett looking back at me: "Don't worry lieutenant, it's going to be a nice ride."

I shook my head and leaned forward. "Don't say that!"

One of the nice things about the pace is that all you have to contend with is setting the speed. The convoy commander has to make the decisions while the trail has to tend to the breakdowns. The first breakdown came just before the top of the pass. By then my truck was about halfway down negotiating the switchbacks. I could see that some gaps were forming, so I told Crockett to slow the speed. Then I called it in to Captain Eiler. The entire convoy was kicking up clouds of road dust that could be seen for miles. I remembered what Sergeant Thomas said in the company office: "We're telling them to come and get us."

Down the road, on the north side of Lang Co, three Vietnamese boys, Phoung, Hoang, and Don, were in a sandy clearing off the road. The boys were clad in shirts, shorts, and sandals. They were being paid in Vietnamese piasters, by a bridge security team, to fill sandbags. So far they had five sandbags filled. They were working on three more when Hoang stopped and looked up.

Three North Vietnamese soldiers emerged from the thick brush. The soldiers were dressed in gray shirts and trousers, wearing pith helmets. The boys dropped their shovels and stood, looking at the soldiers. Nothing was said. The soldier standing in the middle looked south toward the Hai Van Pass and could see road dust swirling skyward. He picked up a shovel and cracked it across Phoung's head, knocking the boy to the ground. Dazed, Phoung got to his hands and knees, making an attempt to stand. The soldier then pulled a pistol from his holster.

As soon as they saw the pistol Don and Hoang bolted and ran into the brush. The soldier moved closer to Phoung, pointed the pistol next to his ear, and pulled the trigger. The blast sent Phoung back to the ground, motionless.

The soldier replaced his pistol in the holster as two more North Vietnamese soldiers appeared. The first was carrying a mortar tube and a base plate. The second carried a pack full of mortar rounds. Phoung's body was quickly moved to the side of the sandy clearing and they began setting up the mortar tube.

Coming up the road I saw villagers walking and running south along the shoulder. This was an unusual amount of villagers out on the road at this time of day. I called in checkpoint five-eight as the pace kept moving toward the bend at Phu Gia Pass. I looked back and noticed a huge gap behind my package. We were really getting spread out, in several packs of eight to ten vehicles. I could see the loss of control. And there was no call from Captain Eiler to slow the speed. We were nearing the top of Phu Gia Pass when I heard the first explosion. Then someone got on the radio, "This is Kilo Three, we're getting hit, we're getting hit!"

I could hear small arms over the radio and then saw more explosions farther back. Jack came on the radio: "Transport Six, this is trail. Someone in the train is being hit. I say again, someone in the train is getting hit."

Captain Eiler came on the radio. "This is Transport Six, where in the train? I need to know—"

More explosions came as Captain Eiler's radio cut out. The first thing I thought of was that his jeep took a hit. I ordered Crockett to pull up and stop. The small-arms fire continued as I called back to Jack: "Trail, this is Pace, what can you see from your pos, over?"

"Pace, this is Trail. I'm coming down from the big pass into Lang Co. I can see the road up ahead and it's blocked. The whole train is halted up ahead; they're under fire, over."

The relay station came on. "Transport Six, this is Defend Alpha. Interrogative your situation, over."

I waited for Captain Eiler to respond. There was nothing. I thought of the worst, which meant that I would have to take command. I keyed the handset. "Defend Alpha, this is Transport Pace. We're halted at checkpoint eight-eight.

I can see explosions about halfway back in the train. It sounds like mortars and small arms, over." I knew we needed a gunship over the ambush zone as soon as possible.

"Pace, this is Defend Alpha, we need to talk with your Charlie-Charlie [convoy commander], over."

I waited for Captain Eiler to come up on the radio. Silence for several moments. "Defend Alpha, this is Transport Pace, Transport Six can't be raised now. Can we get a Cowpoke [Huey gunship] on station? I can supply approximate grid coordinates, over."

"Pace, this is Defend Alpha, roger, wait one, out."

I stood in the sandbagged bed of the pace truck, looking through the binoculars at where the explosions were. I searched for a terrain feature such as a bridge or a bend in the road. I chose a bend in the road, marked it, and wrote down the grid coordinates. Then I called Defend Alpha and gave the six-digit coordinates. All I got was, "Roger, thank you, out." I looked at my watch. More than five minutes had gone by since the first explosions and small-arms fire. It was still going down. I made two more attempts to raise Captain Eiler. By this time I was sure his command jeep had been hit. Then I called Sergeant Thomas in the X-Ray jeep. "X-Ray, this is Pace, can you give me a sit rep from your pos, over?"

"Pace, this is X-Ray. I'm about halfway back. The road is blocked. I'm going to try and get on the shoulder and get back there. Be advised that there are civilian WIAs back here. Don't know how many. And it looks like we have casualties also."

"Roger, keep me posted, out." I had to make a decision when and if I would take command of the convoy and how I would do it. I could stay in the pace truck and command from it or I could transfer to Sergeant Thomas's X-Ray jeep and run it from there. I tried to raise Captain Eiler again. And again, nothing. *My God*, I thought, *Sergeant Thomas called it, the bend at Phu Gia Pass.* We rode right into it.

I tried Kilo Three, one of the infantry security trucks. The small arms seemed to be sporadic now. I didn't get anything because of double transmissions. The firing continued. It was now almost ten minutes from the opening of the ambush. It seemed like ten hours. I tried Kilo Three again. "This is Kilo Three. We've got people down back here, over."

Then I suddenly heard, "Kilo Three, this is Transport Six, get the hell out of that area!" I couldn't believe what I was hearing. "Transport Trail, give me a sit rep, over."

Jack responded. "This is Trail. Be advised that the wagon train is halted back here. Request permission to go forward with the trail package."

"This is Transport Six. That's negative. Maintain your position, Six out."

I keyed the handset again. "Transport Six, this is Pace. Interrogative, did you leave the net, over?"

"Pace, this is Six. That's negative. I had comm problems, over."

"This is Pace, I made a request through Defend Alpha to have a Cowpoke on station, over."

"This is Six. Roger to that, out."

I held the handset, looking at the radio. Crockett turned and looked at me. "What happened to the captain, lieutenant?"

"I wish I knew," I said. I stood again and looked through the binoculars. The small-arms and mortar fire had ceased. It looked like the enemy had broken contact. I scanned both sides of the road and the halted convoy, realizing that they let my package go through and took advantage of a gap. That was one of the most important things that I had heard—how dangerous the gaps could be. I recalled it from my first convoy with Gordon and Parker. There wasn't just one gap here; there were several. I wondered what the fallout of this would be.

Cowpoke, the Huey gunship, never did get cleared. The damaged vehicles and the wounded men were all U.S. Army, about two-thirds of the way back right at the opening of a gap. The NVA soldiers timed it perfectly. None of the wounded required a medevac. In addition to Phoung being killed, eight local villagers were wounded by mortar and Claymore mine shrapnel. The MPs, who had halted the convoy after the enemy broke contact, gave Jack the report of what Don and Hoang told them. Phoung's body was found in the sandy clearing, a fatal gunshot to the head. The MPs reported that twenty undetonated Claymore mines were found in the immediate area. It was impressive how the NVA soldiers set up that ambush in such a short timeframe.

It was less than an hour later when I got the word to move out again. When we reached the gate at Phu Bai, checkpoint three-eight, there were several MPs along the road observing our arrival. Because of the radio traffic everyone in the area knew that the convoy from Danang had been ambushed. After the pace truck pulled into the airstrip staging area I began making notes of what happened for the AAR. I also gave release signs to the Army and Seabee trucks. Then I made a note of Captain Eiler's absence off the net, which had to be explained. I was still writing when Captain Eiler's command jeep pulled in. I got out of the pace truck and approached his jeep. I noticed the look on his driver's face. Lance Corporal Albert Dawson appeared tired and a bit in shock. Captain Eiler was giving a transmission, so I waited until he finished. He finally replaced the handset on the MRC–109 radio. "All the casualties were Army. We were lucky in that regard."

"What happened back there, captain? You were off the net for about ten minutes," I said.

"I was in a bad area. I couldn't receive or transmit anything," he replied.

I looked over at Dawson. He grimaced and looked away, saying nothing.

"I'll need you, Sergeant Thomas, and Lieutenant Carmetti to write up what you saw from your vantage points," said Captain Eiler.

"Yes, sir," I said. "But what happened to your radio?"

"I have to clear up some details with Defend Alpha. We'll talk later."

I nodded and went back to the pace truck. I didn't like any of this. And I didn't like the facial reaction of Lance Corporal Dawson, his radioman-driver.

Sergeant Thomas's X-Ray jeep arrived, followed by Jack's trail package, his radio jeep, and a wrecker (tow truck). We quickly exchanged notes. This is when I learned about the Vietnamese boys and the damaged Army trucks that were left with a bridge security team. We then approached Captain Eiler, who was sitting in his radio jeep making notes.

Captain Eiler said, "Operations wants a complete report when we get back. So each of you will have to write up what you saw. The final report will come from me."

"Captain, I tried to get a Cowpoke on station back there. And Defend Alpha kept wanting to talk with you. I could have relayed if you were having radio problems," I said.

"That will come later, Lieutenant McAdams. In the meantime I have to talk with battalion on a landline." Captain Eiler gave a nod to Dawson and they headed off.

The three of us stood there looking at each other, still wondering what Captain Eiler's problem was. "Jack, about how many minutes was the captain off the radio net?" "At least ten, maybe more," said Jack. "When I came out of the pass the convoy was stretched all over hell and gone. There was no control."

"Those were ten crucial minutes," said Sergeant Thomas.

I looked at Sergeant Thomas. "What do you think?"

Sergeant Thomas shook his head. "With due respect, lieutenant, I'd rather not say."

After displacing the trucks for the night Sergeant Thomas, Jack, and I headed to the 1st Medical Battalion Staff/Officers club near the airstrip. Upon entering we had to check our weapons at a table near the door. It reminded me of a saloon in a 1950s western. I placed my unloaded shotgun and bandolier on the table along with my .45 sidearm. Jack and Sergeant Thomas did the same with their weapons. As we headed to the bar a chief petty officer turned and gave me a stare. I stopped, giving him a wondering look. And then I realized who it was: Nyman Harris from the *Ticonderoga*. He was a petty officer first class back then. Almost six years had gone by since I left the ship. We quickly exchanged greetings and caught up on each other's recent doings. Harris told me that two other corpsmen from the *Ticonderoga* were stationed nearby. As we were catching up I heard loud talking coming from the bar. It was Captain Eiler with a convoy control officer from Phu Bai. I shook hands with Harris and told him that we'd catch up on my next convoy.

Sergeant Thomas, Jack, and I edged in at the end of the bar and ordered beers. We spent the next twenty minutes listening to Captain Eiler give his account of the ambush. His voice went up and down the bar—how he was out there alone, trying to get communications with the rest of his convoy as the NVA hit us with Claymores, mortars, and small arms. He had the attention of everyone in the club, Navy corpsmen and Marines alike. "We tried to get a Cowpoke on station but it never happened," he said. "We were out there, fending for ourselves!"

Jack and I exchanged looks. I gave him a headshake, motioning to a backdoor. He nodded. We stepped outside with our beers. I remember it as a clear, warm night. The lights from the airstrip were off in the distance. We stared at the other side of the airstrip, staying silent for several moments. Then I broke the silence. "What do you think of the way he uses the pronoun *we*?"

"Are you thinking what I'm thinking?" asked Jack.

I nodded. "Maybe we should talk to his driver."

"Eiler will cover himself. He'll tell his driver not to say anything," I said.

"What are you going to write for the after-action report?" asked Jack.

"What I saw and heard," I said. "I actually thought he was hit and that I'd have to take command." I paused, thinking. "You know, Kilo Three was in the same section of road and I heard him perfectly."

"We were lucky today. Think what it's going to be like when we get another convoy order," said Jack. We exchanged dreaded looks and returned to the bar.

Captain Eiler was still holding court, giving his "John Wayne" account of the day's ambush. Jack and I ordered more beers.

The return convoy was uneventful. When we passed through the ambush site the damaged Army trucks were on the side of the road. *Waiting targets for booby traps*, I thought. Closer to the Hai Van Pass the village of Lang Co seemed peaceful. It was remarkable how that village could pass for a vacation spot in a travel agency's brochure.

Lieutenant Colonel Arnold and Major Ashworth were waiting at the front gate of 11th Motors when my pace truck rolled in. While standing in the bed I gave them a salute. Colonel Arnold nodded, returned the salute, and signaled for us to stop. He approached me and said, "Have Captain Eiler report to S-3 operations when he arrives."

I nodded, "Yes, sir." Colonel Arnold turned and walked off with Major Ashworth.

I notified Captain Eiler as soon as he pulled into the compound. We didn't see him for about two hours, all that time locked into a meeting in the operations office. Sergeant Thomas, Jack, and I busied ourselves with cleaning up and then catching up on reports and memos that had gathered during the previous two days. We also had to begin writing our after-action accounts to be included in Captain Eiler's final report. Top Duncan and the office staff wanted to know about the ambush. Different accounts were already circulating around the company and battalion. Rich Cobb and Gunnery Sergeant Rayhorn said that it was pretty quiet while we were gone. "I'm sure that's going to change now," said Rayhorn.

The following morning Jack and I turned in our handwritten ambush reports to be typed. When I joined Sergeant Woodard in the motor pool he asked me about the ambush. "We were lucky," I said. "It could have been a lot worse."

"It's all over the motor pool about Captain Eiler," said Woodard.

"What do you mean?" I asked.

Sergeant Woodard looked around, making sure this was a one-on-one conversation. "The word is that the captain ran out on you guys."

"Who told you that?" I asked.

"Rumor mill, lieutenant," he answered. "Anyway, glad that you made it back."

I decided to make a quick walk to the communications shack, where I found Lance Corporal Dawson, Captain Eiler's radioman-driver during the convoy, inside working on a radio. I asked him to step outside. He followed me outside and we stood next to the screen door. "First off, this is between you and me." Lance Corporal Dawson nodded. "What happened out there on the convoy when Captain Eiler went off the net?"

"Uh, I'm sorry, lieutenant, but the captain ordered me not to say anything to anybody until he finishes his after-action report."

I slowly nodded. "So, it's like that."

"Yes, sir, I'm afraid it is." My stomach was turning over with anger at this point. I thanked Dawson and headed back to the company office.

When I got back to the office I saw Captain Eiler in his cubicle writing something. "Did you get our ambush reports?" I asked.

He didn't even look up. "Yes, they're right here. I haven't read them yet." He put down his pen and looked up at me. "You have to report to S–1 Personnel. You've been appointed to prosecute a special court-martial."

I knew it would come sooner or later. "What's the charge?" I asked.

"Possession of marijuana. And it's one of our own, Lance Corporal Davis," said Eiler.

Even though Davis was in one of the other platoons, I knew him. He was a tall, dark-haired young guy from the south. "Was he smoking down on the perimeter wire?"

"Doesn't make any difference. He was using. And he needs to be busted, big-time," said Captain Eiler. "Get down to personnel, get the appointment order, and serve charges." He paused. "Since he's from our company I'm going to be watching this . . . very closely."

I walked with dread to the personnel office. Lieutenant Grunwald handed me the charge file. I was being given two weeks' preparation time. There would be three to five members sitting on the court-martial board. The president of the board would be a captain or major yet to be named. I sat at a nearby desk and read the file. Lance Corporal Davis had left his footlocker open while writing a letter. One of the sergeants happened to walk through the hooch and saw a plastic bag in the footlocker. The bag contained what turned out to be king-sized marijuana cigarettes, the kind available on the black market. He was brought up on office hours with a recommendation for a special court-martial. When I finished the file I signed for it and left the office. I was told that Davis was doing a stint in the mess hall. So I headed over there, pulled him out, and showed him the charge sheet. I read him his rights, according to procedure. Then I had him sign two copies of the charge sheet, giving him one. "What will happen now, lieutenant?" he asked.

"The only thing I can say at this point is that you'll be contacted by Lieutenant Carmetti. He'll be your defense counsel. Be honest with him." I took the file and left the mess hall, still angry that I was being a lawyer without going to law school.

I spent the next two days preparing the case, recalling the weeklong course in military law at TBS. As prosecutor I had to prove the elements of the offense to the court-martial board. If any one of the elements was in doubt an acquittal was likely. The burden of proof would rest on my preparation. And I knew that Captain Eiler would have me under the proverbial microscope.

During this time the battalion began getting convoy orders to support an Army Special Forces camp out in Thuong Duc Valley, southwest of Danang. The area was ripe with NVA activity. The convoys were small, less than twenty vehicles, each without a wrecker because of the thick terrain and the soft, unpaved roads. The first convoy of twelve vehicles was ambushed on the way out, with mortars, a .50-caliber machine gun, and small arms. Five Marines were killed. The convoy commander and his jeep driver were among the wounded. The command was transferred to a truck and the convoy got through to the Special Forces camp. The next morning the convoy commander was evacuated to the NSA facility in Danang. It was evident that more convoy orders to Thuong Duc were coming.

I began trial preparation. The next morning I was reading the *Marine Corps Manual for Courts-Martial* when Gunnery Sergeant Rayhorn came in the company office and stood at the counter. He asked to see me. I approached him and said, "Come on in the back to my desk."

He shook his head. "Uh, lieutenant, we should talk outside."

I grabbed my soft cover and went outside with him, sensing something serious. I thought he had something to tell me about Lance Corporal Davis's upcoming special court-martial. We began walking down to the company sector at the perimeter wire. "One of the trucks on deadline had a transmission problem and I needed to check it out." I nodded, listening. "I got on a creeper and slid under to look at the crank shaft. I was under the truck for a couple of minutes. Then I noticed a couple of sets of feet nearby. I didn't think anything of it. Then I realized that I was hearing something."

When Sergeant Rayhorn said this, the hairs on the back of my neck stood up. "What did you hear?"

Sergeant Rayhorn took a breath. "Lieutenant, there's a $2,000 price on Captain Eiler."

We stopped talking. For several moments both of us looked out at the rice paddy. Finally I asked, "Did you confront these men?"

He shook his head. "No, they didn't know that I was under the truck. I stayed there, on the creeper, listening to everything."

"What did they say?" I asked.

"Some of them have put up MPCs. They'll wait until the next convoy goes out. If an ambush goes down one of them will take out the captain." He paused. "The shooter will get the two large." Another pause. "It will be written off as a KIA."

"Did you recognize any of the voices?" I asked.

He shook his head. "No, they didn't even know I was there. I waited until they walked off. Then I got out from under and thought about it for a while. I heard about the convoy ambush and the scuttlebutt going around. That's why I decided to come to you."

"Do you think that this might be a lot of hot air, troops blowing off steam?"

"In another company, maybe, lieutenant. But this captain, in all honesty, sir, got off on the wrong foot. He made it worse with the Bobby Kennedy remark, right in front of the office staff. And now there's the other day and what happened out on that road," explained Rayhorn.

I said nothing for several moments. "All right, for now let's keep this between you and me. I'll try to figure something out. In the meantime I have to prepare for a court-martial date."

"Yes, sir, we heard about Davis," said Rayhorn. "Too bad, he's a nice kid."

When I got back to the office Captain Eiler was gone. First Sergeant Duncan told me that he was called to operations. "He got a convoy order to Thuong Duc."

I cringed at the words Thuong Duc. The troops referred to it as "Fuck Duc" because it was a hot area. This might play right into the planned hit on Captain Eiler, I thought. A few minutes later, as I was reading the *Manual for Courts-Martial*, the landline phone rang. First Sergeant Duncan picked it up and spoke for a few moments. He hung up and said, "Lieutenant, that was operations."

I looked up. "Now what?"

"Your presence is requested at operations," said the First Sergeant.

When I got to operations Captain Eiler was sitting in front of the I Corps map with Major Ashworth. Ashworth was tracing a route on a map. Captain Eiler made some notes and looked over at me. "You will be commanding a convoy to Thuong Duc in the morning."

I looked at him. "Captain, I'm in the middle of preparing for the Davis court-martial."

"Lieutenant, didn't they teach you how to juggle assignments at The Basic School?"

"Yes, sir, but a convoy will take me out for two days, maybe even more," I said. "I'm on a deadline."

"Nonetheless, you'll be in command tomorrow," said Captain Eiler.

I glanced at Major Ashworth, expecting some sort of reaction. Nothing from him. Then I looked at Captain Eiler as my stomach turned, recalling those ten to twelve minutes where he left the radio net at Phu Gia Pass. I didn't need to have a wall fall on me to know why I was getting this convoy order. Captain Eiler avoided my look, turning to his notes.

"It will be a small one, nineteen vehicles," explained Major Ashworth. "Instead of a radio jeep you'll be in a command truck with an MRC–109 mounted radio."

"Major Ashworth will explain the full order," said Captain Eiler. "I still have to work on my after-action report from the Phu Gia ambush." He got up and left the office.

For the next fifteen minutes Major Ashworth explained the convoy order as I took notes. This run was in support of the second phase of Operation Mameluke Thrust. Mameluke was the name of the Marine officer's sword worn at ceremonies and parade formations. Instead of a platoon of security this convoy would take a company. That spoke volumes to me. This would be the third convoy to Thuong Duc from our battalion. The previous two had been ambushed on the way out. The cargo would be bunker beams, C–4 plastic explosive, small-arms ammunition, grenades, flares, radio batteries, and C-rations. The infantry company and the FAC would join the convoy at Hill 52. We would then proceed to Hill 65. From there we would head southwest along Route 4 to Thuong Duc. I would also be given a grenade package, which contained two thermite grenades and various smoke grenades. The pace and trail vehicles would be equipped with .50-caliber guns on ring mounts. We stood at the map as he showed me the route of the convoy and the checkpoints. My call sign would be Transport 5. Riding in the trail vehicle would be Sergeant Woodard, also with a radio. Walking back to the company office my mind was reeling from this one-two combination. I had a two-week deadline to prepare for and prosecute a court-martial, for which I was not qualified. And now I was going back on the road, commanding a convoy that was a surefire bet to be ambushed, a convoy that was initially assigned to my company commander. What good would it do now to tell Captain Eiler about the $2,000 contract on his head? I decided to put the court-martial preparation and the $2,000 contract on the backburner. The front burner was the convoy to Thuong Duc.

7

Thuong Duc

Before giving my convoy briefing that evening I met with Sergeant Woodard and explained where he would be in the convoy line and that security would be a company picked up at Hill 52.

"Then we'll be the first Rough Rider convoy to carry a company of security instead of a platoon to Thuong Duc," remarked Sergeant Woodard.

I nodded. "You got that right."

I realized the increased odds. On the previous convoys the security unit was a platoon commanded by a lieutenant. This was a small convoy according to the order, nineteen vehicles, without a wrecker (M-543). The fact that security on this one was an entire company spoke volumes to me. Translation:

They're waiting for us but we're going out with more weight.

As I began my convoy briefing I noticed Captain Eiler sitting in the back of the conference room, taking notes. This meant that he would be giving me a critique of the briefing. Naturally, it would be negative. I began the briefing, outlining the mission: The convoy order was to resupply a Special Forces camp in Thuong Duc Valley. The Special Forces camp was set up there specifically to blunt NVA operations in the valley and along Song Vu Gia River. I added that this was in support of Operation Mameluke Thrust. I gave the route, heading out of Danang to the southwest, first to Hill 52 to pick up the security troops, then proceeding to Route 4 and Thuong Duc. I added the total amount of vehicles and radio call signs with checkpoints called in to division.

During the execution phase of the briefing I explained that the two previous convoys on this operation were ambushed on the way out. Those had a platoon of security; ours would have a company from the 1st Battalion, 7th Marine Regiment. I added that because of the terrain we would be without a wrecker. Someone asked what would happen if a truck became damaged or hit a road mine.

"Our policy is to leave nothing behind that can aid the enemy." I remember looking around the room and then to the rear at Captain Eiler. "That decision will rest with me as convoy commander." How prophetic that would be.

Another question came up. "What's the latest on enemy activity?"

"There are at least three company-size NVA units, from an NVA regiment, working in that valley according to the latest intelligence reports. I'll have an update on that before we leave."

Someone asked, "What about air cover?"

"There will be a Huey on call through a forward air controller." Again I looked around the room. "Hopefully we won't need him." I knew full well that we would need him as well as preset artillery targets.

After I dismissed the briefing several people approached me with follow-up questions. I could sense their necessary concern. I noticed Captain Eiler leaving the room. With each answer to the follow-up questions I managed to contain my anger knowing that Captain Eiler should be commanding this convoy.

When I returned to my hooch I saw the Davis court-martial file where I had left it on my bunk. I picked up the file and stared at it, still upset at having this convoy thrown at me by my company commander. I put the file in my locker, sat on my bunk, and wrote a letter to Patty. I remember keeping an upbeat tone to the letter, all the time wondering if this would be my last letter to her and where I would be in twenty-four hours. It made me reflect on my three-hour epiphany at Camp Hansen on Okinawa. The things that run through your mind on the eve of battle can almost cause a complete breakdown. My thoughts then went to OCS and the fact that I applied to the Marine Corps with open eyes, going into a combat zone knowing what the odds were. And tomorrow I would be facing the odds.

I was just about finished with the letter when Corporal Adair knocked on the rear door of the hooch. He apologized for the late hour and added that Captain Eiler wanted to see me in the company office immediately. All I could do was sigh, put pen and paper aside, gather my soft cover, and head to the company office. When I entered Captain Eiler's cubicle he was reading one of his paperback detective novels and smoking a cigarette. He set the novel aside and pulled out his notebook. "I noted some discrepancies in your convoy briefing."

I stood in front of his desk. "Captain, it's been a long day and I have a convoy tomorrow. Can't we do this at another time?"

He shook his head. "Negative, we'll do it now." He glanced at his notebook, stubbing out the cigarette. "You neglected to state the convoy speed and the distance between vehicles. You also neglected to state the chain of command."

"I explained that the checkpoints would be called into Defend at division convoy control."

He shook his head. "Not good enough. The chain goes from your command vehicle to battalion to division."

"Correction, captain. On the road my direct contact is with division convoy control. Convoy control is where I call in the checkpoints with battalion monitoring."

He glanced at his notebook again, ignoring my correction. "Still, there was no mention of chain of command and distance between the vehicles."

I took a deep breath, taking the shortest point to end this senseless meeting. "Yes, sir." He closed his notebook and leaned back in his chair. In that moment I thought of telling him of the price on his head. Instead, the convoy was my priority. If he was in command of the convoy I would have definitely told him at this point. *There will come a time*, I thought. "Will that be all?"

"One more thing," he said. "Make sure you check the G-2 intelligence reports in the morning."

I glared at him, remembering the June 10 preparation where he neglected to check the intelligence reports and reprimanded me for being late into the motor pool. "Yes, sir, it's the convoy commander's responsibility."

"That's all, Frank." I left the office and he resumed reading his novel.

That night I tossed and turned the first few hours. Then I drifted off. When first light came through the nearby screens my eyes opened. *This is it*, I thought. Might as well dress, get to the mess hall, and put down a hardy breakfast. Since I was the first one in the officer's mess I ate alone. Upon leaving, outside, I ran into Major Ashworth. I saluted and said, "'Morning, major."

He returned the salute, walking to the door. "Lieutenant McAdams, have you checked the morning intelligence reports?"

I nodded. "I'm on my way to do that now, major."

Major Ashworth turned, holding the door. "Make sure that you do."

Here I am commanding a convoy into a valley with noted NVA activity. Like always, before any convoy, I will check the latest intelligence reports. It suddenly dawned on me that Major Ashworth, since reporting into the battalion, had never been on a convoy, either down south or through the Hai Van Pass.

Upon entering the battalion commander's office I went right to the G-2 clipboard. The latest reports had been posted from 1st Force Reconnaissance Battalion and division headquarters. The three enemy units were still operating in the valley and along Song Vu Gia River. These sightings were on both sides of Route 4, where the Song Vu Gia intersects with the Song Con. The convoy would be heading right into that—fullback up the middle. It hit me that I could have NVA on both sides of that road. No wonder they were giving me a company of security.

I met Sergeant Woodard in the motor pool. Because there were no jeeps on this run he would be in the trail truck with a PRC-25 radio tuned to my frequency. I placed my command truck one-third of the way back, about the fifth truck. I had a radioman, Lance Corporal Roger Sillcox, and a mounted MRC-109 radio. I also had an M-60 machine gun with a gunner, Corporal J. R. Forsythe. The pace and trail trucks had swing-mounted .50-caliber guns.

I climbed aboard the command truck and did a radio check. Then I pulled out the Thuong Duc map and did a quick recon. I went right to Route 4, along Song Vu Gia River, and then worked backward to Danang. About twenty minutes later we got the word to head out to Hill 52 to pick up the security company.

As we headed out of the battalion compound Lieutenant Colonel Arnold and Major Ashworth were standing by the gate. Standing in the truck bed, I gave them a salute and they returned it. It was then when I noticed that Captain Eiler was nowhere to be seen. I shook my head. My own company commander hadn't even thought to see us off on a convoy that he should be commanding. By the time we reached Hill 52 the temperature had cracked 90 degrees. Many of the drivers had a rag or a towel stuffed in the necks of their flak jackets to absorb the heavy perspiration. I used a second T-shirt. I checked in with Defend—division convoy control—and said that I was waiting at the Pennywise Hill (meaning Hill 52). Pennywise was the radio call sign for the 1st Battalion of the 7th Marine Regiment. I was also getting radio traffic on a force logistics convoy going north through the Hai Van Pass.

I met the CO of Alpha Company, Captain John Craig, a stocky man who recently took over as company commander. His call sign would be Pennywise Alpha. He introduced me to his gunnery sergeant. And then the security troops began boarding the trucks. It was a light company, approximately seventy-five total troops. In motor transport parlance we were "loading for bear." We had as many security troops on trucks as we did cargo, pound for pound. I watched as the troops—teenagers, most of them—boarded and checked their weapons. I began to think that my fears were unjustified. Maybe this will be a milk run, that I'll have the first Rough Rider convoy to reach Thuong Duc without being ambushed. Less than an hour later we got a green light to Hill 65. We moved off the hill in the morning heat. At Hill 65 we checked in and got the okay to head out to Thuong Duc.

The road going southwest out of Hill 65 had long been secured for daylight traffic. But once we made the turn that led to Route 4 we all knew that we were leaving safe confines and heading into dangerous territory. At this point I could hear the clicks as the troops began inserting magazines into their M-16s. For some reason I recalled a line from an old John Ford cavalry movie as a column of troops was leaving the fort: "If you see them they aren't Apaches." After a while we made a slight turn and headed northwest. I called in a checkpoint and looked around, studying the terrain. Then I used my binoculars, scanning the hills and knolls along with the distant ridgelines. It all seemed peaceful enough. But I still kept wondering if there was a mortar team setting up somewhere out there. The NVA was notable with mortars, par excellence.

We continued along the road keeping Song Vu Gia River on our left. I called in another checkpoint as the convoy slowed for a left turn. This was a perfect spot for an ambush, I felt, with the convoy slowing almost to a crawl. The area had become thicker with swamplike terrain. This was the reason why we didn't have a wrecker; the mere weight of the vehicle would cause it to sink into the ground, thereby slowing the convoy.

The heat became more intense as we moved southwest. The absence of any breezes brought up a pungent fish odor. Across the river was the first of three hamlets where the villagers did their day's toiling either in the rice paddies or fishing in the river. We passed a primitive waterwheel on our right that was pumping water from a nearby creek into a lower level of rice paddy. Even though it was primitive construction, going back hundreds of years, it still had a look of efficiency. Farther out I saw a farmer working on a rice-paddy dike. I raised the binoculars for a closer look. I had heard stories how a farmer in the paddies was a lookout, somehow giving information to the enemy as to our direction, speed, and size. From my position on the road, however, he had the appearance of a farmer and nothing more. The convoy continued as the heat became stifling, mixed with the stench of fish. Everybody on the command truck had taken salt pills at the start of the day. And now we were finishing off the first of our two canteens as the sweat was literally pouring out. I knew that at the end of the day I would have salt stains on my utility blouse.

We continued on Route 4 as I called in another checkpoint. There was a hamlet on our left that bordered the river. Several villagers, wearing cone hats, were in small skiffs out in the river lightly sculling with the current, which was moving east toward Danang. I always found the resiliency of the villagers brave and fascinating. Here they have two armies fighting in their locale, in skirmishes and battles day and night, and they calmly continue with the day's work to feed their families. For some reason I thought of Lieutenant Colonel Arnold's observation that he made on our first meeting: "They're really a childish people." These villagers were anything but childish.

About a half-hour later we passed an airstrip on our right. It was a small strip obviously designed for light fixed-wing aircraft. The strip was a paved tarmac, about two football fields in length. We slowly crossed over Song Con River where I called in another checkpoint, still looking around, studying the terrain and wondering where the hell the NVA was lurking and when would they hit us.

They never did.

Within another half-hour we were rolling into the Special Forces camp. Our only enemy on this Rough Rider convoy was the intense heat, which now had to be hovering between 110 and 115 degrees. I called in our arrival at the Sierra Foxtrot (Special Forces) destination, feeling that the third time was the charm. Transport 5 had become the first 11th Motors convoy to get into Thuong Duc without being hit on Operation Mameluke Thrust. The CO of the Special Forces camp was an Army captain. He was about my size with a tanned face, salt and pepper gray hair, and a gunfighter's mustache. I expected the commander to be at least a major or lieutenant colonel. He congratulated me on getting in safely, which surprised him. As we shook hands the troops began dismounting from the security trucks. Captain Craig approached me, and we began discussing the nighttime perimeter defense and where I would position my trucks with the .50-caliber gun mounts.

Then somebody cracked a Budweiser can and handed it to me. I cocked my head, held the can up, and let the beer cascade into my mouth, splashing a bit on my face and flak jacket. Naturally the beer was warm. To me it was a "cool one." To this day I consider it the best beer I ever tasted.

The Special Forces captain explained what the terrain was like outside the perimeter and where the NVA had made probes during previous nights. Based on the captain's recommendations I positioned our .50-caliber gun trucks so that they would "interlock" on our side. Two of their bunkers with M-60 machine guns were already in position on the other side. I placed my command truck, with its M-60, in between the two .50-caliber gun trucks. Even though we made it safely into the camp, we now had to contend with an NVA specialty—the night attack.

I remember doing another map recon for the return convoy, looking at Route 4 and making mental notes where an NVA officer would choose for an ambush zone. Then I grabbed a quick C-ration meal. After that I jumped back in the bed of the command truck and took a quick "recon nap," knowing that I would be awake most of the night checking our side of the perimeter. In a situation like this you grab sleep piecemeal.

Corporal Forsythe shook me in what seemed like minutes later. I got about a ninety-minute respite and opened my eyes to a fast-fading twilight. I put on my flak jacket and assembled some hand flares in the truck bed. As soon as darkness came that eerie jungle silence settled in. This is where the moon becomes either friend or foe. On this night the moon started out as a friend. Because of where we were I knew the troops would be on edge as the night wore on, all the time wondering if they were hearing something while seeing nothing. I thought of a line from the classic western film *The Searchers*: "It's quiet out there . . . too quiet." We popped a few flares periodically, but they showed no movement.

With first light I had the feeling that the Divine Providence was watching over us. It was as peaceful as a summer night on a Southern California beach. And it put most of us in a good mood for the return convoy. After checking in with DCC I shared some coffee with Captain Craig. We had to wait for Route 4 along the Song Vu Gia to be swept by a detail of two tanks. This gave the troops time for C-rations and to clean their weapons. And the day was going to be another oven. I met with my drivers and emphasized to watch the road ten to fifteen yards in front, to stay in the tracks of the vehicle in front of them. I could see the seriousness in their faces. I didn't need to tell them who might be lurking in the next tree line. We went back to the trucks and waited for the green light from division. Once more, I used the time for a quick recon nap.

About ninety minutes later we got the word to move out along with a report that one tank had struck a road mine but was being towed by the other. They were nicknamed "Fred" and "Ginger." I found the Special Forces captain and said that we were cleared to leave. He thanked me and wished us well. I boarded my command truck and ordered a moveout. As soon as we cleared the camp the troops began putting magazines into their weapons. For some reason I thought back to what Bob Gordon said on the first day that I reported in: "We're like the Eighth Air Force in England during World War II . . . and we're out there, bare-assed and rolling." We met the tanks, Fred and Ginger, about fifty yards out, where they fell in to guide us back. Just the sight of the tanks gave off a safe feeling.

As we headed northeast on Route 4 I called in a checkpoint and studied the map. I noted the right turn that we had to make that would cause the convoy to slow. Our speed was 10–15 miles per hour. That turn was also the closest point that the convoy would be to two ridgelines on our left. I remembered those coming out, but now I was looking at them even closer. Once we passed that point we were home-free.

Even though we were close to the river on our right, the area on our left was thick with foliage and undergrowth. Suddenly I heard a Huey coming in over the right side of the river. With choppers, you hear them before you see them. It was always a welcome sound, this time making me feel more secure as I continued watching for the pace truck to make its turn.

And then it came, a loud explosion not at the front but from the rear. *Ho-ly shit!*

I turned and saw a black cloud and knew instantly that one of our trucks had hit a road mine. I called the pace truck and told them to stop and swing the .50-caliber gun around to face the ridgeline. The tanks also halted. I could hear screaming and yelling. A few troops were cranking off rounds into the tree line to our left.

I told Sergeant Woodard to meet me with his PRC-25 radio and I got off the command truck. Captain Craig checked in, notifying me that the mined vehicle, from the 7th Marine Regiment, was about third or fourth from the rear. He told me that the truck looked demolished. I fast-walked down the convoy line, leaving Sillcox in the command truck. My first thoughts went to casualties and snipers.

Sergeant Woodard met me at the damaged truck. The first thing I noticed was the gaping crater hole. The device had to be a huge box mine or a 155-millimeter artillery round. It most likely was command-detonated, which meant that we had company in the tree line. I realized that they allowed two-thirds of the convoy to pass and hit the one with the most troops aboard. One of the security squad leaders told me that we had taken seven wounded. Captain Craig arrived in front of me. I said to keep his men on the trucks but also to cover the tree line. The force of the explosion had lifted the truck off the road to the right. The undercarriage took the brunt of the blast, which probably saved some lives. One of the front tires was in shreds. The frame was bent and there were shrapnel holes in the floor of the cab. The black powder smoke lingered in the area like a bad cigar. Captain Craig said that he would transfer his men to different trucks and moved back up the convoy line. The driver was wounded but not seriously.

I now saw why the Huey was in the area. He was making a gun run on the other side of the river where a firefight was. I grabbed the PRC-25 handset and called Defend at DCC, reporting my position and that I had taken seven wounded from a command-detonated road mine. I added that a Huey was in the air across the blue line (Song Vu Gia River) covering another unit in contact.

"Interrogative, Transport 5, what is the condition of the vehicle, over?"

I gave a quick damage assessment, adding that, in my opinion, the vehicle was beyond repair and should be blown in place so that we could move out of the area as we didn't have a wrecker.

"Roger, Transport 5, you're requesting to blow the damaged vehicle in place, over?"

Before I could respond Captain Craig's troops began firing into the tree line. Then I heard more fire, not from the river but from the tree line on our left. I realized what was happening. It was another "*Oh, shit!*" moment. My convoy was caught in between two firefights—a classic pincer with us in the middle.

I keyed the handset again. "Defend, this is Transport 5, that's affirmative on the request. Be advised that I have two firefights, I say again, two firefights moving in on my pos, over."

From Defend I heard, "Roger, wait one." I could sense the growing uneasiness with the security troops on the trucks, a natural reaction. For the next several minutes they continued transferring the casualties to other trucks. I found a corpsman working on one of the wounded. "Anything for a medevac?"

The Corpsman kept working on the Marine, shaking his head without looking at me. "No, they'll be able to make it."

I radioed back to the pace truck to send a runner with two thermite grenades and a red smoke grenade. Captain Craig come running toward me as the firefight across the river got louder. The Huey had now turned around and was coming back on another gun run. "Lieutenant, we gotta get the hell outta here. And now!"

I nodded to him and called Defend again. "This is Transport 5, requesting an answer to the request." I quickly scanned the tree line and the two ridges, hearing rounds coming from that direction. *Shit*, I thought, *both firefights are moving in on us.* I not only had my drivers to worry about; I had a company of infantry security as sitting ducks in the truck beds.

From Defend I was told, "Roger, wait one."

I notified the FAC that there was an enemy force moving in on my right "approaching the blue line"— the Song Vu Gia. I knew if the enemy began crossing the river I could be under fire from two sides. Corporal Forsythe arrived with the grenade package.

It was now about twenty minutes from the time of the explosion. The only sounds came from the firefight across the river. The Huey was still in the air making gun runs, trying to prevent the enemy force from approaching the edge of the river. I keyed the handset and requested an answer from Defend. The response came quickly, "Roger, Transport 5, wait one, out."

I gave the crater hole another look. The mangled truck was resting on the road side; what a mess. I recalled convoy doctrine, leave nothing behind to the enemy. And I remembered hearing about the Army trucks that were booby-trapped after being left behind at Phu Gia Pass. I wiped my forehead and looked at Sergeant Woodard standing nearby. Down the truck line Captain Craig kept his security troops in place. What the hell is taking so damn long? I thought of the air-conditioned offices back at division headquarters. I grabbed the handset again and keyed it. "Defend, this is Transport 5, be advised of my situation. I need an answer ASAP, over!"

"Roger, Transport 5, wait one." This was becoming ridiculous. The firefight on the other side of the river continued with the Huey up in the air.

I could see Captain Craig approaching again. The expression on his face said it all. "Lieutenant, what the hell is the holdup?"

I stood there, feeling both angry and foolish, holding the handset. "I'm trying to get an answer from division to blow the truck so we can get out of here."

"Once again, as convoy commander, you have my security troops in a vulnerable position. We need to get out of here ten minutes ago!"

I looked at my watch. It was now a half-hour since the explosion. I keyed the handset again. "Defend, be advised if I don't get an answer within two minutes I will blow the damaged vehicle in place. I say again, two minutes, over."

"Roger, wait one, out." I nodded to Captain Craig. He turned and walked down the convoy line, saying something to his platoon commanders.

The closest security truck had a .50-caliber mounted gun. I knew that the tracers would ignite the diesel fuel if it came to that. Several of the security troops began firing into the tree line. Then they were told to cease fire. Finally, the two minutes were up. I keyed the handset again. "Defend, this is Transport 5. Interrogative on my request, over."

"Transport 5, stand by. We're waiting for a committee decision, over."

I couldn't believe what I was hearing. *A fucking committee decision?* It was well past the thirty-five-minute mark at this point. I keyed the handset again. "Defend, be advised I am not going to keep this convoy in a vulnerable position. The damaged vehicle will be blown in place, do you roger, over?"

"Transport 5, this is Defend, wait one, out."

I reached into the bag and pulled out a thermite grenade. Its composition, when armed, is not explosive but causes intense heat, high enough to melt an engine block. All I had to do was pull the pin. Sergeant Woodard and I went to the nearest security truck. I had the gunner get down off the ring mount. Then I took his position. I moved the gun to get an angled line of sight on the truck and the fuel tank. Then I yelled, "Stand aside at the truck!"

I cocked the gun twice, as required for a .50-caliber. Then I held the two handles and slowly pressed the butterfly trigger in between. I was prepared for the heavy recoil as the rounds went out, tracers hitting the fuel tank, which smoldered at first and then ignited as more tracers hit. As the flames came up I nodded to the gunner and jumped off the ring mount. Then I approached the truck, holding the thermite grenade, as the flames got more intense.

The hood was already ajar, popped open by the force of the explosion. I pulled the pin on the thermite grenade. The fuse started with a hissing sound. Then I placed the grenade on top of the engine block. I stepped back a few feet and stared at my work. As I recall it took less than ninety seconds. And I heard nothing from Defend or what the so-called committee was deciding.

I looked at the driver of the pace truck and gave him a circle signal with my right hand—get ready to roll. Captain Craig came fast walking up the road. He nodded to me, "I agree with what you did, lieutenant. Now let's get the fuck outta here!"

Forsythe and I climbed aboard the command truck. I gave the order to move out. Then I turned and looked at the smoke coming from burning truck. The firefight was still on the other side of the river and the Huey was still making gun runs. What seemed like two hours was actually less than forty minutes. And there still was no decision from DCC.

As we continued back down Route 4 Defend called and said, "Do not, I say again, do not blow the damaged vehicle."

I remember chuckling to myself with the choice of words, *don't blow the damaged vehicle*. The truck had been totaled by the damn mine! I keyed the handset, "Defend, be advised that the vehicle was blown in place." There was a long silence on the net.

And then came, "Transport 5, this is Defend. Roger, out."

We continued along Route 4 and soon arrived back at Hill 52 where Captain Craig's company was headquartered. As his platoon commanders were taking count of the troops and casualties being moved to the battalion aid station, Captain Craig approached my command truck. "If you need a statement about this let me know." I nodded and gave him a salute. He muttered something about a committee making a decision and walked off.

I called in to Defend that we were departing Alpha hill for Charlie Papa (11th Motors). Defend responded, "Transport 5, interrogative, you blew the vehicle in place, over?"

"This is Transport 5. That's a roger. The damaged vehicle was blown in place. The seven WIAs are being treated on Alpha hill, over."

"Interrogative, Transport 5, what gave you authority to blow that vehicle, over?"

I was getting pissed at this point. "Defend, be advised that I am the convoy commander. I had two firefights moving in on me, as noted, and was acutely aware of the situation having a company of security in a vulnerable position for an extended period." I paused. "I needed a decision. When no decision came after thirty mikes [minutes] I took the initiative, over." There was silence on the net for several moments. Then I keyed the handset again. "Defend, interrogative, what was the reason for the delay on your end, over?"

"Transport 5, this is Defend. Report to your Charlie Papa, over."

I gave the handset to Sillcox. I remember taking a deep breath, trying to control a seething anger. I had to find out why we were kept waiting. And I knew that headquarters people, both at division and at 11th Motors, were monitoring the transmissions.

When we arrived at 11th Motors I was informed to report to operations. The first thing they wanted to know was the map coordinates of the truck and the condition of the casualties. I explained that they didn't need to be evacuated, that they were being treated at Hill 52. I explained that Captain Craig, CO of Alpha Company, is willing to write a statement for my AAR. "Do I need to talk with Colonel Arnold?" I asked.

"He's not available right now. He's talking with division convoy control."

I left operations, went to my hooch, and proceeded to undress for a trip to the showers. As I stood under the showerhead I reflected on the two days. The first day was easy; the second was exhausting and stressful. I still needed to know what caused the thirty-five-minute delay. After I got dressed I began making notes for my AAR. Then I headed to the mess hall for a hot meal.

Upon leaving the mess hall I ran into Captain Eiler. "I was in operations, listening to everything out there," he said.

"Did you hear anything about division keeping me waiting for thirty-five minutes?" I asked.

He shook his head. "Something about a meeting to decide your request. I wouldn't worry about it. You did the right thing and got the hell out of there."

"That's nice to hear on this end," I said.

I went to the company office and started on the first draft of my AAR. I worked on several drafts then decided to put my notes aside, waiting to see what would come down from division. Besides, I had to prosecute an upcoming special court-martial. I couldn't believe the previous twenty-four hours. So much had changed in a short time.

That night I walked over to the Staff/Officers club. It was the club tradition to take off your soft cover before entering. Anyone who entered wearing either a helmet or soft cover had to buy the entire bar a round. As I went up the steps I took off my soft cover. Upon entering I placed my cover on a rack. When I turned around everyone in the bar—senior NCOs and officers—began clapping and hooting. One of the sergeants gave a two-handed gesture mimicking an explosion and said, laughing, "Lieutenant McAdams . . . boom!"

I couldn't buy a drink that night. The main topic was the thirty-five-minute delay, what caused it, and what kind of combat award I would be recommended for. While this was going on I saw Colonel Arnold enter with Major Ashworth. Both men walked right by me without saying anything and settled in at a corner. *Uh-oh*, I thought, *there's going to be more to this.* Later, with the television in the far corner near Colonel Arnold and Major Ashworth showing a *Gunsmoke* episode in Japanese, I kept looking out of the corner of my eye. If only I could place a recording device under that table. . . .

Throughout the night I kept getting backslaps and handshakes. I heard remarks like, "Fuck division, you're out there and they're back here in an air-conditioned office. . . . A committee is a body of people who attempt to design a horse and come up with a camel."

I walked back to my hooch that night a little lightheaded. Naturally I had no idea what was about to unfold.

8

Investigation

The next morning, upon reporting into the company office to resume work on my court-martial preparation, First Sergeant Duncan informed me that I had to report to Major Ashworth at operations. I suspected that they wanted more information about what happened on the road back from Thuong Duc.

I entered the operations office, where the office clerks were busy with reports and the day's convoys—a line haul down south to Hoi An and a convoy north through the Hai Van Pass. I sat next to Major Ashworth's desk. After several moments he pulled a file and opened it. "I need you to sign this, Lieutenant McAdams."

The memo had an 11th Motors heading. I stared at it, wondering. "Sign this for what?" I asked.

Major Ashworth leaned back in his chair. "I've been appointed investigating officer into the truck-blowing incident on the road returning from Thuong Duc."

"You've got to be kidding, major, an investigation?"

"You destroyed a government vehicle without authorization," said Major Ashworth. "That's a violation of a division order, which is why the investigation was appointed."

"No, sir," I said. "The NVA destroyed the vehicle," I countered. "I blew it in place to leave nothing behind to the enemy after being kept waiting for thirty-five minutes."

"The investigation will state the facts and make recommendations," said Major Ashworth. "Right now I need your signature that you have been advised of the investigation."

I signed the memo and was given a copy. "So I'll have to get statements from those on the convoy," I said.

He shook his head. "That's my job as investigating officer. Yours is to write a statement, have it typed, and submit it to me."

"I'll need to talk with several people about the thirty-five-minute delay," I said. "I still haven't been told what caused it."

Major Ashworth didn't say anything. He placed the appointment order back in the file. Before I left operations one of the clerks informed me that the Special Forces camp out in Thuong Duc got hit with a heavy sapper attack during the night. "They took beaucoup casualties," he said. "The fight went on until dawn, Katie Bar the Door." "Katie Bar the Door" was Marine Corps jargon for hand-to-hand fighting using the K-Bar combat knife.

"What happened to their CO?" I asked.

He shook his head. "No details on the casualties."

Back at the company office I showed Captain Eiler the memo. "I have to write a statement," I said.

"That's standard procedure," said Captain Eiler, looking up from reading a detective novel.

I said, "I remember what you said at the mess hall yesterday, not to worry about it."

He set the novel aside. "What do you mean?"

"Yesterday at the mess hall when we met. You said not to worry about it. You added that I did the right thing and got the hell out of there," I explained.

Another stare, this one was longer. "I never said that you did the right thing." He paused and then asked, "Did you tell Major Ashworth or Colonel Arnold that I said that?"

"No," I said. "But I remember you telling me—"

He interrupted. "Let's get this straight right now. I never told you that you did the right thing. I do remember saying that it was good that you got out of there."

The proverbial winds were shifting, big-time. "Don't you have a special court-martial to prepare for?"

"Yes, sir," I said. "The Davis case."

"Well, get to it."

At this point my head was spinning. I was halfway through outlining *Elements of the Offense* for my special court-martial prosecution. All I could do was stare at my handwriting. My thoughts were 180 degrees from the upcoming Davis trial. Here I was, the appointed battalion prosecutor, and I was now under a separate investigation for allegedly violating a division order. Again, I made an attempt to calm my anger. But that's all it was—an attempt. I knew that the anger was going to be there until Major Ashworth's investigation was resolved. Beyond that, I was going to be judged on how well I prepared for this special court-martial.

I remember taking an early lunch at the mess hall, sitting alone trying to organize my thoughts, when Lieutenant Andy Garrison entered. He came right to my table. "Mac, I've been transferred to the S–1 personnel office. And I just saw a copy of the investigation appointing order."

I nodded. "I had to sign a memo," I said. "I'm told that I violated a division order, acting without authority. They kept me waiting out there for more than a half-hour."

"Have you found out why?" asked Andy.

I shook my head. "Not yet. I'm heading up to division to check the radio log. They should have a record of the transmissions."

"I can't believe this shit," said Andy. "Let me know what happens." He walked over to the food line.

When I returned to the company office Sergeant Woodard was waiting for me. "Can we talk somewhere, lieutenant?"

I nodded and we stepped outside, walking to the command bunker down by the perimeter wire. The last time I took a walk like this it was with Sergeant Rayhorn—who had informed me about the $2,000 price on Captain Eiler's head. Transport Company was turning into a daytime soap opera.

"Major Ashworth wants me to write a statement on Thuong Duc," explained Sergeant Woodard.

"I have to write one, too," I said.

"What do you think I should say?" he asked.

I stopped, quickly replaying the scenario in my head. "Write it exactly as you saw it. You can emphasize how they kept us waiting out there, for thirty-five Goddamn minutes!"

"We had two firefights closing in on us," he recalled.

I nodded. "And we had to wait for a committee decision, a committee sitting back here in an air-conditioned office."

"The infantry captain agreed that you did the right thing," said Sergeant Woodard.

"Did you hear him say that?" I asked.

Sergeant Woodard nodded. "I was on my way back to the trail vehicle, passing his truck when he said it."

"Put that in your statement," I suggested.

"Lieutenant, what are they trying to do?" he asked.

"Between you and me, battalion is covering its ass with division. They're contending that I violated a division order, blowing up a truck without authorization," I explained. "I tried to get in to talk with Colonel Arnold but he won't see me."

"Don't they realize that the damn truck was already blown by the NVA?"

I nodded. "That's the catch. And it might work in my favor."

How wrong I was.

I returned to the office and continued outlining my prosecution case. When Captain Eiler came in from lunch he called me to his cubicle. "I understand you're writing a statement for the investigation."

"Yes, sir, I have to check out the radio transmissions up at division. It will document the time from the explosion to when we finally got back on the road."

"What are you going to say about our conversation at the mess hall?" he asked.

"That you said not to worry about it, that I did the right thing," I answered.

Captain Eiler gave me a long stare. Then he stood. "We had this discussion, Frank. I told you that I never said that you did the right thing." Another pause. "Why are you countering me on that?"

"Because that's the way I remember it, captain."

He sat back down. "For your own sake, don't put that in your statement. It will work against you."

"In what way, captain?" I asked.

"In ethics and truthfulness. Remember, I'm the one who will be recommending your fitness report."

I stared at him for several moments. *You two-faced, lying son-of-a-bitch.* "Yes, sir, I know."

He nodded. "I know you have trial preparation to do." As I walked out of his cubicle he picked up another of his paperback detective novels.

I left his cubicle, went back to my desk, and looked at my trial preparation pages. I remember staring at the first two paragraphs. Five minutes later I was still looking at them with glazed eyes. Whiskey Tango Foxtrot. In the military this is phonetic alphabet for the universal question. "What The Fuck [is this all about]?"

That night I went over to the Staff/Officers Club. They had a Peter Sellers comedy on the screen out on the patio. I ordered a beer and looked around. Then I realized that since the first time I reported into this battalion I was drinking alone. No more backslaps, no more laughing, no more talking about which combat medal I would be recommended for. I drank my beer slowly that night, at the end of the bar, hearing the laughing coming from a movie whose title I have since long forgot. For some reason, today, I can still hear the laughter.

The next day I told Captain Eiler that I had to check out a jeep to drive over to division legal to meet with one of the lawyers on a prosecution point in the upcoming Davis special court-martial. He nodded to me with a smile. "Get a conviction and a worthwhile sentence for that pot-smoking doofus fuck."

I walked out of the cubicle, leaving him to sign training reports and catch up on his paperback detective novel. Then I signed out a jeep and drove out of the compound to the division legal office. There was a captain there whom I had heard about, Carl Davidson. He was a broad-shouldered guy, a little taller than me, sandy red hair with glasses, who some people called an "Intellectual Gyrene." He was a product of the Platoon Leaders Class–Law. The Marine Corps selected law-school students who would do their active duty as lawyers. The PLC-Law Candidates had to do two summers at Quantico and then would be commissioned as first lieutenants upon graduation from an accredited law school. After TBS graduation they would report to their first assignment, to prosecute and defend general courts-martial. Captain Carl Davidson was my designated mentor to guide me through prosecuting a lower special court-martial.

In his office I explained the facts of the case and then the elements of the offense as I saw them. He explained what I had to do for a thorough prosecution. The first element was to convince the tribunal beyond any reasonable doubt. Next were the acts and the mental state of the accused. This was followed by the elements of the offense that were in violation of the *Uniform Code of Military Justice* (*UCMJ*). I had to prove all of these before a tribunal. If the accused was convicted, I had to make an argument for sentencing.

I now had a clearer path to my prosecution. It was a short meeting and I thanked Captain Davidson for his time, opinions, and suggestions.

When I left his office I went to the true mission of my trip: to visit DCC and acquire a copy of the radio log, documenting the thirty-five-minute delay on the Thuong Duc convoy. I met Lieutenant Robinson, who, ironically, was the same lieutenant that picked me up months before when I first landed at the 15th Aerial Port. He had been transferred to the Convoy Control section of Division G–4. Further, he was the voice to whom I was talking during the thirty-five-minute delay. We sat at a counter in the small radio room. Above us, on a shelf, were several radios that monitored convoys on numerous frequencies throughout the First Marine Division's area of responsibility (AOR). Each radio was dialed into a different frequency. Along a wall was a bunk on which the night clerk could grab a recon nap. I explained to Robinson why I was there, that I needed to check the radio log for June 22. I remember him shaking his head, giving off a slight laugh. "You've got to be kidding."

"I need to document that thirty-five-minute delay," I added.

He pointed to the shelf above our heads where the radios were perched. "You see those radios?" I nodded. "They cover the entire division AOR, anything where rolling stock is involved, from Force Logistics, to the Hai Van Pass, south to Hoi An, then over to An Hoa and Thuong Duc. Once the roads get swept I have to monitor every convoy that goes out." He paused, picking up a wire notebook. "Yours was just one convoy under fire that afternoon. A Force Logistics convoy up in the pass was taking sniper fire at the same time." Robinson then began paging through the notebook. "Yeah, here it is, Transport Five, Route Four, Thuong Duc Valley."

He passed the notebook over to me. I looked at a half-page of quickly scrawled notes indicating "seven WIAs" (wounded in action), the grid coordinates, and that all the wounded were from Alpha Company, 1st Battalion, 7th Marine Regiment. Underneath that was written *Damaged Vehicle/Request to Blow In Place . . . Denied.* I stared at the handwriting, suddenly realizing that no detailed radio log had been kept. "This is it?" I asked.

Lieutenant Robinson nodded. "Yours was just one incident that afternoon. And yes, you were in the middle of two firefights along that river. We had to monitor those also."

I shook my head. "I can't believe this. At 11th Motors, even when we send an observation post to Hill 364 we keep a radio log, incoming and outgoing messages."

"And that's 11th Motors," said Robinson. "You have what, one observation post and a perimeter around that rice paddy? We have this little room and all sorts of shit going down at the same time. We're not required to keep a detailed log, just to monitor the convoys and if they step into some shit to get them out of it with support."

"Well what about the thirty-five minutes where my convoy was kept waiting with an infantry company in a vulnerable position?" I asked.

Robinson shook his head. "You should have just left the truck there."

"What about leaving nothing behind to the enemy, Rough Rider convoy doctrine?" I said.

"You got an answer."

"Yes, after thirty-five Goddamn minutes!" I was getting hot at this point. I breathed a deep sigh. "I'd like to talk to Major Bradley."

"Stand by." Lieutenant Robinson got up and left the room. I picked up the notebook and looked at the June 22 page again. There was no documentation on the crucial thirty-five minutes, just notes on the landmine incident, the wounded, a request to blow the damaged vehicle, and the denial of the request. I was still looking at the page when Robinson returned. "Major Bradley is tied up in a conference over at Third MAF [Marine Amphibious Force] for the entire day. It might even run over to tomorrow." Third MAF was the headquarters in Danang. It was the center of all Marine Corps operations in the Republic of South Vietnam (RVN).

"Somehow I want to get documentation for that thirty-five-minute delay. You were here monitoring my convoy. You went through the delay with me," I said.

Robinson nodded. "That's right. I'm a conduit with these radios. And I was monitoring four convoys that afternoon. I don't remember exactly how long it was on your convoy. What I do remember is your request to blow the vehicle and that you were denied." He paused. "And you went ahead and blew it anyway. That's why there's an investigation. Are you aware that the investigation could recommend a court-martial?"

Again, I couldn't believe what was happening. So much for getting documentation. I was beating the old dead horse here. I stood. "Okay, thanks for your time."

Robinson nodded. He then went to his notebook and turned to a fresh page, getting ready for the day's convoys once the road sweeps were complete.

Driving back to 11th Motors I analyzed my options, which were getting smaller. What I had to do now was get out to Hill 52 and have Captain Craig write a statement. He would definitely be supporting my position. One thing that Lieutenant Robinson said opened up a new avenue: that Major Ashworth could recommend a court-martial. This added further irony to my prosecution of Lance Corporal Davis. Once I prosecute the accused, from my own company, I stand to be the accused in another court-martial. Whiskey Tango Foxtrot. Welcome to the war.

I spent the rest of the day at my desk preparing for the special court-martial. Another irony was the defense counsel, Lieutenant Jack Carmetti, one of my hoochmates. Even though our bunks were feet away from each other we chose not to discuss the upcoming trial or anything about our preparation.

At mail call that afternoon I got a quick note from my brother Dennis, an Army draftee, who was stationed at the Central Highlands Headquarters of II Corps down in Qui Nhon. He got a three-day pass and would be flying up shortly.

I began the next day outlining my statement for Major Ashworth's investigation. After an hour I went down to the armory and checked out my favorite

12-gauge shotgun with a bandolier. Then I took a company jeep, drove down to the dispatcher shack, and checked to see if any vehicles were heading to Hill 52. Three six-bys, from another company, were scheduled to leave on a line haul to Hill 52 within the hour. I doubled back to the company office and signed out to Hill 52. It was an easy, uneventful ride. The convoy commander was a staff sergeant. I simply followed the third truck and before long we were at Hill 52. The headquarters of 1st Battalion, 7th Marine Regiment looked the same as it did June 21. But a hell of a lot had gone down since. They were mostly set up in medium general-purpose tents.

I checked into 1st Battalion headquarters and asked where Captain Craig's command post (CP) was located. The adjutant pointed toward the tent flap. "Out there somewhere, lieutenant."

"Is he still on the hill?" I asked.

The adjutant shook his head. "Alpha Company is out on a search-and-clear. They're not scheduled to be back until the end of the week, if that. Depends on what they run into."

"I need to get a written statement from Captain Craig about a landmine incident on the road to Thuong Duc," I explained.

The adjutant thought for a moment. "Then I'd wait a week or so. Give us a call on our landline and make sure Alpha Company is here. Sorry that you made a trip for nothing."

Disappointed, I waited until the three trucks were ready to make the return trip. My options were running out, with no detailed radio log at division and not being able to locate Captain Craig. I figured that I'd spend the next few days in trial preparation and working on my investigation statement.

When I pulled up in front of the company office First Sergeant Duncan was out in front talking with Gunnery Sergeant Rayhorn and Staff Sergeant Thomas. As I shut down the jeep and grabbed the shotgun Duncan approached me. "Major Ashworth wants to see you immediately, lieutenant." Staff Sergeant Thomas added that another convoy had towed in the damaged truck from Thuong Duc. "The engineers found two booby traps the next day."

I shook my head. "Why am I not surprised?"

What now?, I thought. I went to the armory and turned in the shotgun and headed to Major Ashworth's office. He waved me to a chair and continued talking on a landline phone. I immediately noticed that since he was promoted to major he had some work done to his office space. He hung up the phone and opened the investigation file. Right away I could see it had grown since I had signed the memo. "I understand that you went out to Hill 52."

I nodded. "Yes, sir, I wanted to secure a written statement from Captain Craig. He commanded the security troops on my Thuong Duc convoy."

"Lieutenant McAdams, there's only one investigating officer here. And it's not you."

"Major, Captain Craig supported my decision out there."

"Did he give you a statement?"

"No, sir, his company was out on an operation. They're not scheduled to return until about a week. I'll have to call on a landline before I go out there again."

Major Ashworth shook his head. "Lieutenant, until this investigation is complete you'll confine yourself to trial preparation. That takes precedence over all your other duties. And that includes jaunts out to Hill 52."

"Major, it wasn't a jaunt. I need Captain Craig's statement as to what he saw and said during those thirty-five minutes."

"I've spoken with Captain Eiler. You're to confine yourself to trial preparation." He paused. "You're dismissed."

Less than five minutes later I was standing in front of Captain Eiler's desk. "Frank, it would behoove you to let the investigation take its course. That's what investigations are for, to determine exactly what happened, who saw what, and to make recommendations."

"Who saw what is why I went out to Hill 52, captain. The infantry captain supported my position. I need his statement."

"And you're needed in this company to prepare to prosecute a special court-martial. Can't you get that through your head?"

I thought for a moment. "When you gave me the command for the Thuong Duc convoy you wanted to know if they taught me how to juggle different assignments at The Basic School. That's what I've been doing—juggling assignments."

He gave me a studied look. "Then continue to juggle the assignments." He pointed a finger in the air. "Here, in this office."

Later that day I went down to the mess hall. Parked on the side of the mess hall was the damaged truck from the Thuong Duc convoy. I remember staring at the burned and battered hulk, realizing what that NVA landmine had caused and was continuing to cause.

I continued with trial preparation, analyzing how I would present my side, looking at the preceding office hours that had recommended the special court-martial. (In Marine Corps legal procedure office hours have to be held first to determine if a court-martial is warranted. In the Navy it is called "Captain's Mast.") I began to see an irony in the Davis case. He made a judgmental error and opened himself up for a bust in rank and loss of pay. Likewise, I was now hearing how I made a judgmental error on the road back from Thuong Duc. I kept telling myself that all I could do was put everything down in a statement and submit it. In the meantime I had a court-martial to prepare for as trial counsel, and possibly another one where I would be the accused facing a conviction and a sentence.

It was afternoon when a call came through to the company office. My brother Dennis was down at the dispatch shack at the front gate. I grabbed my soft cover and did a sprint down to the shack. Dennis had hitched a ride on a C7-A Caribou flying up from Qui Nhon. At the 15th Aerial Port he hitched a ride to 11th Motors. And now he was on the downside of a second tour. After his first tour, being informed that he was going to Fort Polk, Louisiana, heading into a blistering summer, he signed a waiver. Then he took a thirty-day leave and returned to Qui Nhon, in a relatively safe area. His rationale was that despite being in a combat zone in Qui Nhon, the weather in Vietnam was better than at Fort Polk in the summer. Fortunes of war.

The first thing I did was pull a cot from company supply. Andy Garrison helped me set it up in our hooch. Then I had Corporal Adair take Dennis to the mess hall for the evening meal while I continued preparing for the court-martial. The next morning I checked out a jeep and we spent the day at China Beach. We started talking about family. After a while I related my dilemma—being investigated for blowing up a truck that had already been totaled—while I prepared to prosecute a special court-martial. It was the first time I had been to China Beach since the Sunday before the June 10 convoy that got hit at Phu Gia Pass. So much had gone down in a fortnight. As I was explaining this I recalled that Captain Eiler hadn't commanded a convoy since. Each time the rotation came down to Transport Company one of the lieutenants was given the command. It was a standard pattern now.

We shared some beer and treated ourselves to hamburgers and French fries. On the way back to the jeep I approached a young lance corporal and asked him to take our picture. This was to document that the Brothers McAdams were in Vietnam at the same time. If we survived the doubters would be proven wrong.

The day after I drove Dennis to the 15th Aerial Port and said goodbye I carried a white vinyl notebook into the battalion conference room, which had been converted into a courtroom. The president of the court and the two members had yet to be seated. Corporal Forsythe, who was on the Thuong Duc convoy, was the court reporter. He was setting up a recording device whereby he spoke into a rubber cone to tape-record the trial for the transcript, which would be reviewed by a convening authority at a later date. I settled in at the prosecution table and began going over the opening script from the pages in front of me. Jack Carmetti and Lance Corporal Davis then entered and sat at the defense table. I exchanged nods with Jack, still amazed that we were even here, that we were opposing each other in a military court of law without even going to law school or being members of the bar. To this day I feel that was a breach, perhaps necessary at the time, but still a breach.

I was going over the script pages when Captain Corliss, from S-3 operations, entered followed by the two court members. The first court member was a first lieutenant. The other was the enlisted member, a staff sergeant. This was an option for the accused, where one member of the tribunal could be enlisted.

Captain Corliss waited for the court members to be seated. "This special court-martial will come to order." He nodded to me. "Trial counsel will now swear in the court."

Captain Corliss and the court members stood and raised their right hands. I read from the notebook, as required, swearing in the president and the members while Corporal Forsythe repeated my words into the recording device. After swearing in the court I turned to Jack and swore him in as defense counsel. Next was the accused, Lance Corporal Robert Davis, USMC, service number 218-96-54.

Since there were no challenges by the defense to relieve any member of the court, I went to the charges and specification. The charge was illegal possession of marijuana in violation of a First Marine Division order. I then read the order number. The specification was that on May 23, 1968, in the 11th Motors compound the accused was found to be in possession of approximately twenty marijuana cigarettes contained in a plastic bag. I added that the charge and specification were in violation of Article 92, *Uniform Code of Military Justice*, failure to obey an order or regulation; and Article 112a, *UCMJ*, wrongful use or possession of controlled substances.

Captain Corliss then asked, "How does the accused plead to the charge and specification?"

Jack stood and said, "To the charge and specification the accused pleads not guilty."

"The plea of not guilty has been entered," said Captain Corliss. He looked at me. "Trial counsel will make an opening statement."

I stood, glancing at the notes in front of me that I had rewritten more than a half-dozen times. Out of the corner of my vision I saw Captain Eiler sitting behind me, notebook and pen at the ready. I quickly realized that I would not only be reviewed by a convening authority; I would be critiqued by my company commander at his choosing and according to his agenda.

My opening statement summarized the scenario where Lance Corporal Davis had an open footlocker on the afternoon of May 23, 1968. And on that afternoon, in Lance Corporal Davis's hooch Sergeant James Grant, during a walkthrough, noticed a plastic bag containing what looked like contraband marijuana cigarettes. Sergeant Grant immediately confiscated the plastic bag and notified the company security NCO. The plastic bag was then marked for evidence to be sent to First Division Headquarters for analysis. The cigarette samples later tested positive, for cannabis, tetrahydrocannabinal (THC). The accused then stood office hours where a special court-martial was recommended. I paused, looking at my notes. Then I continued explaining that the prosecution witness, Sergeant James Grant, will testify that he saw and confiscated the plastic bag in Lance Corporal Davis's footlocker. I then concluded the opening statement.

"Call your first witness," said Captain Corliss.

Sergeant Grant entered from the back of the room and walked to the witness chair. I swore him in and he sat down. I went right to the afternoon of May 23, 1968, and had Sergeant Grant explain what he saw and what he did. When he finished his testimony I entered prosecution exhibit number one, the analysis from First Marine Division Headquarters confirming that the cigarettes in question contained marijuana. Then I nodded to the president, finishing my questioning. Jack stood, looking at his notes, preparing to cross-examine.

"Sergeant Grant, was the accused smoking a marijuana cigarette at this time?"

"No, sir, the cigarettes were sealed in the plastic bag."

"Sergeant Grant, did you at any time see the accused smoking a marijuana cigarette?"

Sergeant Grant looked at me then back to Jack. "No, sir."

"Were you sure that it was the footlocker of the accused where the plastic bag was resting?"

"Yes, sir, it was his footlocker," replied Sergeant Grant.

Jack paused, looking at his notes. "Sergeant Grant, isn't it possible that even though the marijuana cigarettes were in the footlocker of the accused the plastic bag could have belonged to someone else?"

I felt that this was coming. I stood and said, "Objection, Mr. President. This calls for a conclusion."

Captain Corliss nodded and said, "Sustained."

"Defense has no further questions," said Jack.

At this point I felt that my case had been presented, simply and succinctly. I stood and said, "Mr. President, the prosecution rests."

Captain Corliss nodded and looked at Jack. "Defense will now make its opening statement." Jack stood and explained to the court that the accused was "not a smoker, per se." He emphasized that the accused made the mistake of keeping the sealed plastic bag for another Marine while that Marine went on R&R. Since the investigation began the accused had steadfastly refused to identify that Marine. "Because of this element the accused has chosen to plead not guilty."

When Jack finished his opening statement he called his first witness, Lance Corporal Davis. I stood and swore Davis in and he sat down in the witness chair. "Lance Corporal Davis, will you tell the court how you came into possession of the sealed plastic bag that contained the marijuana cigarettes?"

"Yes, sir. One of my friends in the company came to me explaining that he was going on R&R and that he didn't want to take the plastic bag with him. He also felt that several others in the hooch knew of the bag. That's when he asked me to hold it for him until he returned."

"Did you ever smoke any of the marijuana cigarettes?" asked Jack.

"No, sir. I don't smoke at all," said Davis.

"When you took possession of the plastic bag was it sealed?" asked Jack.

Davis nodded. "Yes, sir. And it was sealed when Sergeant Grant took it."

Jack looked at the court then back to Davis. "So you did not, at any time, open the plastic bag or smoke any of the contents?"

Davis shook his head, looking at the court members. "No, sir." Jack nodded to me. "No further questions."

"Trial counsel may cross-examine," said Captain Corliss.

I stood at the table. "Lance Corporal Davis, did you at any time reveal the identity of the Marine who asked you to keep the plastic bag?"

"No, sir."

"Why?" I asked.

At this point the court members were looking at Lance Corporal Davis. He looked at me, directly in the eye. "Because, sir, we were friends."

I let a few moments of silence pass, thinking of my decision to blow up the truck—a judgment call. Then I asked, "Were you aware that by accepting the plastic bag you were placing yourself in jeopardy?"

Davis nodded. "Yes, sir."

"Lance Corporal Davis, you now have a chance to identify the Marine who gave you the plastic bag while he went on R&R." I paused and added, "Will you name him?"

Davis looked over at Jack then back to me. "No, sir, I will not."

"Are you aware of what this decision may result in?" I asked.

"Yes, sir."

"Prosecution has no further questions." I sat down.

Captain Corliss paused, looking at some notes. "Does any member of the court wish to ask anything of the witness?" The court members shook their heads. "I want to stress to the witness, who is also the accused, the seriousness of the charge and specification before this court. You were in possession of marijuana cigarettes in violation of a division order and the Uniform Code of Military Justice. I want you to reconsider, before this court, to identify the true owner of that plastic bag."

The room was silent again. Davis looked right at Captain Corliss. "Sir, I will stand on what I have said."

"If there are no further questions, the witness is excused." Davis got up from the chair and returned to the defense table. "Does trial counsel or defense wish to recall any witness at this time?" Jack and I both shook our heads no. "Trial counsel will now make a closing argument."

I stood, taking another glance at my notes. "Mr. President and members of the court: What we have seen here is a lance corporal, who, in an act of friend-ship, made the decision to keep in his possession a plastic bag of contraband marijuana cigarettes in violation of a First Marine Division order. This decision was also a clear violation of Article 92, *UCMJ* and Article 112a of the same code." I took a pause, glancing at my notes. This was what I spent the most time on: the closing statement. "The accused has admitted that he was aware of placing himself in jeopardy in accepting to keep the plastic bag of marijuana cigarettes. He was clearly violating a First Marine Division order and two arti-cles of the *UCMJ*. The elements of the offense are clear, that the accused knew that he would be brought up on charges if the plastic bag was discovered. And that is exactly what transpired on 23 May 1968. In view of the foregoing it is the recommendation that the accused be found guilty as charged." I sat down.

Captain Corliss nodded and said, "Defense counsel will now present a clos-ing statement."

Jack stood and looked at the court members. He walked from the table fac-ing the tribunal bench. "Mr. President and members of the court: There is a dictionary definition of common sense. It states that common sense is sound and prudent judgment based on a simple perception of a situation or facts."

Jack made a gesture toward the defense table. "Lance Corporal Davis had an admirable record before this incident. Yes, he made a serious mistake in judgment. And yes, he was aware of the consequences. In doing so he shielded an unidentified friend." Jack took a pause and added. "This is an unusual circumstance. Lance Corporal Davis has testified that he does not use marijuana. He does not even smoke legal cigarettes. And that is why Lance Corporal Davis has entered a plea of not guilty." Jack took another pause. "The division order and the *Uniform Code of Military Justice* are clear. However, because of the unusual and unfortunate circumstances the defense implores this court to consider common sense." Jack turned and walked back to the defense table. I gave him a quick glance and a nod, feeling that he gave a better closing statement than I had.

Captain Corliss then said, "In view of the time the court will recess for the midday meal. The court will then reconvene at 1300 hours to consider a verdict." He paused and added, "No member of this court, trial or defense, will discuss with anyone these proceedings until they are concluded." Jack and I walked to the mess hall and sat at the same table. We discussed convoys and the weather. As I was leaving the mess hall Captain Eiler passed me, giving off a stern glare. I went back to my hooch and grabbed a quick nap knowing that my duty as trial counsel on this one was in the record.

At one o'clock in the afternoon (1300 hours) the court reconvened. Captain Corliss noted that all the members who were previously present were again present in the court room. He then asked the court members if they had any follow-up questions. The lieutenant and staff sergeant looked at their notes. They shook their heads no.

"At this time the court members will remain in the room to decide a verdict based on evidence and testimony. All others will vacate the room to reconvene on call."

I used the time to return to the company office, working on a final draft for my convoy statement to be submitted to Major Ashworth. In less than ten minutes First Sergeant Duncan received a call that the court was ready to reconvene.

Several people were waiting outside the courtroom. Captain Eiler was among them. I tried to hide my uneasiness for the way in which Captain Eiler was judging my every move. We moved into the courtroom and settled into our chairs. Captain Corliss glanced at his notes. "This court is now in session. Let the record show that all members who were previously present are now present." Captain Corliss looked over at the defense table. "Will the accused stand?" Jack and Lance Corporal Davis stood at their table. "Lance Corporal Robert Davis, USMC, 218-96-54, it is my duty to inform you that this special court-martial board, on secret written ballot with two-thirds majority consenting, has found you guilty of the charge and specification." Jack and Davis remained standing at the table. "You may sit down." After Jack and Davis sat down Captain Corliss turned to me. "Trial counsel will now make an argument concerning sentence."

I stood and glanced again at my notes. "Mr. President and members of the court: In view of the circumstances surrounding the charge and specification prosecution recommends a sentence of one month brig time . . . to be suspended." When I said "suspended" someone behind me gasped. I had an idea who it was. I continued, "It is further recommended that the accused be reduced in rank to PFC, E-2 pay grade, forfeiting two-thirds of base pay for a period of three months."

Jack stood to give his argument. He requested that the court consider the pay forfeiture to be two months instead of three.

Captain Corliss then ordered another recess for extenuation and mitigation. This was for the tribunal to consider the record of the accused. We waited outside the door while the court members decided on a sentence. Out of the corner of an eye I could see Captain Eiler glaring at me. I was preparing myself for another session in his office. A few minutes later we were summoned back into the courtroom.

Captain Corliss reconvened us for the record. Then he asked the defense team to stand. This was it—the final phase. Hopefully justice would be served. "Lance Corporal Davis, it is my duty to inform you that this tribunal, on secret written ballot with two-thirds majority consenting, has conferred the following sentence. You are hereby sentenced to one month in the Danang brig, to be suspended. You are also to be reduced in rank to PFC, pay grade E-2. Further, you will forfeit two-thirds of your base pay for a period of three months." Captain Corliss paused. "Do you understand the sentence?"

Davis nodded. "Yes, sir."

"You will report to battalion personnel to sign the necessary papers. With no further business before this court we stand adjourned to meet on further call."

I closed the white vinyl notebook and gathered my notes. Then I approached Jack and shook his hand. "Good closing argument." He smiled and nodded.

Outside Captain Eiler approached me. "Ten minutes, Frank! In my office." He turned and stormed off.

I went to the personnel office and handed in the white vinyl notebook and signed a form for the review process. Then, with dread, I started the long walk to the Transport Company office.

At the company office I entered the backdoor and placed the trial notes on my desk. First Sergeant Duncan said, "The captain is waiting for you, lieutenant." I nodded and went to Captain Eiler's cubicle.

Captain Eiler waved me to a chair while he was writing something on a three-by-five card. He finished writing, put the card in a small metal file box, and placed the box in his deep desk drawer. "I'm flabbergasted at what transpired in that courtroom. You had several weeks preparation for that trial." He shook his head. "That kid should have gotten six months in the fucking brig for what he did. Christ, a suspended sentence!"

"The court could have sent him to the brig, captain. They chose not to," I replied.

"Because of your Goddamn fucking recommendation!" snapped Captain Eiler.

"He got a bust and a forfeit of pay," I said.

"Are you aware of what the maximum sentence is for possession of unlawful drugs?" He didn't wait for an answer. "Ten years in confinement!" His voice boomed through the office. "We have a growing drug problem in Vietnam. And this sends a message to those kids that if they get caught smoking pot to get Lieutenant McAdams as a prosecutor for a light sentence." He glared at me. "You're not a defense counsel. You're supposed to prosecute for the Marine Corps, Goddamn it!"

"And that's what I did, captain. My case met the elements of the offense. I made recommendations both for a guilty verdict and a sentence," I explained. "And the court went along with both."

"The punk got off with a slap on the wrist because of you!" He shook his head again. "I'm not going to forget this."

My ears perked with this statement. This could be considered as a fitness-report threat. "Forget what, captain?"

"Your lack of preparation. In presenting the Marine Corps' case you had a clear responsibility to press for a maximum sentence." He stood at his desk and leaned forward. "And you ducked it!"

I shook my head. "Captain, I didn't duck anything. I prosecuted Davis. He was convicted, reduced in rank, and gave up two-thirds base pay for three months."

Captain Eiler let out a deep frustrated sigh. Then he sat down. "We'll see what happens in the review process. That's all, you're dismissed."

I spent the rest of the day rewriting my Thuong Duc convoy statement. Then I sat at a typewriter and banged out a draft, double-spaced to make corrections. The next morning I signed out a jeep and drove down to division legal for an appointment with Captain Carl Davidson. I showed him my statement, which was almost four pages. "Why don't you take a walk outside while I read this?" he suggested.

Not a bad idea; I went out and stood on the edge of the legal office parking lot. Down below was the headquarters of the 1st Force Reconnaissance Battalion. I watched as a helicopter came in and off-loaded what looked like a recon squad coming back from a night insert. *What a different war,* I thought. I'm watching these guys returning from a night mission up in the mountains somewhere and I'm at division legal getting advice for an investigation statement on a convoy where I was kept waiting for thirty-five unexplained minutes. On top of that I had just prosecuted a special court-martial, getting a conviction, and my company commander has given me a veiled threat that this would reflect on my upcoming fitness report. *Semper Fi, Mac.*

After looking at my watch I walked back inside to Captain Davidson's desk. He was finishing the last page. Then he nodded and handed me the pages. "Good job. It's clear, logical, and succinct."

"Would you have any recommendations?" I asked.

He thought for a moment. "On the last page you refer to complications at division at such a crucial time." I nodded. "You might get some flak with that."

"In what regard?" I asked.

Captain Davidson smiled. "You're a lieutenant, a junior officer. And you're criticizing division convoy control for lack of a timely response."

"Well, it was thirty-five minutes when it should have been less than five," I said.

"Still, you're criticizing higher headquarters in a combat situation," said Davidson. "But you have one element on your side."

"What's that?" I asked.

"The truth. You've written this exactly as it happened," he said.

"Captain, from where you're sitting where do you think this will end?" I asked.

"It will end with the judgment of the investigating officer," said the captain.

I said, "I've been told that it could lead to a court-martial."

Captain Davidson shook his head and smiled. "They won't court-martial you."

"Why?" I asked.

"Because everyone connected at division convoy control that afternoon would be called to testify. And you're talking media, *Pacific Stars and Stripes.*" He paused, thinking. "But if it does come down to an appointed court-martial consider me for your defense counsel." Another smile. "I would love that."

On the drive back to 11th Motors I felt more confident. This convoy investigation experience still had me spinning. I thought back to my return from

Thuong Duc that afternoon, how Captain Eiler told me that I did the right thing, then being greeted in the Staff/Officers club as a hero, followed by a 180-degree turn within forty-eight hours. Hero to goat. And then Captain Eiler denied that he told me that I did the right thing.

When I returned to the office I sat at the typewriter again and wrote the final draft of the statement, single-spaced, with a carbon copy for my files. I was typing the second page when Gunnery Sergeant Rayhorn came in and asked for some time. One look said it. *Here we go again*, I thought.

I grabbed my soft cover and we took another walk down toward the perimeter wire. Before he started I mused, "We have to stop meeting like this."

"Everyone's talking about the Davis court-martial," said Gunny Rayhorn. "He dodged a bullet for brig time."

"That was part of my argument. And I got called on it by Captain Eiler," I said.

"That's why I need to talk with you," said Sergeant Rayhorn.

"About the court-martial?" I wondered.

"No, sir, about Captain Eiler."

I took a deep breath. "What now?"

"Between us, again?" I nodded. "Last night I was the company duty NCO. After sunset I had to check our truck line down in the motor pool. Then I came back to the company area to make a final check of the hooches." He paused. I could tell this was difficult for him. "I found Captain Eiler in between two of the troops' hooches . . . on his hands and knees."

"What was he doing?" I asked.

"He was lifting up a canvas flap on the side of one of the hooches." Another pause. "I couldn't believe what I was seeing. Lieutenant, he was spying on the troops."

"Did you say anything?" I asked.

He nodded. "I thought something was wrong. I said, 'Captain, is everything all right?'"

"What was his reaction?"

"He jumped up and walked over to me. He said that everything was okay, that he had dropped his pen. Then he turned and walked off."

"He didn't say anything more?"

"No, sir. But after he left I went to the spot where he was on his hands and knees. He had unbuttoned the clips on the canvas flaps to listen to the troops. The clips were still unbuttoned."

I remember wiping my forehead in the afternoon heat. Here I was, finishing my convoy statement. And Patty and I were scheduled to meet shortly in

Honolulu for a six-day R&R. And now I'm treated to a company spying sce-nario. "He was very upset with me that Davis didn't get any brig time."

"Apparently he told you that in a loud voice, lieutenant. It went from the office to the company, then to the rumor mill." He smiled. "And lately all the rumors are true."

"Whatever possessed him to get down on his hands and knees to eavesdrop on the troops?"

"I wish that was all, lieutenant."

"It's not?"

He shook his head. "It's about us NCOs and you junior officers."

"And?"

"The captain is keeping card files on all of us. You, me, the other lieutenants, and the NCOs. He keeps these cards in a small metal file box locked in his desk drawer." *Oh, shit!*, I thought. That was what he was doing when I entered his office after the Davis court-martial. He was probably marking something down on my card. "How did you learn this, about the card file?"

"The office clerks," said Gunny Rayhorn. "They can't stand the man, espe-cially after the Bobby Kennedy remark." He looked out at the rice paddy. "And the price on his head is still standing. He hasn't taken a convoy since Phu Gia Pass."

"If this gets any worse I'm going to have to do something," I said.

"Yes, sir, you're the number-two but you have to stay loyal," said Gunny Ray-horn. "Lieutenant, you're in a tight squeeze. Anything I can do—just let me know."

We walked back to the office in silence. I thanked Gunny Rayhorn for his confidence and went inside to my desk. I finished typing the pages. Then I decided to set them aside until after I returned from R&R. I remember looking around the office. Corporal Adair and the other clerks were busy. I got up from my desk and sauntered into Captain Eiler's cubicle. There were no papers in his in-box; he always kept a neat desk. I walked around and attempted to open the deep desk drawer. It was locked. I stared at it for a moment. *In that drawer,* I thought, *are the contents of a major leadership problem. Keeping secret files on sub-ordinates is not right.*

I went back to my desk and finished typing my convoy statement. I was glad to be doing the last paragraph with no changes from the previous draft. My mind was elsewhere, knowing that Captain Eiler's character traits were going south at flank speed. I had just told Gunnery Sergeant Rayhorn that if this gets worse I'll have to do something. *How in the name of God will I be able to any-thing with this man?* I was realizing there was a part of me that wanted to let the troops get their pound of flesh and then the whole damn drama would end. *Or would it?*

My welcome R&R would take me away from this ugly environment for a week. As I typed the last sentence my mind was doubly on Patty and Honolulu.

Later that afternoon I was summoned to operations and was informed that the officer assigned for Officer of the Day (OOD) had come down with stomach flu and was ordered to bed with a fever. So I was plucked to be the OOD, which meant that I'd be up all night, monitoring radios and making line checks down at the perimeter. I was initially headquartered in the Comm shack (Communications) with a lance corporal radio operator. I had never met him before. His first name was like his rank, Lance Corporal Lance Jenny. I introduced myself being from Transport Company. He gave me a suspicious look and said, "Yes, sir, Captain Eiler's outfit." I let that go, not knowing what he meant.

Later, I met the OP, which had a new lieutenant going up to Hill 364. One of the troops smiled at me. I recognized him as being on the patrol where I got my first "kill"—the rock ape that probed our wire.

The night started out peaceful enough. There was a bright moon at first, as I recall. Each hour or so I made the rounds to the respective company command bunkers. After the third round I returned to the Comm shack. Lance Corporal Jenny had just received a check in from the hill, all safe and secure. I remember sitting down on a nearby cot, taking a rest before my next round out on the perimeter. Jenny turned and asked me, "What's it like working with Captain Eiler?"

What a question, I thought. I didn't want to reveal too much, although I knew of the rumor mill and how the troops got their scuttlebutt. "In one word: challenging."

"He hasn't commanded a convoy since Transport Company got hit at Phu Gia Pass," commented Jenny.

"How do you know that?" I asked.

"Because all the comm-radio drivers know the convoy commanders, the convoys, where they go, and which companies take what convoys. We know all about your problems coming back from Thuong Duc."

"You got that right," I said.

"Captain Eiler has quite a reputation in the Communications section," said Jenny.

"Like what?" I asked.

"Can I speak freely, lieutenant?" asked Jenny. I nodded. "Dawson was his radio driver on that convoy. Dawson told us that when the ambush went down

Captain Eiler turned down the volume control on the radio. Then he ordered Dawson to get over on the shoulder of the road. He didn't take any transmissions until they got out of the ambush zone. Then the captain turned the volume back up. He told Dawson to keep his eyes on the road while he fiddled with the volume control."

"I remember the look on Dawson's face when he pulled up in Phu Bai," I said.

"Captain Eiler ordered him not to say anything, that it was a combat situation," said Jenny.

I was about to say something else when we got a radio transmission. It was security out on the road to Khon Son. During the night the road was closed with a barricade, secured by a sergeant and a four-man fire team. They called in saying that they were hearing moans coming from a nearby ditch. I told Jenny to tell them that the OOD was on the way. I grabbed two hand flares and an M-16 rifle, jumped in the duty jeep, and headed to the main gate. At the main gate I went out on the road heading down to the barricade.

The sergeant in charge of the detail said that the moans were still coming from the ditch. I instructed him to take two men and check it out. Then I repositioned the jeep to give those men the headlight beams. They walked to the edge of the road then went out of sight, into the ditch. Within seconds one of them came running back up and approached me. He was out of breath. "Jesus, lieutenant, it's a village woman! She's pregnant and the baby's head is coming out!"

I got on the radio, called into Jenny, and said to contact the Battalion Aid Station: "Get an ambulance down here ASAP!"

The troops were carrying the young woman out of the ditch when the lights from the ambulance came flashing toward our position. In the front seat were two corpsmen. They were out in a moment with a stretcher, took a quick glance, and set up a blood pressure cuff and an IV—all in record time it seemed. I told them I'd follow them back to sick bay. One corpsman got in the back with the woman while the other drove.

When we pulled up in front of Battalion Aid Station two more corpsmen were waiting. Both had that "bed-head look," being jostled out of a bunk in the middle of the night, wearing only T-shirts with jungle trousers. They got the woman inside, moans and all. One of the corpsmen told me that Dr. Hoffman was on the way. I told them that I'd check back later.

I went back to the Comm shack and made the necessary entries in the radio log. I reflected on the loose way that the radio logs were maintained at division. Then I went down to the wire and walked the battalion perimeter again.

I returned to the Comm shack with first light. And suddenly it was "Good morning, Vietnam!" After signing out I grabbed a quick breakfast. And then I realized that I hadn't had any sleep in the last twenty-four hours.

Upon leaving the mess hall I headed back to Battalion Aid Station. When I entered, the duty corpsman told me that by the time Dr. Hoffman arrived nature stepped in and beat him to it—the birth of a healthy boy. Mother and baby were doing fine. She and the newborn were resting in the ward area. I walked into the ward area and approached her bed. The young woman, with short black hair, was resting with the sleeping baby in the crook of her right arm. Right near the woman's head was an ashtray with a burning Salem cigarette. The woman smiled at me, took a drag on the cigarette, and placed it back in the ashtray. I asked the nearby corpsman, "Should she be smoking, after giving birth?"

I remember a shrug coming from the corpsman. "These are hardy people lieutenant."

"Where's the father?" I asked.

Another shrug from the corpsman. "Probably out there." He pointed to the rice paddy in between us and the village of Bong Mui to our left. *Okay, I thought, fine. My tour as OOD is over.* I headed to my hooch as the morning convoy trucks were revving up in the motor pool. After all, there was a war going on.

I went to my bunk and crashed until about two o'clock in the afternoon. Then I pulled myself up, still groggy, got dressed, and returned to the aid station. The first thing I noticed was that the young mother was gone; the bunk had been made up. I asked the duty corpsman where the mother was. He walked me to the door. We stood outside looking at the rice paddy. "She's out there, lieutenant. Didn't want to miss a day's work just because she gave birth."

"God, these people," I said. "They gather wood up in the mountains and work the rice paddies until the sun goes down."

"They're a tough stock," said the corpsman. "How many American women would give birth during the early morning and then head back to work that afternoon?" He paused and added, "Not just office work but back-breaking physical work."

Lieutenant Commander Frank McAdams. My father in his Navy Class A uniform, circa 1946, while still being treated at the Great Lakes Naval Hospital. As commanding officer of the LSM-201 he suffered serious wounds on October 21, 1944, the second day of the Leyte invasion in the Philippines. The nerves in his right arm never responded. The arm was amputated below the elbow in 1950. (Frank McAdams)

Mrs. Irene McAdams. My mother imparted her lifelong triangular doctrine on each of us: you get out of this life what you put into it; if you start something, finish it; and don't ever be called a quitter. I still hear her words. (Frank McAdams)

USS Ticonderoga (CVA–14). *The attack aircraft carrier is being refueled from the USS Ashtabula (AO–51), in the South China Sea. This was my home from the fall of 1960 to the fall of 1962, as a Navy Corpsman. During Christmas 1962 we were extended in Wes Pac (Western Pacific) because of the Laos Crisis. The planes involved in the Gulf of Tonkin incident were launched from its flight deck in 1964. (Official U.S. Navy Photo)*

OCS, Quantico. Golf Company, 4th Platoon, 42nd Officer Candidate Class. *Our platoon commander, First Lieutenant John Rowe, front row, far left; Staff Sergeant Lee Parrott, front row, second from right end; Gunnery Sergeant John Doucette, front row far right. I'm in the front row, fourth from left. Our class reportedly had a 34% attrition rate. The program, fall 1966, emphasized leadership and physical stamina. (U.S. Marine Corps Photo)*

The Basic School. 3rd Platoon, Hotel Company, Class 4–67. Our platoon commander, Captain Michael Downey, is seated in the second row, center. I'm in the front row, second from right. On my left is the late First Lieutenant Alexander Scott Prescott, Xavier University, who distinguished himself with the Third Marine Division. (U.S. Marine Corps Photo)

An Hoa Combat Base. This aerial photo shows the air strip, just behind the northern perimeter, which was a constant target for NVA rocket and mortar crews. My hooch was along the southwestern sector, which got hit periodically. The road going in, center, was often a mud field during the heavy rains. To the right is Graves Registration. (Charles Soard, Charlie Company, 1/5)

Khon Son Courtyard. The village was about 400 meters in front of our perimeter wire. First Lieutenant Andy Garrison headlined our "Psy Ops" program, which included the building of an orphanage, in this village. The villagers loved the Roadrunner *cartoons. (Andy Garrison)*

Hair Pin in the Hai Van. This angle shows how treacherous the road and the turns were in the Hai Van Pass. The speed in the pass was kept to 10 m.p.h. but gaps often occurred. With the gaps came the vulnerability of ambushes and sniper fire. (Frank McAdams)

Under Full Sail. An earlier photo of the Brigantine Yankee *before it became part of the Windjammer Cruises fleet. The famous ship, under Captain Irving Johnson, made five round-the-world cruises with amateur crews. On the Galapagos Island voyage, the work was never ending, eight hours on, four off at $75 per month. In July 1964 the ship ran aground on a reef in the Cook Islands, Rarotonga. The hulk is still there. (Courtesy of Captain Irving Johnson)*

A Mangled Mess. This was the result of Sergeant Krasny's tragic accident that happened while negotiating a sharp turn in the Hai Van Pass. My first assignment in Transport Company was to inventory his personal gear to be sent to his family. (Andy Garrison)

Village Children. The village children would often line the road in hopes that the convoy security troops would toss C-ration cans to them. The C-rations would either be taken to the family (note the elders in the hut) or sold to the black market. (Frank McAdams)

Command Truck. Lance Corporal Roger Sillcox, left, and Corporal J. R. Forsythe, right, in my command vehicle on the way to Thuong Duc. It was an uneventful convoy going out, and a very eventful convoy coming back. (Frank McAdams)

The Road to Thuong Duc. This primitive paddle wheel is used to transfer water from one rice paddy level to another, a practical expedient in rice farming for hundreds of years. I was told that farmers out on the paddy dikes could also be lookouts for NVA forces. (Frank McAdams)

Patty and Diamond Head. We met for R&R, six days in Honolulu. And we had no idea what the next month would bring: the chaos at the Democratic Convention for her and the village of Hoa Vang and Cam Le Bridge for me. We were half a world apart, witnessing one of the most pivotal years in the 20th Century. (Frank McAdams)

The Brothers McAdams. Brother Dennis caught a flight from Qui Nhon to Danang to spend a few days while I was preparing for the Davis Special Court-Martial. This was taken as we were leaving China Beach. I wanted some documentation to prove that two brothers did serve in a combat zone at the same time. I'm still wearing that watch, after forty-three years. (Frank McAdams)

The German Hospital. One of the contradictions of this war was a neutral country establishing a fully-staffed hospital to treat soldiers from both sides. The two vehicles on the right are Land Rover ambulances. It was reported that after a firefight the ambulances would head into the field to aid wounded North Vietnamese soldiers. The hospital staff took their meals at our mess hall in An Hoa. (Frank McAdams)

A beverage on the seven-mile stretch. Lance Corporal Lance Jenny, right, and I are taking a well-deserved breather in between convoys on the seven-mile stretch from Phu Loc 6 to An Hoa. Jenny was with me every day, on every run. (Corporal Robertson)

Operation Taylor-Common. The hooches were put together to support the Fifth Marine Regiment, commanded by Colonel James B. Ord, and Task Force Yankee, commanded by Brigadier General Ross T. Dwyer. The ridge line in the background is a section of the notorious "Arizona Territory." (Charles Soard, Charlie Company, 1/5)

Delta Company. This was one of the Infantry Training Companies I commanded while at Camp Pendleton, summer and fall, 1969. I'm in the center, first row. To my right is Sergeant Richard Rodriguez. Warrant Officer Tom Farrington is to my left. To his left are Gunnery Sergeant Charles Roundtree and Sergeant Allan Forrester. To the far right, first row, is PFC Victorian wearing the Company Guide brassard. I have often wondered how many of these young Marines survived Vietnam. (U.S. Marine Corps Photo)

Company Commander. As a First Lieutenant I was fortunate to be assigned as a
company commander, usually a captain's billet. For a company-grade officer it's one of
the best jobs in the Marine Corps. One year after leaving active duty I was promoted
to captain in the reserves. I still consider Second Lieutenant (Butter Bar) my favorite
officer's rank. (U.S. Marine Corps Photo)

ĐÀ NẴNG

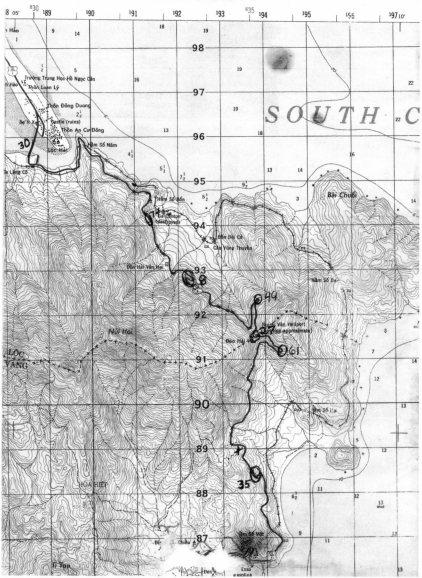

Danang Map. This shows the road's steady climb where the Rough Rider convoys would head into the Hai Van Pass. The dark line marks the treacherous hair pin turns along steep ridges. The narrow, unpaved road dictated that the speed through the pass be 10 m.p.h. Check Point 27 was the top of the pass dominated by an old French fort from the Viet Minh days. (Vietnam, Sheet 6641, III)

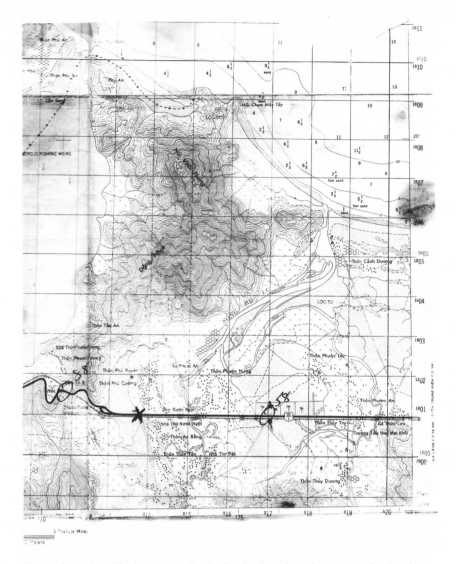

The Bowling Alley. Check point 58, "Ambush Alley," is where the overturned railroad car was located. The "X" is the approximate center of the controversial June 10th ambush. My pace truck was farther up the road where I saw the whole shebang. Captain Eiler never took a convoy after that afternoon. (Vietnam, Sheet 6641, I)

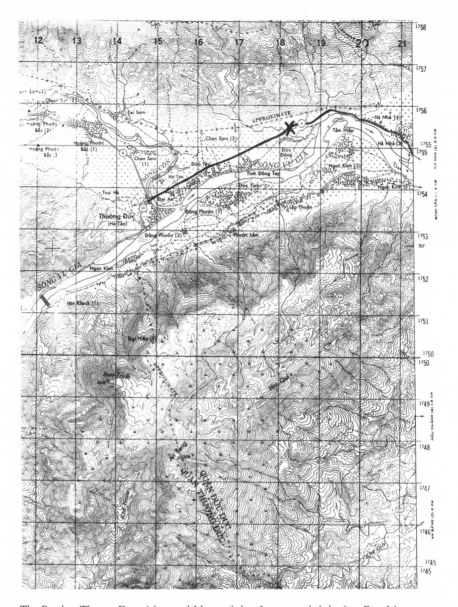

The Road to Thuong Duc. Afterward I learned that I commanded the first First Marine Division convoy that got through to the Special Forces camp at Thuong Duc without being ambushed. After an uneventful night we were hit on the return convoy (X, approximate location). At that position I found my convoy in the middle of two fire fights, one off the southern bank of the Song Vu Gia and the other in the rice paddy between Route 4 and the ridge line. I was kept waiting thirty-five minutes, forcing me to make a decision to blow a damaged truck "in place." This caused an investigation that resulted in a non-punitive letter of censure. After reading the letter I tore it up. (Vietnam, Sheet 6540, I)

DEPARTMENT OF THE NAVY
HEADQUARTERS UNITED STATES MARINE CORPS
WASHINGTON, D. C. 20380

IN REPLY REFER TO

The President of the United States takes pleasure in presenting the NAVY AND MARINE CORPS MEDAL to

FIRST LIEUTENANT FRANK J. MC ADAMS III
UNITED STATES MARINE CORPS RESERVE

for service as set forth in the following

CITATION:

For heroism while serving as Motor Transport Officer of the Eleventh Motor Transport Battalion, First Marine Division in the Republic of Vietnam on 22 January 1969. At the An Hoa Combat Base, a Marine entered the tent of the Advisor Team, First Ranger Group, where several United States Army and Vietnamese officers were billeted, and threatened the occupants with a loaded rifle. From an adjacent billeting area, First Lieutenant McAdams heard the disturbance and rushed to the tent to investigate. Rapidly analyzing the situation, he began to stealthily move up behind the intruder, who was aiming his rifle at an American Officer. As First Lieutenant McAdams approached, the armed Marine turned around and faced him. With complete disregard for his own safety, First Lieutenant McAdams fearlessly grabbed the man and his weapon, thereby enabling the other officer to disarm him. As a result of First Lieutenant McAdams' heroic action, none of the threatened personnel was injured or killed during this potentially dangerous situation. His courage, bold initiative and sincere concern for his fellow men were in keeping with the highest traditions of the Marine Corps and the United States Naval Service.

For the President,

Commandant of the Marine Corps

Navy-Marine Corps Medal

The Secretary of the Navy takes pleasure in presenting the NAVY COMMENDATION MEDAL to

FIRST LIEUTENANT FRANK J. McADAMS III

UNITED STATES MARINE CORPS RESERVE

for service as set forth in the following

CITATION:

"For meritorious service while serving as Division Loadmaster with the Eleventh Motor Transport Battalion, First Marine Division in connection with operations against the enemy in the Republic of Vietnam from 27 December 1968 to 27 March 1969. Throughout this period, First Lieutenant McAdams performed his duties in an exemplary and highly professional manner. Demonstrating superb leadership and resourcefulness, he skillfully supervised the expeditious accomplishment of all assigned tasks and consistently provided his command with outstanding support. Exhibiting an exceptional knowledge of motor transport operations, he constantly ensured the maximum utilization of available motor transport assets and effectively coordinated the movement of vehicles, thereby ensuring minimal interruptions in service. Tasked with the organization of at least two convoys a day comprising approximately fifty vehicles each, his able planning resulted in a minimum of turn-around time. On several occasions, he exposed himself to hostile mortar and small arms fire while serving as Convoy Commander between An Hoa and Phu Loc. By his superb leadership, professional ability and loyal devotion to duty, First Lieutenant McAdams contributed significantly to the accomplishment of his unit's mission and upheld the finest traditions of the Marine Corps and of the United States Naval Service."

The Combat Distinguishing Device is authorized.

FOR THE SECRETARY OF THE NAVY,

H. W. Buse jr

H. W. BUSE, JR.
LIEUTENANT GENERAL, U. S. MARINE CORPS
COMMANDING GENERAL, FLEET MARINE FORCE, PACIFIC

Navy Commendation Medal (with Combat V)

9

Honolulu

Two days later I made another trip to Battalion Aid Station. The corpsmen and the Navy physician, Dr. Allan Hoffman, who was a full lieutenant, had just returned from a MedCap out in Khon Son, during which they hold a village sick call, treating anything from infected feet, to cuts and bruises, to influenza and other maladies. It was diplomatic in nature, letting the local populace know that despite the combat situation we were here to help. These forays, by each battalion, probably accomplished more with the villagers during this time than all the convoys and infantry operations in the I Corps area.

"Doc" Poppell again came to my rescue. I explained I was going to be "leaving on a jet plane" from Danang to Honolulu for a certain period. And I knew that I'd have trouble sleeping with the excitement of seeing Patty and balancing the convoy investigation with Captain Eiler's recent shenanigans. He had just the thing: one Nembutal, a little white pill. Poppell smiled, "Enjoy the flight and enjoy your wife." Poppell added that all I needed was one, that Nembutal was one of the drugs discovered in Marilyn Monroe's system following her overdose in August 1962.

My group assembled at the 15th Aerial Port on a late June morning. It was evident that we were headed for R&R, decked out in our Class-B short-sleeve uniforms. As we were waiting to board the 707 that would take us "back to the world" someone had a portable radio tuned into AFVN. We stood there waiting for the signal to board as The Cascades were heard singing "Rhythm of the Rain," one of the ballads from the pop chart. It made me aware of how fast things had changed in the four months since my staging company flew out of California. In that time I had stopped counting the convoys and the ambushes along with the road mines. I arrived as a hard-charging second lieutenant. Now I was a combat-tested first lieutenant. It all seemed secondary to what I would

141

be coming back to: an investigation and an unstable commander in a company with a severe morale problem. I was beginning to doubt what we were actually accomplishing in Vietnam as a fighting force. Yes, we defeated the enemy at each turn. And yes, we were facing a formidable and determined North Vietnamese Army. I couldn't help but wonder if the U.S. Military Assistance Command Vietnam (MACV) was going to be able to hand over South Vietnam to a rightful and corruption-free government. I was still in those thoughts as the jet lifted off. As the plane banked out of its takeoff pattern I looked out the window. Down below was the Hai Van Pass, where a convoy would soon be passing through. I settled back until we got to our cruising altitude. Then I got up, went to the lavatory, took a drink of water, and swallowed the Nembutal.

The time seemed to fly faster than the plane. Before I knew it somebody was jostling me out of a sound sleep. A smiling flight attendant said that we were beginning our descent into Honolulu. I remember blinking my eyes and nodding, my head a little fuzzy.

Most of us just had a carry-on bag, what the military called an "AWOL bag." So there was no waiting for baggage to clear. As we came down the ladder we were greeted by a welcoming committee—girls in grass skirts. Each of us got the traditional Hawaiian lei. And then we boarded buses to be taken to the Rest and Recuperation Center at Fort DeRussy.

Fort DeRussy's history began in 1911 when it was built to protect Honolulu and Pearl Harbor from any threat of attack to the Territory of Hawaii. A lot of good that did in December 1941. And now the installation served as the R&R Center for Hawaii. An Army major came on board with a booming voice: "Gentlemen, you have arrived at Fort DeRussy for six days of well-deserved R&R. You'll be getting off this bus to complete your residence information. If you see your honey along the way, grab her, and take her along!"

This was a marked contrast from getting off the bus at the Quantico Marine Corps Base to begin OCS. I stood, grabbed my AWOL bag, and moved in line down the aisle. As we got off the bus and proceeded through a breezeway, with people lining both sides, I suddenly saw Patty, in a bright orange and red print dress, jump out and wave her hand. I ran to her, threw my arms around her, and suddenly it was our first date in college.

Patty had arrived the afternoon before and changed our hotel from the Ilikai to the Outrigger. The Ilikai had just opened its doors and wasn't completely finished. So she took the initiative and made the change, especially when she discovered there would be no TV in the Ilikai room. After filling out the necessary forms we grabbed a taxi for the short ride to the hotel.

I couldn't believe how fast everything was happening. It was surreal. Hours before I was in a combat zone, and now I was standing at the window of a luxury high-rise hotel with a sweeping view of Waikiki and the ocean. Patty even had a chilled bottle of Vouvray, a dry French white wine. After putting down my AWOL bag I took my dopp kit into the bathroom. Within moments I was flushing the toilet just to see the water swirling. For the next six days I wouldn't have to rely on wooden four-holers or expedients in the field such as a cat hole.

We pulled the cork and sat at a table, catching up on Chicago, friends, and family. It was here where I learned that the brother of one of my high-school wrestling teammates had drowned in Lake Michigan the week before. He was with friends out on a sailboat at night celebrating the birth of a son. Patty also told me about her application for the Operation Head Start program and the intention of doing volunteer work at the upcoming Democratic National Convention. I don't remember finishing the Vouvray. But I do remember both of us suddenly standing and staring at each other for a few moments, hearts pounding. We grabbed each other and fell into bed. It was one o'clock in the afternoon.

By 3 P.M. we were both asleep when the phone rang on the nightstand next to my ear. I picked it up, "Hello?"

"Lieutenant McAdams, this is Commander McAdams!" It was my father calling from Chicago. Perfect timing.

"Dad, how did you find me?"

"I got in touch with the R&R Center and they gave me your hotel and the phone number. You're not the first one in this family to come out of a war zone and land in Hawaii," he said.

"I'm a short distance from Aiea Heights," I said.

"That's where they had me after I got hit," said dad. "October 1944."

"It's a hotel now," I said. "Not a naval hospital."

"Times change. And how are you?" he asked.

"I'm fine," I answered. "I got in this morning. And we have a great view of Waikiki."

"Are you keeping your butt down out there?" he asked.

I laughed. "When I have to. I'm okay."

"How's Patty?"

"She's fine. We're, uh, enjoying each other," I said.

"Nothing wrong with that, especially when there's a war on."

"This one is a bit different than yours," I said.

"No doubt about that," said Dad. "But you still have to keep your butt down."

We chatted for a few more minutes. I asked how mom was. The last thing he said to me was, "Take care of your men."

I replaced the phone and stared at it. *Take care of your men*—one of the primary tenets of good leadership. And back in Vietnam I was under the command of someone whose primary concern was to take care of himself. But this was something that I didn't have to worry about for six days.

Patty rolled over and smiled. "I bet if you were in some mountain outpost in Katmandu in subzero weather your father would find you."

"I'm not the first McAdams in uniform to land in Hawaii."

"Then let's make a wish that you're the last," said Patty. I leaned over and kissed her.

That afternoon we dressed for the beach on Waikiki. I recalled the days on the *Ticonderoga*, at how surprised I was that Waikiki was such a short beach. But still it was Hawaii, and we took a walk on the sand under the looming mountain of Diamond Head. I thought of telling Patty about my leadership dilemma with Captain Eiler and the convoy investigation along with prosecuting a special court-martial but decided to hold off for the appropriate time. Besides, I was looking forward to hearing about her upcoming position with Operation Head Start and the convention in Chicago. Naturally, neither of us knew at the time how the coming third week of August 1968 would unfold not just in history but with each of us half a world apart. Returning to our room we began dressing for dinner. Patty brought some extra clothes for me—two dress shirts, a tie, and a blazer. We made reservations at the rooftop restaurant. And money would be no obstacle. This was R&R. We anticipated an enjoyable dinner with a view that night. We did get a view, Waikiki with night lights. Coming with it was an extremely irritating middle-aged waiter who rightly suspected that I was on R&R from Vietnam. He quickly went over the line, pushing for a big tip. His theatrics were obnoxious—yes, sir this . . . yes, sir, that . . . oh yes, sir, marvelous choice! After the fourth or fifth blustery inquiry at our table I finally had to say, "We're fine, could you leave us to our entrees?" It was only then when he backed off. I purposely left a modest tip, thereby earning a glare from him as we left.

The next day we rented a 1968 Chevrolet Impala convertible. Looking back at this car today I remember it being as big as a small cabin cruiser. But it served our purpose—seeing the noted tourist sites on the island. After picking up some sandwiches and drinks, our first stop was at Holana Cove. The beach had gained movie notoriety for the "kissing in the surf scene" with Burt Lancaster and Deborah Kerr in the 1953 film adaptation of James Jones's World War II novel *From Here to Eternity*. The film swept the Academy Awards that year with Daniel Taradash winning an Oscar for Best Screenplay.

After negotiating a winding, steep path down to the beach we settled in, enjoying the picnic and looking at the waves lapping up several feet from our blanket. The irony was perfect. Here I was, telling my wife of the goings-on in my battalion in Vietnam on a beach made famous by an Oscar-winning World War II film. I stayed away from describing the actual combat situations, centering on Captain Eiler's character traits, with me in the middle as the number-two officer in the company. And then I explained the thirty-five-minute delay out in the Thuong Duc Valley and the subsequent investigation that had yet to be concluded. She turned out to be the perfect therapist—a good listener. We capped the day off by taking a drive up the Pali Highway. It had been seven years, almost to the month, when I stood at Pali Lookout with several shipmates from the *Ticonderoga*. I recall that a new guardrail was installed. But the wind was just as stiff. That night we decided to take in the Don Ho Waikiki show. It was a good idea, but only halfway. It turned out to be Don Ho's night off. We never did see him or hear his signature hit, "Tiny Bubbles."

We used the next day for a drive around the island, leaving Honolulu for the Dole Pineapple Plantation, and enjoyed a leisurely lunch. The drive made me aware of using each precious day for something different.

On the way back we made a brief stop at Pearl Harbor. We didn't stay long because everywhere we looked was the theme of war, graphic reminders to where I would be returning.

Patty explained how she turned in an application at the Operation Head Start office in Chicago, part of President Johnson's War on Poverty. As an education major at Loyola University she was also certified in the Chicago Public Schools system, perfectly cast for this new program. The objective for the coming school year was to center around K–6 schoolchildren from the inner city, mostly minorities and recent immigrants. She was being prepared for going into these neighborhoods, knocking on doors, and getting the suspicious populace to enroll their children into the program. But first was the volunteer work at the Democratic National Convention. This made me feel that we were both products of our generation. And we were doing something, although I was beginning to have doubts about what I was doing. After dinner, on another night, we went into the cocktail lounge for an after-dinner drink. A group of soldiers and Marines was holding forth at several tables with wives and girlfriends. They asked us to join them. I looked at Patty. She smiled and gave me a slight headshake. We declined, preferring to stay to ourselves and then go back up to the room. We were both aware of the ticking clock.

On our last day Patty made an appointment to get her hair done at the hotel's beauty salon. As it was a two-hour appointment, she suggested that there was a new film I should see. It was playing at the Ala Moana Shopping Mall, within walking distance. She told me that the film was directed by the same man who directed *Who's Afraid of Virginia Woolf?*–Mike Nichols. The name of this film was *The Graduate*.

"It's not really about a graduate; it's about the challenges and situations that a young man faces today," explained Patty. "It's funny and sad because of the generation gap."

Because we shared mutual opinions about films going back to our dating days I trusted her insight. I wasn't disappointed. After leaving the theater I felt that I had seen something new, a breakthrough film with a message for our generation. I hadn't seen a film like this since *Bonnie and Clyde*. Walking back to the hotel I realized why Patty had urged me to see the film. Hollywood was turning a corner; it was the onset of a new generation in story and character. I remember hoping that I would live to see more films like these. Here I was, in my late twenties, hoping that I would live simply to see films that made important statements.

Before leaving the shopping center I stopped at a floral shop and picked up a gardenia. We would be taking an early dinner before our flights. And at the dinner I gave her the gardenia, a remembrance of six days that went by in a flash. In the cab on the way to the airport I remember telling Patty that I had no idea what was waiting for me upon my return. She grabbed my hand and repeated what she had said before: "Keep your boney butt down."

We went through a tearful goodbye at the airport. I watched her walk to the gate, wondering once more if I would ever see her again. I learned later that she was prevented from taking the gardenia with her–something about a state botanical statute.

I had some time before my plane left, so I called my mother. We chatted briefly. She told me to keep writing to her and to stay safe. She also told me that she was glad Dennis had flown up to see me.

The only thing I remember about the return flight was looking out of the window as we flew over Iwo Jima. I remember reading someone's account that the island was shaped like a pork chop. I also thought of the 6,821 Marines who paid the ultimate price on that little pork chop.

It was dark when the personnel carrier dropped me off at the 11th Motors compound. I quietly entered the hooch. My bunk was exactly as I left it; I was back in the war.

The next morning I reported for work at the office. Jack Carmetti and Gunnery Sergeant Rayhorn were in Phu Bai on a convoy. The first memo I saw was from division legal. The court-martial conviction was upheld by the convening authority. It gave me a sense of justice.

We had a new second lieutenant, Bob Greene, a tall guy who was with the Phu Bai convoy as an observer. Captain Eiler was at his desk signing a report. "Glad to see that you didn't pull a Mark Wilson." Lieutenant Mark Wilson was the battalion supply officer.

"Pull a Mark Wilson?" I asked.

"Exactly, he came back from R&R a day late." Captain Eiler shook his head. "If you pulled anything like that you'd be facing charges."

I let that remark go. "The court-martial conviction was upheld by division legal."

He shook his head and sneered. "Yeah, I saw that. So what?"

I walked out of his cubicle. His mood was uglier than usual. I was about to learn why.

10

A Letter

It was quiet for the rest of the day, although I did feel some tension. The office seemed to continue with the day's routine, the clerks typing memos, First Sergeant Duncan answering the landline phone and organizing reports for the captain to sign.

I remember being in a down and depressed mood returning from the mess hall. I suppose it was natural, coming back to Vietnam after six wonderful days in Hawaii and hating to leave Patty. Staff Sergeant Thomas caught up with me before I got back to the company office. He asked me how R&R was.

"All too short," I said. "But I'll get over it."

"We had another event while you were gone."

"Another convoy ambush?"

"I wish." He shook his head. "No, the event was here, down at the perimeter."

I dreaded asking, "What happened now?"

"Captain Eiler was checking the line one night," explained Staff Sergeant Thomas. "He came across a mound of earth. At one end of the mound was a wooden marker."

"A wooden marker?"

Staff Sergeant Thomas nodded with a frown. "It had Captain Eiler's name on it in heavy black ink." He paused. "The marker was a fake gravestone."

I was speechless for several moments. "What happened next?"

"He stored the marker in a locker in our supply shed. The next morning he called a staff meeting and went into a rage, calling for an in-house investigation. Lieutenant Carmetti explained that battalion would have to be notified. Captain Eiler didn't want battalion headquarters informed. He said that he would conduct this investigation himself, that he already had ideas of who was behind this."

"Is the marker still in the supply shed?" I asked.

Staff Sergeant Thomas shook his head. "Captain Eiler took it down to CID

[Criminal Investigation Division, a branch of the division legal office] to have it checked for fingerprints. I told him that it wouldn't turn up anything because the marker was wooden. A clear print can't be drawn from a piece of rough wood. He wouldn't listen."

"Who does he suspect is behind this?"

Sergeant Thomas threw up his hands. "He won't say. He swore us all to secrecy, to say nothing to anyone outside of the company while he conducts his investigation."

"Does battalion know about this?" I asked.

"No, sir. Nobody has said a thing," said Sergeant Thomas. "Lieutenant, this is getting out of hand. I've been in this Corps eighteen years. I've served under a lot of officers, including Chesty Puller at the Chosin, but none like this man."

"To repeat one of Captain Eiler's phrases, tell me something I don't know. I'm his XO and have to keep this company together while he's making the job more than difficult."

"You should know something else," said Staff Sergeant Thomas.

"Christ, now what?"

"Rumor mill has the price on his head being upped to five thousand, from two thousand. Welcome back from R&R."

When Jack Carmetti, Rich Cobb, and Bob Greene returned from Phu Bai we talked in our hooch about the false grave marker and the company morale problem. Jack explained what it was like the morning after Captain Eiler discovered the grave marker. "His rage was Hitleresque, yelling and pounding on the desk. He kept saying that he knew who was behind all this but he never named any suspects. He referred to them as 'that pot-smoking group.'"

"I've never seen him so mad," commented Cobb. "Out of control."

Staff Sergeant Thomas was right: This was getting out of hand. The next afternoon I turned in my Thuong Duc statement to Major Ashworth and sent a copy to Patty in Chicago. Then I called an impromptu meeting, in one of the hooches, with the officers and senior NCOs—buck sergeant and above. I timed it for when Captain Eiler would be attending the daily company commander's meeting in the conference room. First item was the company morale problem and that as leaders we had to take some initiative. I went around the room, listening mostly. The Bobby Kennedy remark surfaced again. Then I had to hear about the captain sneaking around the troop's hooches at night. I cringed when it was mentioned that Captain Eiler was now sleeping in his flak jacket with a loaded .45 nearby on a map stool. This sent the meeting into silence. I let a few moments pass and said, "Regardless of how we feel about the man he is our company commander. And we have to hold this company together while the convoys go out, despite how we personally feel."

One of the sergeants said, "Lieutenant, that man hasn't taken a convoy since Phu Gia Pass. And we all know what happened that afternoon."

I held up my hand and nodded. "That's all behind us." This was one of my most hateful phrases—*that's all behind us*—used too often by weak leaders and ruthlessly ambitious politicians in a time of crisis. And now I was using it. "We're talking in the present. We're being tested and have to prove our stripes and bars or we'll go downhill fast."

More silence. I was about to add something when the rear door opened. And in came Captain Eiler, carrying the company logbook. The company commander's meeting had ended earlier than expected. "What's going on here?" he asked.

I stood, thinking fast. "We're discussing morale issues, captain. I, uh, felt it might be good for the NCOs to air some opinions." He looked around the room. Several of the sergeants looked away. Their facial expressions said it all. The tension was building. *Damn it*, I thought, *I organized this with the best intentions.* And now it was falling apart . . . in seconds.

Captain Eiler turned to me. "I need to see you right away." Then he looked around. "And this meeting is concluded." He turned and walked out of the hooch.

I shook my head, angered and frustrated again. One of the sergeants patted me on the shoulder. "Nice try, lieutenant."

I thought I was going to get another reaming from Captain Eiler for calling an impromptu meeting while he was gone. For whatever reason he let that go. Then I found out why. "You have a convoy to Hoi An tomorrow. You depart at 0700."

"Hoi An?" I wondered.

He nodded. "Carmetti and Cobb just came back from Phu Bai. Greene is still snapping in. And the Thuong Duc run is still going on. You're up next."

I thought of trying something new: I asked, "Captain, any thought of taking this one yourself?"

"What, you have a hearing problem? I said *you* have a convoy to Hoi An. It's a short line haul, leaving from here, about ten trucks with small security, a wrecker, and a corpsman. Sergeant Thomas will be your X-Ray and trail. I'm sure you can handle it." The meeting ended.

Before the evening mess that night I got the convoy order at operations. It was nine trucks heading down to an artillery battery near Hoi An. We were hauling C-rations and 105-millimeter ammunition, Claymore mines, and radio batteries. The only differences were that we'd be leaving earlier than usual and wouldn't have to wait long for a road sweep by the engineers. Our security was one .50-caliber gun on the pace and a fire team on one truck. I went to the armory and drew my 12-gauge shotgun and a bandolier.

After breakfast that morning I went to Lieutenant Colonel Arnold's office and looked at the G–2 overnight intelligence reports. The messages were all about enemy movement up in the Hai Van Pass and Thuong Duc—lots of activity in both areas. There was no mention of the road down to Hoi An, which was Highway 1 and then branching off on Route 608. I didn't like it.

As I walked with my convoy bag down to the motor pool I remember having so many mixed and conflicted feelings. My first was to get the convoy off and back in the same day. Next, I was angered at my company commander for ducking so many convoy orders, diverting them to us junior officers while he sat in his cubicle signing reports and reading detective novels. Ever since I was informed about the false grave marker I had visions of him in his hooch sleeping in a flak jacket with a loaded .45 nearby. *Should I feel sorry for the man?* To top it off I was still waiting for the final investigation on the Thuong Duc convoy.

I met with Staff Sergeant Thomas and we quickly went over the convoy route. Highway 1 in that area was fairly safe. I figured that the time to worry was when we peeled off to Route 608 heading into Hoi An. There wasn't much time to talk. I gave the order to move out precisely at 0700. When we passed through the front gate nobody was there, not even our company commander. Along Highway 1 our first major landmark was the Danang garbage dump, which was undergoing its daily pilfering by local villagers. You always knew that the garbage dump was coming up. And then you had to hold your breath while passing it. I remember on this morning it had an unusual pungent odor, old garbage mixed with dead rodents. Next was the bridge at Cam Le, which would be a tragically important landmark for me and many others, before the summer months ended.

By the time we took the turn off to Route 608 the troops had already loaded magazines into their M–16s. After calling in a checkpoint I thought to myself that this would be a quick milk run. Why did I even think that?

It was less than a minute later when the truck in front of my jeep detonated a road mine and was lifted off to the side of the road. Several troops opened fire as I ordered my driver to pull up behind the damaged vehicle, which was still smoking. I grabbed the shotgun and moved along one side of the truck while the troops were still firing. Then, as quickly as it started, it ended. By the time I called a cease-fire a corpsman was inside the cab administering to the wounded driver, who took shrapnel wounds in both legs. It didn't look like a medevac was needed. I went back to the jeep and called in the situation with grid coordinates. Defend asked me about the condition of the truck. I shook my head. I had a wounded driver and they were worried about the Goddamn truck. I explained that the device looked like a box mine and that the undercarriage of the vehicle was a twisted mass; the truck was a total loss. He gave me a roger. And I ordered the truck's cargo to be transferred to another truck bed and the wrecker to carry the damaged truck, a bit different from Thuong Duc. I gave the area a quick once-over. As soon as the cargo was transferred we'd be on our way. There were no firefights moving in on me this time, so there was no urgent need to get out of the area. Sergeant Thomas approached me and we looked at the crater, knowing that the mine was most likely planted during the night. "You lead a charmed life, lieutenant."

"What do you mean?" I asked.

"Command-detonated. I'd say that they were going for your jeep, with that whip antenna swaying in the breeze. Whoever it was hit the button too soon," explained Sergeant Thomas. "There goes another of your nine lives."

We pulled into the artillery battery compound, off-loaded our cargo, had lunch, and headed back. The damaged truck was left at the compound. The wounded Marine had his dressings changed and returned with us. I made sure that the corpsman made the notation for the Marine to get his Purple Heart. It was an uneventful ride back to 11th Motors.

Afterward I checked in with operations, confirming the location of the mine and that the damaged truck was at the artillery battery. I was then informed that Lieutenant Colonel Arnold wanted to see me. I deposited the shotgun at the armory and reported in at battalion headquarters. Colonel Arnold asked me to sit down. I assumed that the file in front of him was the Thuong Duc investigation. "I've read your statement, Lieutenant McAdams." I nodded. "And I think you should give some thought to rewriting certain phrases."

"Which phrases?" I asked.

"You used the phrase 'complications at division at such a crucial time.' That's your opinion and I certainly don't agree with it."

I suddenly heard Captain Davidson's voice, at division legal, predicting that I would be called on this. "Colonel, I was kept waiting in that situation for thirty-five minutes. I have yet to hear why that happened. I made an attempt to contact the infantry officer who had the security detachment on that convoy and was told by Major Ashworth that he would be gathering the statements. That captain told me that I did the right thing and he would support that."

I expected Colonel Arnold to respond. Instead, he opened the file and looked at the first page, which I recognized as my statement. "I also think you should eliminate the phrase 'wise and prudent under the circumstances.' I don't think what you did was either of these."

"I had Captain Davidson, at division legal, look at that statement. He saw nothing wrong with it," I said. "He added that it was logical and succinct."

He glared at me for several moments. "That's his opinion. Your statement needs a serious rewrite." Then he handed the two pages to me.

I looked at the first page, containing my anger. Then I handed the pages back. "Colonel, I'll stand by these pages."

Several more moments went by in silence. "Are you planning on remaining in the Marine Corps after Vietnam?"

"I don't know. I'll make that decision when the time comes," I said.

"Lieutenant McAdams, are you aware that this statement, and the investigation, could affect your promotion to captain?"

"I'll take that chance," I replied.

He closed the file. "I'll tell you what. I'm going to pass on this. After thirteen months in this Godforsaken combat zone I'll let my successor sign off on this."

"Your successor?"

Colonel Arnold nodded. "Major Rip Pearson is coming down from up north. Change of command will be on the fifteenth. It will be his decision to sign off on the investigation." He paused and pushed the file aside on his desk. "That's all, lieutenant."

The rest of the week went by as normal routine. The convoys kept going out, down south, to Thuong Duc and through the Hai Van Pass. Battalion headquarters was now preparing for the change of command. All that we knew about our incoming battalion commander, Major R. I. "Rip" Pearson, was that he was with a motor transport battalion up near Quang Tri and was on his second tour.

On the afternoon of July 15, 1968, the companies assembled in mass formation in the motor pool and the change of command took place with the reading of orders and transfer of colors. At the conclusion of the ceremony Lieutenant Colonel Arnold and Major Pearson, a short, stocky man with thinning hair, repaired to the headquarters hooch to sign formal papers. Corporal Forsythe then drove Lieutenant Colonel Arnold to the 15th Aerial Port in Danang.

On the way, a village woman squirted her sentiments to our former battalion commander. As Corporal Forsythe drove through Khon Son, with Lieutenant Colonel Arnold in the passenger seat, the village woman stepped into the road, lifted her blouse, and cupped her right breast. She then squirted mother's milk on the passenger side of the jeep windshield. Corporal Forsythe said later that when he made the turn onto the main road leading to First Marine Division Headquarters Lieutenant Colonel Arnold was "visibly shaken."

We now had a new leader. But for me he was a battalion commander who was going to make a decision on the Thoung Duc investigation. During this time Andy Garrison was still doing double duty. His primary assignment was psychological operations officer. But now he would also be the acting battalion adjutant until a new one reported in.

Several days later I was called to the S–1 personnel office and handed an envelope. I had an idea what it was. I went to the hooch, sat on my bunk, and opened the envelope. I went right to the subject line: *Non-Punitive Letter of Censure.* It was signed by Major R. I. Pearson. Lieutenant Colonel Arnold was right; he passed it off to his relief, a man I hadn't even formally met. The letter contended that, *without proper authority,* I destroyed a Marine Corps vehicle that had the value of $9,700. It did not mention that the vehicle had already been totaled by a command detonated enemy road mine and that my convoy had two firefights moving in on our position. The last paragraph stated that, according to Judge Advocate General's instructions, this nonpunitive letter of censure would not be a part of my permanent record, nor would it be quoted in or appended to any fitness reports. I stood for several moments looking at the last paragraph. Then I tore the letter into little pieces.

To this day I regret tearing up the letter; I should have kept it as a badge of honor. As it was said by a wise gunnery sergeant in World War II, "A letter of censure is better than no mail at all."

11

The River

The rest of July and early August 1968 were spent adjusting to the command style of Major Pearson. Like any new battalion commander he wanted to know the situation of each company under his authority. This meant scheduled inspections for each company, starting with administration and then supply. Transport Company was slated for the second week of August. Suddenly the emphasis was taken off of the battalion's primary mission: supporting the infantry and artillery units in the First Marine Division's AOR. In his first company commander's meeting Major Pearson explained, "There's more to being a company commander than running convoys."

This statement confused some of the junior officers. As a group we felt running Rough Rider resupply convoys was the primary mission of 11th Motors. The battalion crest, in front of the dispatcher's shack, carried the motto: THE ROLLING 11TH. I even recalled my first-day orientation at the division chief of staff's office, where he said that the Rough Rider resupply convoys were "the lifeblood of the division." Almost overnight we had to concentrate on administration and supply, coordinating office memos and reports along with counting "jocks and socks." Captain Eiler wasted no time in preparing for Major Pearson's inspection. As XO I was to coordinate with First Sergeant Duncan and supervise the organization of the company office, memos, and reports. Gunnery Sergeant Rayhorn and Staff Sergeant Tonto Garrido were to coordinate the supply section with Jack supervising, ensuring that everything was accounted for on paper. During this time I learned that the false grave marker was returned from Division CID with negative results for fingerprints. When Gunnery Sergeant Rayhorn told Captain Eiler that the grave marker was being stored in the supply hooch Captain Eiler ordered him to burn it. Captain Eiler added that irritating and timeworn phrase, "That's all behind us." In the meantime Rich Cobb was transferred to an artillery battalion as a motor transport officer.

155

After a week of preparation Captain Eiler scheduled a late-afternoon meeting in the company office, where he would be given updates for the coming inspection. As he sat at the First Sergeant's desk I outlined how the company records—weekly and monthly reports—were filed. Then I explained how the company memos had been reorganized in chronological order. Jack gave an introductory presentation for supply followed by Gunnery Sergeant Rayhorn going into more specifics. Rayhorn then turned it over to Staff Sergeant Garrido, who had only been in-country less than a month. Sergeant Garrido, who came from a large Guamanian family, had a habit of speaking in a staccato-type voice when he got excited.

As he began with his supply presentation Staff Sergeant Garrido broke into his staccato tone. Captain Eiler suddenly slammed his fist on the desk and interrupted him. "Goddamn it, I don't understand Spic. Speak English!"

The office fell silent. I lowered my head and stared at the floor, stinging with embarrassment. I exchanged looks with Jack, mortified. Staff Sergeant Garrido looked around the room, took a pause, and continued with his presentation in a slower voice.

The meeting broke up just before mess call. I caught up with Captain Eiler outside of the office. "Uh, captain, a follow-up on Sergeant Garrido."

Captain Eiler turned and looked at me. "What about him?"

"It's about the remark that you made, about not understanding Spic." Captain Eiler nodded. "Sergeant Garrido is not Hispanic; he's Guamanian. And Spic, as we know, is a derogatory racial term."

"What are you saying?" asked Captain Eiler.

"That Sergeant Garrido deserves an apology."

"You're suggesting that I apologize because I couldn't understand him?"

I shook my head. "It's not that you couldn't understand him. You used the term 'Spic.'"

"Frank, at the first formation I said that I'm a book man. I don't apologize to sergeants." Once more, I couldn't believe what I was hearing. "I've got to get a lax company ready for an inspection."

He turned and headed to the mess hall. A feeling of disgust welled up in my stomach as I watched him walk away. He was not only walking away from me; he was showing another negative character trait—the inability to admit being wrong.

I found Sergeant Garrido at the supply hooch with Gunnery Sergeant Rayhorn. I took Sergeant Garrido outside and explained my situation. "The captain made a mistake in using that term." Sergeant Garrido nodded with a serious expression. "And I want to apologize for what you had to hear."

Sergeant Garrido said, "Thank you, lieutenant, I understand." He walked back into the supply hooch.

Within the week the company inspections were complete. The next day a battalion memo came out with the results. Two of the truck companies received excellent ratings—Alpha and Transport. At the afternoon company formation Captain Eiler stood in front of the troops and read the memo. Then he added, "Every man here should know that without the proper preparation we would not have attained this rating. When I assumed command of this company I vowed that I would make it better." He paused and looked around. "And I have. This inspection proves it." Without mentioning any of the staff work, he turned the company over to me for dismissal and went back in the office.

Later that week I was writing a letter to Patty after the evening formation. Corporal Adair knocked on the hooch door and said that I was to report to operations immediately. At operations Major Ashworth explained that I was to command a reaction convoy to the village of Hoa Vang on the south side of Song Cau Do River at Cam Le Bridge. "This is a line haul," said Major Ashworth. "You'll pick up Alpha Company, First Force Recon, at their headquarters, transit them down to Hoa Vang, and return here. It's that simple."

I nodded and made some quick notes. "Take them down there, drop them off, and return here."

"Exactly, Lieutenant McAdams, nothing more. We've been notified that there's a possibility of a VC sapper squad attempting to make a run across the river into the south end of the airbase. They want a reaction company ready."

"When do I leave?" I asked.

"You don't," said Major Ashworth, meaning that a depart time had not been set. "Get your gear ready, report to the dispatcher's shack, and await orders. Your convoy will be six trucks, with drivers and A-drivers [the Marine Corps term for "assistant driver," a second trooper in the cab]. No need for a corpsman. You'll have a PRC-25 radio, call sign Transport 5."

"Is there anything in the G-2 reports on enemy movement down there?" I asked.

"The standard alert, nothing more. Your people should be back here for noon chow, which is why a convoy briefing isn't necessary," said Major Ashworth. "It will be a routine line haul."

When I left operations I had no idea that I was riding into the biggest fight I would see in Vietnam, what came to be known as the '68 Summer Offensive. Yeah—a routine line haul.

I went back to my hooch and quickly finished the letter to Patty. Then I got my gear ready: helmet, .45 sidearm, and flak jacket. Because it was a short line haul I didn't think it was necessary to draw the 12-gauge shotgun from the armory. How wrong I was.

Shortly after ten o'clock that night I went down to the motor pool and met my drivers and A-drivers. Like many of the convoys, the drivers were pulled from the various truck companies. Some of them I knew by face; others I had never met. One of the negative aspects of Rough Rider convoys was that the drivers you worked with filtered in from the other truck companies. We would never fully get to know each other. I explained that we were taking a reaction company from 1st Force Recon down to Hoa Vang. We'd drop them off and be back for a hot meal in the mess hall. I remember a few of them smiling. It was a warm night. The last thing I told them was to return to their trucks and get what sleep they could; we would be called on a moment's notice. Then I went back to the dispatcher's shack and used my convoy bag as a pillow. I pulled my helmet down over my nose. Within minutes I was asleep.

"Lieutenant McAdams, Lieutenant McAdams!" I cocked my helmet above my eyes. It was Corporal Ronald Profitt, the company dispatcher. I nodded to him. "Your reaction convoy has a green light. They need you down at 1st Force Recon for a pickup ASAP."

I stood and could see streaks of the first light in the sky. "What have you heard so far?"

"All hell has broken loose down at the river," said Corporal Profitt. "They need 1st Force Recon *hai ah-ku.*" *Hai ah-ku* was Asian slang for "right away." As I went into the motor pool I had a sinking feeling in the pit of my stomach. *We're riding into some deep shit.* And Major Ashworth said that there was no reason for a corpsman. Too late now.

I assembled the drivers and A-drivers—about ten Marines total. I explained that this was classified as a line haul, that the pace truck would also serve as my command truck. They would follow closely. At 1st Force Recon we would load Alpha Company and take them down to Hoa Vang. I would give further instructions at that point. While they were warming up their engines I placed my PRC–25 in the cab of the pace truck and did a radio check with Defend at division. I got out on the running board and gave the sign to move out. The first light of day was coming in over the Gulf of Tonkin along with the hot rays of a tropical sun. We headed out of the main gate. Once again the cavalry was leaving the fort.

At 1st Force Recon we pulled off on the left side of the road. Within minutes Alpha Company was climbing into the truck beds. I met the company commander, Captain F. J. Vogel, a stocky redhead who was wearing a United States Naval Academy ring, and his gunnery sergeant. Captain Vogel told me that he just received an update from G-2. It wasn't a sapper squad coming across the river; it was a reinforced unit, "possibly a fucking NVA battalion." I paused and took a deep breath—*holy motherfucker!*

Back on the trucks, we headed south along the road that paralleled the airbase. I noticed two Huey gunships making gun runs and firing rockets. I got out on the running board to see where the rockets were landing. Then I ducked inside the cab and reported my position to Defend, adding that air cover was off to my left.

I instructed my driver to pull up at the intersection. As the troops began off-loading I smelled something wafting in the air, like scrambled eggs and bacon. And it was. Nearby was a line of Air Force barracks. Several airmen were out on the balcony, towels hanging around their necks, holding dopp kits for their morning toilette. Several of them raised clenched fists, encouraging us. A few more yelled phrases like "Go get 'em, Marines!" and "Semper Fi!" Then they filed inside for morning breakfast. In the meantime Alpha Company was off-loading and checking their weapons, a marked difference between service branches.

A sergeant, holding his M-16, came running up to me, his face streaming with sweat. "You the reaction convoy commander?"

I nodded. "11th Motors."

"You need to report in to the CP down the road. It's set up in an AmTrac [Amphibious Tractor]. You'll get a frag order there." He turned and ran off.

A "frag order" meant fragmentary order, an addendum to the previous one. In this case I already knew what was in store. We would be under operational control of whoever is running things down here. So much for the noon meal back at 11th Motors.

I had the trucks follow me in an easterly direction along a road that bordered a rice paddy. On the other side of the rice paddy was the south fence of the airbase. I had my driver pull up at the AmTrac CP. Inside the AmTrac was a temporary communications hub. Several radios were set up on field tables, frantic transmissions coming in and going out. A burly major approached me: "You with the reaction convoy?"

I nodded. "Lieutenant McAdams, 11th Motors. Six trucks. I just dropped off Alpha Company, 1st Recon Battalion."

"Your convoy is attached to me, 1st MPs. We need to get wounded and dead off the streets down there." He walked me several yards down the road. "Go straight down this road. When you get to the intersection, turn right. That's south, into the village." I nodded. "Keep your butt down because it's house-to-house fighting. They came across the river during the night, infiltrated that ville [village] and two others. They took some of the villagers out in the streets and mass-executed them."

"Where do I take the casualties?" I asked.

The major pointed to my rear. "1st Tanks has a compound back there. They set up a field hospital and Graves Registration."

"Will I be able to turn around once I get into the village?"

"It's house-to-house fighting. I can't guarantee anything. From the radio traffic it's a clusterfuck!" He wiped his forehead. "Get in there and get the wounded and the heat cases out first. The dead are secondary." I nodded dreadfully. "And good luck!"

I returned to the trucks and stood off at an angle giving the assemble sign, circling my right index finger in the air. The drivers and A-drivers approached me. The Hueys were still in the air making gun runs, so I had to talk loudly. I told them to follow my lead truck, that we were going into a hot village, house-to-house fighting, to get the wounded and heat cases out. "Leave the dead bodies for now." A few nodded; the others just stared at me. "Okay, let's get it done!" I took off my helmet, wiped my brow, returned to my lead truck, and climbed into the cab. I checked the radio and suddenly became aware that all I had was a .45 sidearm. *How Goddamn stupid!* If only I had thought to bring that 12-gauge shotgun. I then reached into my convoy bag, pulled out a pair of binoculars, and strung it around my neck.

We moved out, slowly heading toward the intersection. I saw that Alpha Company had already started down the road, in files, bypassing the intersection, continuing east to come around Hoa Vang from another direction. By now I could hear sporadic small-arms fire. As we got closer to the intersection I saw several dead bodies on both sides of the road. We made a right turn and headed south into the village.

The street was littered with debris and bodies—Marines and NVA mixed with villagers. I looked farther down the street. Black smoke had mixed with the intense heat. Down at the end it was worse: more debris and dead bodies. I had the driver pull over. *We'll start from here*, I thought.

As soon as I got out of the cab a rake of automatic-weapons fire came from an angled position. Marines were firing on the run, going back and forth from house to house. I hugged the right-front fender, trying to determine from where the enemy fire was coming. Then more fire came from a row of houses off to our left. *Oh shit*, I thought, *we're in a crossfire!*

By now the drivers and A-drivers were out of their trucks huddled along the passenger sides. I grabbed the radio from the cab, adjusting it on my left shoulder. Across the street was a well. On the other side of the well was a brick wall where several Marines had taken cover. I quickly moved down the truck line. "Make a run for the wall!" I yelled.

We made an infantry-type charge across the street and reached cover along the wall. Wherever the enemy was, they saw us and opened fire. I could hear rounds hitting on the other side of the wall and dinging off the well. Somebody yelled, "Where's that fucking gun at?"

I yelled above the gunfire, "Stay put, don't move! Alpha Company is coming around the other side!"

A Marine down the line yelled, "Those motherfuckers!" There was more fire and then I heard a loud "*Unnh!*"

I grabbed the radio handset and keyed it, trying to contact Defend and tell them our situation. "Be advised, we're in the ville near the blue line, taking enemy fire from two directions. Do you copy, over?" All I heard was crackling and static. I didn't get through.

Then I looked over at the well. There was a redheaded Marine, propped up on his back against the well. He had taken a round in the forehead that had knocked off his helmet. His glasses were still perched on the edge of his nose. It was senseless: The poor guy didn't keep his head down.

The Hueys were still in the air, making gun runs. I looked up and down our section of the wall. My guys were snug, waiting for the all-clear. *How long would it be?* More rounds came in on the other side of the wall. I made another attempt to call in to Defend. More crackling and static. By now I was tempted to lift up and take a peek over the wall. I cast another look over at the dead redheaded Marine. It was at that point where I ironically realized something: I couldn't move and neither could he. I kept my head down knowing that I'd be pushing fate. *Where the hell is Alpha Company?!* It seemed like an hour before the reaction force came in on the other side. At first all we heard was more small-arms fire punctuated with explosions. Then we heard shouting and yelling. I popped a quick look over the wall and saw Marines moving along a street on the other side. We waited for another five minutes. Then I slowly stood. We were clear. But there was still more fighting down at the south end at Cam Le Bridge. My troops were still huddled along the wall. I looked at my watch. It had been only about twenty minutes—twenty minutes of intense, tragic hell.

"Okay, back to the trucks. Load up the wounded and heat cases and let's get the hell out of here."

It took another half-hour to get casualties loaded onto the trucks. My drivers helped the walking wounded. The stretcher cases took more time. Slowly the truck beds filled up. While this was taking place I went back to the well to confirm the redheaded Marine. Someone had put a white handkerchief on his face. There was nothing I could do. His M-16 was lying next to his right leg. I picked it up. Then I took a bandolier off of the Marine's shoulder. At least I had a rifle and ammunition for the duration. I had no idea how that rifle would come to affect me in the aftermath, a good omen gone bad.

With trucks loaded we went through the turnaround process, moving up and back so that the convoy was pointed north to head back down the street. Meanwhile, fighting was still going on down at the bridge. I gave the signal to move out. As we headed back to the intersection in the dusty heat a villager came running past the truck line on our right. He angled off into a field heading toward a rice paddy. Suddenly a shot rang out. I had no idea from where it came. Then I saw part of the villager's head explode; a dark mass flew off. But the villager didn't go down right away. His legs kept pumping along the ground. Then his arms went up and he fell and rolled. We went right by him; there was nothing we could do.

My trucks pulled into the tank park where a temporary aid station was set up. Stretchers and body bags were lined on the ground in separate sections. My drivers helped the Navy corpsmen get the casualties off the truck beds. Two drivers carried a stretcher right by me when a corpsman told them to put it down. The corpsman bent over the Marine, examined the eyes, and felt the carotid artery. He shook his head and pointed toward the body bags. "Put him over there."

I made another call to Defend. This time I got through. He asked for a sit rep and I summarized what we did so far and that the convoy was now "Op-Conned" to Whiskey Point, call sign for 1st MPs. I concluded, "The enemy force was much larger than first anticipated." And I assumed that battalion was monitoring my transmissions.

Defend simply gave me a "Roger, Transport 5, out."

While filling an empty canteen I realized that my utility blouse under the flak jacket was sopping wet. Before getting the trucks ready to return to the AmTrac I stopped in at a field desk of the aid station and got a box of salt pills. When I came out I saw that the Hueys were still in the air making gun runs over the rice paddy and Hoa Vang.

We left the tank park and headed back to the AmTrac CP. I had my driver take the box of salt pills and distribute them. Then I sought out the major. He was inside the AmTrac making a radio transmission. He held up a hand, signaling me to wait. Finally he put down the handset. He walked me out back toward my command truck. "They're still trying to get the bridge back."

"Get the bridge back? I could see the bridge from my end of the street," I said.

"There's an old French bunker on the south side of the river with a .50-caliber gun. They took over the bunker and have the .50," said the major. "It's going back and forth." He paused. "We need you to make another casualty run."

I remember swallowing and giving him a long look. "We were lucky the first time. They had us pinned down for a while."

He nodded. "Alpha Company got you out of there. Now get back in there and get our people out."

"Any chance that I can get a corpsman to go in with us?"

"That's negative, they're all committed." He turned and headed back to the AmTrac. *Thank you, Major Ashworth, for telling me that I wouldn't need a corpsman.*

I assembled the drivers again, explaining that we were going back in. Nobody said anything. I looked at their sweaty faces. This time we knew exactly what we were going into. "I'll take a volunteer to be my driver in the lead truck." One of the drivers raised his hand. "I'll go in with you this time, lieutenant."

"What's your name?" I asked.

"Walker, sir. Bravo Company."

"Okay, I'll transfer my radio to your truck." I added that my command truck would head out last in line. We would go past the intersection and stop when the command truck came abreast to the intersection. At that point we would back into the village, command truck first for a quick getaway. "When I stop that's the point from where we'll load the casualties." I paused. "Any questions?"

A Marine asked, "How long will we be doing this, lieutenant?"

"As long as they need us. The NVA still holds the far end of the village. Stay tight and keep a round in the chamber."

From the previous truck I grabbed my radio, the M-16, and my convoy bag. The binoculars were still around my neck. I placed everything in Walker's cab. Then he pulled his truck out of line to the rear. The trucks moved out slowly. When my truck came alongside the intersection the convoy stopped. I got out of the cab, stood on the running board and signaled them to go in reverse.

We made the turn at the intersection and began backing into the village. The first thing I noticed was the dead villager who kept running after he was hit. He was lying on his back, sightless eyes skyward. If only the poor guy had stayed put, just like the redheaded Marine whose rifle I was now using.

As we backed into the village I had Walker go a bit farther this time. Then I motioned for him to stop. The drivers began breaking out the stretchers while several walking wounded came limping from the sides of the street. The Hueys were still up in the air but on the other side of the river, blasting away. As we continued loading the casualties I noticed several men, holding cameras, coming up on the safe side of the convoy line. *Now we have the press here*, I thought.

One photographer, wearing a bush hat and a safari jacket, approached a truck while the wounded were being loaded. "Hey, Marine, I'm going to take your picture!" he shouted. He raised the camera and started clicking off frames.

One of the wounded Marines in the truck bed, bleeding from a leg wound, raised his M-16 and pointed it at the photographer. "Back off, motherfucker, or you're a dead man!"

The photographer quickly took the advice. He ducked to the side and continued up the street with two friends. For a moment I thought we'd be carrying out a dead combat photographer. I then went up and down the truck line as the casualties continued to climb aboard. They seemed to be mostly heat cases, heavy breathing, exhausted with that thousand-yard stare.

With all the tailgates up I went to the front truck and told the driver to head to the tank park; we'd follow in line. Back in my command truck I tried to raise Defend again and got more static. *What is it with this area?*, I wondered.

There was more activity at the tank park as we pulled in. While we were off-loading the casualties two mules—platforms on wheels—pulled up. They were carrying stacked ammunition cans. The drivers wanted us to take them in. I gave a quick nod. As the wounded were leaving the truck beds they were replaced with ammunition cans for M-16 rifles and M-60 machine guns. While the ammo was being loaded I got the sense that we were going to be here not only for the rest of the day but for the duration. They needed us—by God they did!

With the ammo cans loaded we headed back to the AmTrac CP. As soon as we arrived my drivers started stacking the cans in an area near the AmTrac. Several Marines came by, picked up some M-16 cans, and headed into Hoa Vang. The major came out and explained that an NVA unit had infiltrated a village just east of us and were moving toward our position. He said, "Have your men take up firing positions behind the trucks. We have sight reports from the Hueys and we're getting sniper fire from across the rice paddy."

He went back to the AmTrac. I grabbed my newly acquired M-16 and took up a position at the convoy midpoint with the radio. With the binoculars I began scanning the rice paddy in front of us. On the far side of the rice paddy was a tree line less than six hundred meters to our front. I passed a slow look in increments going from east to west, all the way to the road where the Air Force barracks were. A Huey came over the rice paddy, took a southerly bank, and headed off to the river. I proceeded to do another scan. And then I saw them: At first it looked like a group of villagers coming out of a tree line, heading west toward the road. I began following them. Then I saw that they were only dressed as villagers, several wearing cone hats. They were carrying weapons. I counted ten of them moving in file, about three or four hundred meters along our front. The third and fourth in line were carrying what looked like a crew-served machine gun. Then I realized what they were doing. They were moving toward the far road where the gun would have an unobstructed angle on us.

"Lieutenant, we've got movement out in the rice paddy!" yelled one of my drivers.

"I see them, enemy dressed as villagers, hold your fire!" I wanted to see if there were more than ten. As they kept moving I knew that they couldn't reach the road and set up that gun. It looked like ten and no more. "Steady . . . steady, hold your fire!" They were more than halfway to the road. And now they were all in the open. "Commence fire!" I yelled.

The drivers opened up while I kept the binoculars trained on the file. The Marine closest to me, Harris, held his fire following the line. They now realized that we spotted them and broke into a run as paddy water kicked up all around them. Several of them went down. Then I saw the last two turn and head for the tree line. By now there was one left, holding what looked like an AK-47 rifle. He kept running through the paddy water until Harris squeezed off one round. The next thing I saw was the AK-47 flying into the air. The soldier was running so fast that when the round hit him, either in the neck or head, his legs went up in the air in a flip. And then he hit the water. By now the last two were gone.

Suddenly I felt someone pulling on my flak jacket. It was the major. "Cease fire, lieutenant, those are villagers out there!"

"Cease fire, cease fire!" I yelled. Then I looked at the major. "Major, they're dressed as villagers, they were carrying weapons. There were ten and we knocked down eight."

"Have your men stand by." He turned and went back to the AmTrac.

I turned to Harris. "One hell of a shot; I saw him go down." Harris nodded and smiled at me. I lifted the binoculars back up. No movement out in the rice paddy. Then I realized that with two words, "commence fire," I indirectly killed eight enemy soldiers.

We held the line along the road as more Marines came by to pick up M-16 ammunition cans. Then we heard a commotion down the line toward the main road. Someone yelled for a corpsman. I checked my troops. It wasn't one of mine. I set aside my M-16 and moved down the line to where a group was forming. A corpsman was working on a young Marine on his back, breathing heavily. Both legs were saturated with blood. A sniper got lucky. With one shot the Marine took hits in both thighs, in and out. I went back to my previous position and told my drivers to stay put at their firing positions.

A few minutes later a Marine approached me. He explained that he was the assistant gunner and needed help carrying M-60 ammo up to a ridgeline where they just set in an emplacement. I looked around, realizing that my drivers were spread out on the convoy line, rifles trained out on the rice paddy. I decided to leave them there. I told Walker to monitor the radio and pulled one of the other men, Allen Widmer, out of line. "Grab some M-60 ammo cans and follow this guy." I set aside my rifle and nodded to Widmer, signaling that we were both going on an ammo run. I left Walker in charge and to monitor the radio.

Each of us took four cans, one under each arm and the second held in each hand. Then we moved down the frontage road to a little cutoff that led up to the ridgeline. The Marine turned to us: "Keep your head down going up to the ridge." I nodded. He went up first with Widmer and me following. Halfway up, I heard a snap overhead, then another and another. I had no idea from where the rounds were coming, only that they were hitting the banana leaves above us.

At the top of the cutoff we came out on a clearing. On the edge of the clearing the M-60 was set up with a commanding field of fire of the river and the southern bank. The gunner had just laid out the spare barrel as we set down the cans. The assistant gunner opened the first can and began feeding a belt into the gun. "We're going to need more ammo," said the gunner.

I looked at Widmer. Both of us were breathing heavily with sweat streaming down our faces. "You've got ten cans right here," I said.

The gunner nodded. "Yeah, and that'll last us about twenty minutes."

"Okay," I said. "We'll be back." Widmer and I turned and headed back down the cutoff to the frontage road. Again, rounds snapped over head. *Where the hell is that sniper?*, I wondered.

Back at the AmTrac Widmer and I loaded up more ammo cans, four each. Then we headed back to the cutoff and up the trail. As soon as we began climbing up the cutoff path more rounds snapped overhead. We came into the clearing while the gun team was laying down fire to the other side of the river. When I saw the empty cans I realized how fast they were going through the ammunition. The assistant gunner gave a thumbs up and said, "We need more!"

Widmer and I exchanged exhausted looks. I wiped my face and said, "Okay, one more run then we have to get back."

The assistant gunner nodded, holding a belt while the gunner continued firing in short bursts. Widmer and I headed back down the cutoff. And we were greeted with more rounds snapping overhead. *This is getting old fast*, I thought.

We picked up more M-60 ammo cans and made another run, back to the cutoff, up the trail, and into the clearing. We dumped the cans behind the gun team and fell on the ground like two runners finishing a marathon. I looked at Widmer, who was turning white by now. I wondered what I looked like. "You ready to start back down?"

He nodded in between heaving breaths. "In a minute."

While we waited, the gun team continued firing across the river. I could see people on the other side running back and forth, ugly house-to-house fighting. It made me realize that this fight was far from over, that this offensive was a well-coordinated attack. It made me think of what Major Ashworth said—that a VC sapper unit was expected to hit the south end of the airbase. He didn't mention anything about an NVA battalion or regiment.

I nodded to Widmer and signaled him to follow me. I didn't have to tell him to keep his head down. We inched over to the trail and began running back down. About halfway down the sniping started in again with the rounds hitting the trees and the leaves. We both rolled out of the cutoff and onto the frontage road. We stayed there on the ground for several more minutes, chests heaving, catching our breath in the heat. I turned to him, "You okay?"

Widmer shook his head, "I think I'm going to be sick."

"Hold it in," I said. "That was our last run."

After we arrived back at the convoy line I picked up the binoculars to scan the rice paddy. I could barely hold the glasses! My hands were shaking and wouldn't stop. I put the glasses down and placed both hands on the truck fender. Then I realized that this was a combat reaction. I took a deep breath and waited, looking up and down the truck line. I didn't want anyone to see me like this, no control over my shaking hands. It was a minute or two before the shaking stopped.

A short while later the major approached me. "We need you to make another run into the village. More casualties and heat cases." All I could do was nod. He turned and went back to the AmTrac.

I lined up the trucks again. Walker said that he'd stay with me in the command truck. We went to the intersection and backed our way down the street into the village. The main fighting was still at the south end where the bridge was. There were Marines resting along the street with several more in stretchers. We got out of the trucks, lowered the tailgates, and began getting the casualties aboard. I didn't see any combat photographers this time. Then we moved out, back to the intersection. The dead villager was still in the same spot. However, I noticed some bloating in his body, the result of exposure to the intense heat.

As we were off-loading the casualties at the tank park I suddenly realized that it was late afternoon and I hadn't eaten anything since early morning. I couldn't believe the passage of time. Then I assembled the drivers and passed out boxes of C-rations. We took a much-needed rest, not knowing what the early evening and nighttime would bring. When I took off my flak jacket I saw the salt stains on my utility blouse.

After finishing the C-rations I checked in with Defend and gave a sit rep. All I got back was "roger, out." Then I switched frequencies and made a direct transmission to 11th Motors. One of the sergeants responded, acknowledging where we were and that my convoy was still attached to the 1st MPs. I put down the handset, wondering if 11th Motors knew exactly what we were going through.

That night I put the trucks in a line overlooking the frontage road. We could see flares in the sky and heard more firing. It was evident that the village of Hoa Vang had not been secured. I slept when possible in the bed of the command truck. At various increments I got up and used the binoculars to scan the area, hearing more firing and seeing more flares.

In the morning the CP was transferred to the operations bunker in the tank park. I reported in after a quick breakfast and was told to take the convoy back to the frontage road and stand by. When we got to the frontage road the Am-Trac was gone. My orders now came from the operations bunker. I wasn't a bit surprised when we got another order to go back into the village on a casualty run. This time it seemed easier; there weren't as many casualties. While they were being loaded I walked toward the southern end of the village. A stiff, acrid smell permeated the street in the stifling heat. It was an effort simply to breathe. The enemy had chosen this village as an avenue to the airbase and the city of Danang. It was evident that our side had paid a price. But they paid a much bigger one. And so did the civilians. I noticed the extensive damage to the shops, overhanging doors blown out, shards of glass, and shrapnel bits in the street. Here and there were dead villagers who either didn't get out in time or were executed. Rigor mortis and the heat were taking an ugly toll.

I stopped alongside an open area. I stood there, holding the M-16, looking at the scene in front of me. There must have been about three dozen dead bodies of North Vietnamese soldiers. Most of them were on their backs, riddled with entry wounds, arms stiffened, empty eyes looking skyward. Several of them were wearing swimsuit briefs. I recognized the Jantzen logo. Obviously these were the ones who swam across the river during the night. Others were in gray or green North Vietnamese jungle uniforms. There were several stacks of pith helmets nearby along with captured weapons. I noticed an open kit with two syringes lying next to a body. They were shooting up before they got shot up. I approached a nearby corporal who was sucking on a Pepsi Cola bottle. "What are they going to do with these bodies?" I asked.

"We're still collecting them. They'll go through the uniforms for documents. After that it will be a mass grave somewhere," explained the corporal. We watched as more bodies came in on two mule platforms and were quickly tossed into the pile. I walked out about twenty yards onto the Cam Le Bridge and stood there looking at the brownish water. Then I turned and looked back at the village, trying to visualize how they came across the river at night and took over the French bunker at the south end. Sentries along the bridge were standing there putting random shots into the water if anything looked suspicious. I had a sense that the worst was over.

As I walked back up the street to the trucks a group of villagers approached. They were carrying sections of corrugated tin and plywood boards. I watched as they placed the stiffened dead bodies of their fellow citizens on the tin sections and boards. Then they walked off. Next came several more villagers carrying gasoline cans. They saturated the area where the bodies had been lying. Then they lit it to abate any infestations. The gasoline smell mixed with the heat and the cloying odor of death made me realize how fortunate I was. The rifle I was holding belonged to a young Marine who wasn't as fortunate. Most likely he was in a body bag over at the NSA facility waiting for transfer home and a military funeral.

We made another run into the village that afternoon. There was still sporadic fighting but nothing like the first day. The enemy had definitely lost his thrust. In the operations bunker I was told that my trucks would be on call until the next day. Then I learned what we went up against: the 402nd VC Sapper Battalion combined with the 38th NVA Regiment. This was a marked difference from the first intelligence reports. I wrote down the units, if nothing else so I could include them in my AAR. As I copied the unit numbers I noticed a baldheaded man wearing glasses and one star, sitting next to a radio. He was smoking a thin cigar, staring into space as he listened to transmissions. I knew who he was: Major General Carl Youngdale's assistant division commander, Brigadier General Ross Dwyer. General Dwyer would cross my path several more times in the coming months.

I used the landline phone to call 11th Motors operations. I explained to the duty NCO that the convoy would be spending another night "down at the blue line attached to Whiskey Point." He gave me a roger and asked to be kept informed.

The next morning after breakfast we took up our position on the frontage road. I checked in with Whiskey Point and was informed that my trucks would be released soon. We were still on standby when I saw Captain Vogel and his gunnery sergeant. Captain Vogel and I shook hands. "How did your guys hold up?" he asked.

"The first day was hairy but we got used to it," I said.

"Same with us," he said. "We came in together and now we're going out."

I smiled and breathed a sigh of relief. "Okay, let's go home."

I had the drivers do a turnaround and pull up in line. Then Alpha Company climbed aboard. Soon we were heading back to 1st Recon Battalion headquarters. So much had happened in two and a half days. In my head I was organizing the outline for my AAR.

Lieutenant Colonel L. P. Charon, the CO of 1st Recon Battalion, was standing in the road in front of the headquarters as we pulled up. I got out and saluted him. He shook my hand. "Lieutenant, can't thank you guys enough. I heard the transmissions, what your people did down there at Cam Le."

When we pulled into the 11th Motors compound it was as if nothing had changed. I had the trucks pull up to a stop and assembled the drivers. Then I checked my notebook to make sure I had the correct spelling of their names and different companies. I closed the notebook and looked at them. "You gents should feel proud. We did everything that was asked of us and then some." I exchanged looks with Walker, Widmer, and Harris. "And I'll make sure your company commanders are aware of what *we* did." I emphasized the pronoun *we*.

At Transport Company I entered through the backdoor, set down my convoy bag and the M-16 and took off my flak jacket. I was really ripe, stinking up the place, wearing the same clothes that I left in along with a three-day growth of beard. Corporal Adair and First Sergeant Duncan welcomed me back. I was sitting at my desk, looking at some papers that had piled up when Captain Eiler came through the front door. He nodded for me to enter his cubicle. I went in and stood at his desk. The first thing I noticed was a new paperback detective novel on his desk.

"Explain why you were gone for almost three days," he said.

I was aghast! He knew nothing about where we were or what we did. "When we off-loaded Alpha Company from 1st Recon they attached us to the 1st MPs. They kept us there, making casualty runs in and out of the village."

"Aw, bullshit! You were down there sitting on your asses."

I said, "Captain, do I look like I was sitting on my ass? We were under fire much of the time. The first day we were pinned down for more than twenty minutes in house-to-house fighting."

He held up a hand, shaking his head. "Don't give me that John Wayne crap!"

I stared at him for several moments, realizing his denial and ignorance of what we endured. Then I said, "If you don't believe me, get on the landline phone and call Lieutenant Colonel Charon over at Force Recon. He just welcomed us back." We stared at each other in silence for a few moments. The feeling of disgust came up from my legs to the stomach. I said, "Captain, regardless of what you think, we were under fire several times the first two days." I took another pause while he stared at me. "Goddamn it, we were getting shot at!" I didn't even wait for an answer. I turned and stormed out of his cubicle.

There was silence in the company office. The staff who had heard everything was sitting at their desks, staring into space in dead silence. I walked to my desk, picked up my gear, and went out the backdoor, full of anger. *Yeah, welcome back.*

At the hooch I stored the M-16 in my locker and stripped, pulling out a towel and my dopp kit. Then I spent the next half-hour cleaning off three days of crud and using a razor. While standing under a hot showerhead the dirt and sweat streamed off my body, but the stain of an ugly moral dilemma was going to remain until I did something about it.

Going back to my days with the Marine Detachment on the *Ticonderoga* I saw the camaraderie, the brotherhood of the Marine Corps. It was one of the elements that brought me back on active duty. While in OCS and TBS I knew I was around a special group of men, men I was in training with, men I was going to be in combat with. These were brave, ordinary men in extraordinary circumstances. These were Marines. I now had to realize that my company commander, given his character traits, was not one of these men. He was an anomaly, an officer not of the Corps, and because of his glaring weaknesses he was forcing me to make a decision.

When I returned, Jack Carmetti, Andy Garrison, and Bob Greene were in the hooch waiting to hear what happened at Cam Le Bridge. While I changed into a clean uniform I summarized the events and how I picked up the M-16. I concluded how Captain Eiler had no idea what we did in those three days, including his statement about us sitting on our asses.

The next day I began outlining my AAR. I also drew up a letter of commendation memo for each of the drivers and A-drivers, emphasizing how we suddenly got attached to the 1st MP Battalion and made numerous casualty runs, under fire, into Hoa Vang. I also mentioned being pinned down on the first casualty run. I gave the handwritten memo to First Sergeant Duncan, who made some corrections and additions. He assigned one of the clerks to type it under the Transport Company letterhead. I knew Captain Eiler would see a copy of it and finally realize what we did down there. Another copy would go to the battalion operations office with a copy to Major Pearson.

Later in the day I got three personal decoration forms from the company files. I wanted to write up Walker, Harris, and Widmer for either a Navy Achievement Medal or a Naval Commendation Medal with the attached "V" for "Valor." First Sergeant Duncan explained that I should look at the USMC criteria for each medal. If there was a flaw in the citation the Awards Section at First Marine Division would either reject it or knock it down one level. For example, if a Marine was being recommended for a Silver Star and the citation did not carry the necessary elements, someone up the chain would knock it down to a Bronze Star. We heard about this syndrome endlessly. I spent the rest of the day reading up on combat recommendations.

The following day I was at my desk working on the citations when Captain Eiler approached me. "What are you working on?" he asked.

"I'm writing up several of the drivers for personal decorations for what they did down at the river," I explained.

He shook his head. "That's bullshit, you're wasting your time." He turned and walked to his cubicle.

I looked over at First Sergeant Duncan. He watched Captain Eiler walk to his cubicle then shook his head. He didn't have to say anything more. It was the third week of August.

Several days later, after the noon meal, I was sitting on the steps of the hooch cleaning the M–16. I had intended on turning it into our supply section and signing off on it. Major Ashworth happened to walk by and saw me cleaning the weapon. "Where did you get the M–16?" he asked.

I looked up at him. "Down at the river. I took it off a dead Marine."

He gave me a surprised look. "What? You took it off a dead Marine?"

I nodded. "We were locked into house-to-house fighting. He was shot in the forehead. I'm going to turn it into supply." Major Ashworth shook his head. "Lieutenant McAdams, you never should have done that." He waved a finger at me: "That's wrongful appropriation." He walked off.

I shrugged, not giving much thought to what he had just said. I continued cleaning the M–16, totally unaware of what was about to unfurl with "wrongful appropriation."

12

Chicago

August 30, 1968

Hi Hon,

When I left you in Hawaii I had no idea that in a short time I would be writing a letter like this. Mom and Missy picked me up at the airport. They tried to cheer me up but I just sat in the back seat and cried.

I know you are going through combat situations with your convoys. And now, on the other side of the world, I just witnessed a different side of history. What a time our generation is going through.

Cousins Julie and Nancy Conners and I were volunteering downtown at the Conrad Hilton Hotel on Michigan Avenue where they set up the Democratic Headquarters. Vice President Humphrey had his headquarters there with banners proclaiming The Happy Warrior. Senator Eugene McCarthy's headquarters seemed like a much "cooler" place, headlining Clean Gene.

The first day was an orientation, greeting people, working the phone banks, passing out literature and arranging transportation over to the Amphitheater. We heard the rumors of an anti-war demonstration outside of the Amphitheater and assumed that we would be away from that.

Then we saw the gathering in Grant Park right across Michigan Avenue. They seemed peaceful enough, teen agers and college students from across the country.

We returned the next day (28th) and started our shifts about noon, right off the lobby. At one of the breaks Julie and I snuck up to the mezzanine where Eugene McCarthy had his headquarters. His volunteers were our age and very enthusiastic about McCarthy's chances. To be honest Humphrey just sounds old and past his prime.

Around 3:00 P.M. we came back down to the main headquarters, when things started to happen in the park across the street. We went to the windows and saw that the crowd had gotten larger. This was supposed to be at the Amphitheater across town; suddenly *it was happening right in front of us. They had signs: End the War Now! Power to the People! Down with the Pigs! Pigs are Whores!*

An American flag was flapping from a makeshift pole. Then a chant came up, "The whole world is watching! The whole world is watching!" Initially what I thought was a crowd of a couple hundred was now in the thousands.

Hotel doors were locked, nobody in or out. I called Mom to tell her we were okay but might be home later than expected. The protestors and students were still across the street in Grant Park. The chanting got louder. Several files of Chicago Police officers wearing short sleeve shirts, blue helmets and carrying batons lined Michigan Avenue.

Someone tried to lower the American flag. This started a scuffle with people shoving back and forth. The police were still holding their lines in the street. It was as if they were protecting the hotel. Then the chant got louder as the crowd began advancing through the park right toward us. I think Senator McCarthy spoke to the protestors from an upstairs window.

I had a creeping, ugly feeling. We knew that as soon as the protestors came out of the park the police would move in from Michigan Avenue for a confrontation. My God, I thought, they don't care. They're walking right into it.

We went to the windows. The police still held their lines, even when rocks and pieces of food would come flying from the protestors' ranks. More stuff went into the air, even bags of urine. The police still held.

Then the protestors, right in front of us, began moving toward Michigan Avenue, some locked arm in arm. They kept chanting, "The whole world is watching! The whole world is watching!" More rocks, bottles, urine bags and rotten food went into the air toward the police.

The first police line advanced toward the protestors. It looked like the beginning of a medieval battle. As soon as the protestors got to the sidewalk the first police line charged them, flailing batons to heads and faces. Front line protestors went down, hands over their heads. Some went to the fetal position.

Then the second police line moved forward as the first line began breaking up with officers running into the park as more protestors piled into the street. And then everything broke wild.

What control there was before was now gone. Police were clubbing while protestors ran. The worst a protestor could do, at this point, was stand still. If he did he'd soon go down with two or three police whacking him . . . repeatedly. We kept hoping for it to end. Instead, it continued.

Patrol wagons came up and the police literally began throwing the down protestors into the wagons. One guy was dragged to a wagon by two officers while a third kept hitting him. By the time they got him to the wagon he looked unconscious.

Inside people were walking away from the windows, not wanting to watch the police beatings. Some left for the lobby but quickly returned saying that someone set off a stink bomb in the lobby. Whoever put it together did a real job. It smelled like puke mixed with rotten eggs. And the stink air moved quickly through the red, white and blue banner-filled lobby while the beatings were taking place on the street.

We were watching the demonstrations from two angles: beatings on the outside with a stink bomb on the inside. So much for doing volunteer work at Democratic Headquarters.

When they opened the windows to let the stink bomb smoke filter out we heard the sirens and yelling from the street. And then the lock down was called off.

Now comes the surreal part. We got down to the garage into our car, with me at the wheel, and out to the streets.

We had to go slow because of the rocks, cans and bottles in the street. Even though we were away from the stink of the hotel there were wisps of tear gas in the air. I made a turn to Wabash Avenue hoping it was all behind us. Wrong!

I turned right into a line of National Guard soldiers wearing gas masks and holding M-1 rifles pointed right at us. In the middle of these soldiers was a tank with the cannon tube also pointed at us. Are we the ones in Vietnam?

I've lived here all my life and at that moment I wasn't sure where we should be. Then a guardsman approached our little VW with his hand held up. He asked where we were going. I said, "Back to the south side." He waved us through.

We ended up taking side streets until we got to the Outer Drive. Then we started to breathe again. The rest of the way was easy. Unreal!

It's one thing to write about it now, quite another to have gone through it. We went to Democratic Headquarters as volunteers with the best intentions. And look what we got for it?

You're seeing one thing where you are; I've seen a share back here. Neither of what we have seen is any good. Were the protestors right? Were the police right? Were they both wrong? We won't know for some time. So who's in more danger, you or me?

Poor Mayor Daley. He'll never live this down. His "shoot to kill" statement did not help things. I remember when Mayor Daley sent us a telegram on our wedding day.

My present hopes and prayers are for you to survive, get through it all and return healthy and in one piece. I'm sure it's a mess where you are just as it's a mess back here. I'm not sure what you'll be coming back to—but I can't wait for you to be home.

Be safe. I love you, XO.

Patty

P.S. Operation Head Start should bring new opportunities. I've already started, very interesting.

13

Going to Staff

Within two days I had the letters of commendation and the combat award recommendations in final draft. Widmer, Harris, and Walker would get the award recommendations while the others would receive letters of commendation. As I was the one initiating these it didn't require Captain Eiler's signature. But he would eventually see the carbon copies because they were typed under Transport Company letterhead. Then he would know exactly what went down at Hoa Vang and Cam Le Bridge. I anticipated what his reaction would be as to what happened in those three days: nothing.

Several days later another convoy order came down, Danang to Phu Bai, approximately forty-five vehicles including Air Force and Seabees. When the order came in from division it was assigned to Transport Company (i.e., Captain Eiler). I had also heard that since I received a nonpunitive letter of censure it was recommended that I not participate in any more convoys. The original order from S–3 operations had Captain Eiler in command with Jack Carmetti as trail officer. At this time we had a new second lieutenant, Jim Vodar, who was still "snapping in."

When the order came to Transport Company Captain Eiler wrote in two changes. Jack would be commanding the convoy with me as trail officer. I went to Captain Eiler and asked why the change. "Major Pearson is resetting the company fields of fire down at the perimeter wire. I have to draw up the revised plan for Transport Company."

I said, "Captain, that can be done in a few hours, possibly less."

He shook his head, shuffling memos on his desk. "No, I'm needed here. You and Carmetti will have the convoy tomorrow."

With boiling anger I decided to chance it. "Captain, you haven't commanded a convoy since Phu Gia Pass."

"Frank, I'm the commander of this company, responsible for everything it does or fails to do. There's more to this company than running convoys."

He was echoing Major Pearson's philosophy. "Captain, running convoys, supporting the infantry and artillery units, is the primary mission of this battalion."

"As company commander, I have the option to change the command structure of any convoy that's assigned to us." He paused and looked up. "Jack will be in command tomorrow and you'll ride trail."

"I thought that I wasn't to be participating in any more convoys," I said. Again, he shook his head. "I'm negating that for this convoy." Another pause. "Now, is there anything else?"

I stared at him for a moment, gritting my teeth. Then I softly said, "No, there isn't anything else." I turned and left him to his memos.

That night Jack gave his convoy briefing in the conference room. I sat in the back with Captain Eiler. At the end of the briefing Jack had Sergeant Thomas and me stand to introduce us, respectively, as the X-Ray and trail officer. During the question-and-answer period Captain Eiler got up and left the room.

Instead of going to the Staff/Officers club after the briefing Jack and I got a six-pack of Schlitz and went back to our hooch. Both of us knew that we were on a convoy that Captain Eiler should be commanding. By now we were used to his rationale—coming up with an excuse to remain behind. We cracked a few cans as we prepared our convoy bags for the morning. Jack explained that he had checked the intelligence reports late in the afternoon. There were some NVA sightings along the ridgeline in the Bowling Alley area.

After staging at Red Beach for about an hour we got the green light from Defend. And off we went, climbing up into the Hai Van Pass, winding through the checkpoints that we knew by heart now, not even referring to the maps because we knew the area. Again, I looked down on that beautiful crescent-shaped beach out of a travelogue.

On the north side of the Hai Van Pass a Seabee tractor and low-bed trailer with a heavy load broke down. We were about forty-five miles from Phu Bai. Jack made the decision to leave the tractor-trailer behind at an Army engineer compound. The load couldn't be towed by a wrecker for forty-five miles and we had no "Bob-Tailed" tractors in the convoy. (A Bob-Tail is a tractor vehicle without a trailer load.) I supervised the job, pulling my trail jeep out of line with a truck of infantry security: one squad. In less than fifteen minutes we were back on the road. I had no idea how this decision would later affect me.

At Phu Bai that night we dropped in at the 1st Medical Battalion. Here I got to catch up with Chief Nyman Harris from the *Ticonderoga*. He gave me a quick rundown of what happened to some of the corpsmen from the medical department. It was a nice chat; he wished me well.

Other than the breakdown with the Seabee tractor-trailer it was one of the most uneventful convoys I had been on, textbook up and back. I didn't know it at the time, but it would be the last time I went through the Hai Van Pass.

After returning from the convoy Jack and I grabbed a quick shower and then a meal at the mess hall. We then took in the movie at the club that night. All was well down at the perimeter. I remember sleeping soundly that night.

Several days later I was at my desk going through the monthly training schedule when Top Duncan said that Major Pearson was on the landline phone for me. After I picked up the phone Major Pearson said he wanted to see me in his office immediately and to bring my Officer Qualification Record (OQR).

When I entered the command headquarters Major Ashworth, now the XO, was at his desk looking like a receptionist in a law office. He nodded to me, with a slight smile, and pointed to the next cubicle. "He's waiting for you."

I was about to be ambushed.

I reported to Major Pearson, who directed me to a chair next to his desk. I handed him my OQR. He opened it and flipped through several pages. "I understand that you went on a convoy to Phu Bai the other day."

I nodded. "Yes, sir, I went as trail officer."

"I also understand that you are not to participate in any more convoys."

"Captain Eiler changed the command structure," I explained.

"I'll speak to Captain Eiler about that." He then closed my OQR and handed me a pink two-page form, an officer's fitness report. "I want you to look at your fitness report."

I glanced at the first page then spent several minutes looking at sections C and D, on the second page. The rating grids, from bottom to top were: Not Observed, Unsatisfactory, Below Average, Average, Above Average, Excellent, and Outstanding. My highest rating was Above Average. Most of them were Average and Below Average. The latter two were in Judgment and Presence of Mind. Section D was the remarks section, written in Major Pearson's own hand.

I remember taking a deep breath to calm myself. My mouth went dry. In section D it stated that I was given to making "snap decisions" without thoroughly analyzing the situation. It then mentioned the Thoung Duc convoy and blowing up a Marine Corps vehicle without authorization. It added that I had received a nonpunitive letter of censure following an investigation. It then stated that I had committed an act of "wrongful appropriation" by taking a weapon from a dead Marine. The final incident was making a faulty decision of leaving a Seabee vehicle behind on a convoy.

I slowly looked up at Major Pearson, who barely knew me. "Many of these statements are incorrect, major."

"I don't think so," he said. "I got these items from Captain Eiler. You did blow up a truck without proper authorization. Is that not true?"

"Yes, sir, after being kept waiting in the middle of two firefights for thirty-five minutes. And I was never told why the long wait," I said.

"Well, I wasn't here then," said Major Pearson. I remember being surprised at his casual indifference.

"Taking a weapon from the dead Marine occurred during heavy house-to-house fighting down at Hoa Vang and Cam Le Bridge," I explained. "We were down there for almost three days. Another Marine and I made three ammo runs under fire. When I returned to the battalion I was going to turn the weapon into supply. I had no intention of wrongful appropriation." He stared at me for several moments. I continued, "As for leaving a vehicle behind on a convoy, I wasn't even in command. And Captain Eiler knows that. In addition, the captain didn't even know what we were doing down at Cam Le. He told me that we were 'sitting on our asses.'"

Several more moments went by in silence—nothing from this man. As I sat there, boiling with anger, I assumed that Major Ashworth was behind the louver separator, eavesdropping. "In section F you have the right to make a statement."

"According to the guidelines for a nonpunitive letter of censure it cannot be part of the fitness report. I remember reading that," I said.

"You can take this up with Captain Eiler," said Major Pearson. "Obviously you have a lot to write about."

I stood. "Yes, sir. I'll start on my statement immediately. This is wrong, very wrong!"

A few more moments of silence. "That's all, lieutenant."

My mind was festering with white-hot anger knowing that he signed off on this without making any inquiries or corrections. I turned and walked toward Major Ashworth's cubicle to confront him about mentioning the letter of censure. He was gone.

When I returned to the company office I went right to Captain Eiler's cubicle. The next several minutes were spent going over the inaccuracies of the section D statement. He sat there listening until I got to the Seabee vehicle and then he said, "Still, you supervised it."

"I wasn't the convoy commander. I was the trail officer on your order. Beyond that, it was a sensible and logical decision," I replied.

"Frank, you have the right to make your statement. I suggest you start on it right away."

I stared at him for several moments. "You bet I will!" I turned and walked out.

During the first week of September the battalion had several convoys leaving the compound in different directions. I was taken up with training reports and standing OOD duty. It was in midafternoon one day when a jeep with one star on the front bumper drove through the main gate. The driver was a buck sergeant from division. In the passenger seat was Brigadier General Ross Dwyer, the assistant division commander. Normally, proper military protocol would be that division headquarters would notify the battalion commander that the general would be stopping by on a certain day. This would give the battalion staff an advance warning.

Not so this time. It's what General Dwyer wanted—an impromptu visit.

The jeep pulled up in front of Major Pearson's headquarters. General Dwyer entered and told Major Pearson that he wanted to meet with him and his staff immediately.

In less than ten minutes Major Pearson had the battalion staff assembled in the conference room. All sections were represented: personnel, intelligence/operations, supply, psychological operations, and the command, Major Pearson and Major Ashworth.

General Dwyer began by asking Major Pearson how many officers and enlisted men were assigned to 11th Motors. Major Pearson gave some approximate figures, 425 enlisted with twenty-five officers, adding that they fluctuate from week to week. "I assumed command July 15 and we've gone through some remarkable changes along with a supply inspection."

General Dwyer nodded. "And you get your convoy orders from division G-4, is that correct?"

Major Pearson nodded. "Yes, sir, they usually come down the day before. We have the briefings in this room. For the Phu Bai Rough Riders we stage at Red Beach."

General Dwyer glanced around, then looked at Major Pearson. "How many convoys do you have on the road right now?"

Major Pearson pointed to Captain Corliss, the S–3 operations officer. "Captain Corliss, my operations officer, can supply that information."

General Dwyer shook his head. "No, major, I want *you* to tell me." He took a long pause. "How many convoys do you have out at this moment?"

Major Pearson took a deep breath and cleared his throat. "Well, we have our usual Rough Rider run up north to Phu Bai supporting operations Allen Brook and Mameluke Thrust. That one left this morning." He paused and looked over at Captain Corliss. "And we had another head out to Hill 65. Isn't that right, Captain Corliss?"

General Dwyer looked at Captain Corliss. "Is that correct captain?"

Captain Corliss had a grim look. "The secondary convoy is to Hoi An."

"That's right, Hoi An," added Major Pearson quickly. "And we have another going out to Deep Water Pier."

"That was yesterday, major. The third convoy went to Ap Loc," corrected Captain Corliss.

General Dwyer looked around the room. "Very well, thank you, gentlemen." He got up and left the room.

A strange silence settled into the conference room. Then Major Pearson said, "Let's get back to work, gents."

Several moments later General Dwyer's jeep left the compound. The entire incident took less than twenty minutes. Naturally no one knew how pivotal that meeting was.

The next day we were told that Major Pearson was being transferred stateside. Because there was no scheduled change-of-command ceremony a "Sayonara Party" was held for him at the Staff/Officers club. At the end of the party one of the officers drove him to the 15th Aerial Port, where he was scheduled to fly out early the next morning. He had held command for six and a half weeks.

The following day Lieutenant Colonel John A. Kinneburgh arrived to assume command of 11th Motors. His previous assignment was being the aide to General Leonard F. Chapman, 24th Commandant of the Marine Corps (CMC). He was a man of medium height with short black hair, given to using a stern glare before saying anything. Before putting his personal gear in the battalion commander's hooch he called for a staff and company commander's meeting in the conference room. Colonel Kinneburgh said he was coming in to "clean up this battalion." He added that there were going to be major changes immediately and that if any man, staff, or company commander couldn't measure up to those changes "I'll relieve the whole fucking lot of you. That's not a threat; it's a fact!" He took a stage pause. "Now, get back to your jobs while I unpack."

The meeting ended. We had a new battalion commander without a change of command.

My first handwritten draft of the fitness report statement was three and a half pages, single-spaced. The second and third drafts were just as long. I had expected Captain Eiler to call me in to rewrite certain sections. Surprisingly, that didn't happen. I typed it myself and signed off.

I finally got a meeting with Major Ashworth about the mention of the non-punitive letter of censure in section D of my fitness report. He explained that that was not a regulation, merely a guideline. "Besides, Lieutenant McAdams, that's all behind us." He smiled. "We have a new battalion commander."

Within two weeks I was called to the S–1 personnel office and informed that I was being transferred to Headquarters Company. Lieutenant Colonel Kinneburgh, I was told, had selected me to supervise "an ambitious maintenance and camp update program" that would make our battalion compound one of the best-looking "in the I Corps area."

I cleaned out my desk in the company office. Then I said goodbye to Top Duncan and the office staff. Jack Carmetti was now the XO. I was told that Captain Eiler was doing some work in his hooch, that he'd be gone for the rest of the afternoon. Translation: He was sleeping during the day and working in the office at night. It was just as well; no need to say farewell to him. I'd see him in the club, at a preferred distance.

I walked out of the office with Jack, feeling regretful that I hadn't done anything about my moral dilemma with Captain Eiler. In all honesty I was letting it slide, washing my hands.

"I hate to see you leave," said Jack. "I'm here with Greene and Vodar. And God knows what the captain is going to pull next. It's getting worse with him sleeping during the day, afraid that some troop is going to roll in a grenade at night."

I laughed. "I almost feel sorry for the man."

"I don't," said Jack. "Captain Hansen, the new supply officer, had the hooch next to him. When he heard the scuttlebutt about the price on Eiler he moved to another hooch."

"That's not funny," I said.

"No," said Jack. "But it's reality."

I had an empty feeling as I took my OQR down to Headquarters Company. Previously I had promised to do something about the situation with Captain Eiler. And I was leaving it swinging in the wind. At Headquarters Company I was given the new title as S–4 Alpha, Camp Maintenance Officer. I would have a crew of five Marines and five Vietnamese carpenters.

Lieutenant Colonel Kinneburgh called me in for an orientation. We sat at his desk as he puffed on a cigar, outlining the Camp Maintenance program and told me that I would have "complete leeway" for getting these projects completed. This included extending and improving the Comm shack, making it a reinforced command bunker; updates to the mess hall; a wider stage for the USO shows; upgrading the troops' shower area; constructing a chapel; improving the battalion barber shop; and installing a gift shop inside the main gate. *My God*, I thought, *a gift shop. We're turning 11th Motors into a shopping center.* Colonel Kinneburgh added that he wanted me to use "any means necessary" to get the materials I needed. This included plywood, two-by-fours, bunker beams, paint, and electrical wires.

There was a part of me that was feeling overwhelmed by what he was outlining. I waited for him to get to the end. And then I asked, "Why was I selected for this?"

"I was told about your experience with blowing up the truck. Then I looked at the investigation and the statements," he explained. "Division had you hanging out there for thirty-five minutes."

I nodded. "And I never found out why."

He leaned forward. "How did you blow the truck?"

"The truck was already destroyed. I put a thermite grenade on the engine block. Then I fired tracers into the fuel tank with a .50-caliber machine gun. It did the job."

He nodded. "I can't do anything about the investigation or your fitness report. But I can give you this chance. If it comes off as planned you'll turn some heads around."

The next day I reported down at Camp Maintenance and introduced myself to the crew. My office was carved out of a storage hooch next to the Battalion Aid Station. Most of my crew knew of me. And, like me, they had seen their share of road mines and ambushes; they were thankful to be off the road.

My NCO was Buck Sergeant John McEllany, a stocky, sandy-haired guy from Tennessee. He was chosen because he didn't have a Motor Transport specialty. He was a combat engineer along with being a classic "scrounger."

Someone found an old wooden desk and some castoff chairs to decorate the office. I had Lance Corporal Albert Horse, a slender Arizona Pima Indian, tack a sign to the edge of the desk. I wrote out what I wanted on the sign. In Latin, the sign stated: *Illegitimi Non-Carborundum*. In English it meant, "Don't let the bastards get you down."

I gave Patty a quick update in a letter. I emphasized how fast things had changed, getting a marginal fitness report because of inaccurate information, Major Pearson being relieved of command, and me being transferred to a staff job. The good news for her was that there would be no more convoy duty. How wrong I was with that assumption.

Because I was now attached to the supply section I developed a good relation-ship with Captain Mike Hansen, the new, soft-spoken battalion supply officer. A Yale graduate, he had an easy demeanor and was well aware of what Lieuten-ant Colonel Kinneburgh wanted to accomplish with the Camp Maintenance program. After a ten-day period as Camp Maintenance officer Captain Hansen told me, "You're under more pressure than any officer in this battalion."

I also had to sit in on various staff and company commander's meetings in the conference room. Sitting along the side of the room, away from the table, I watched as Lieutenant Colonel Kinneburgh, at his choosing, chewed out either a staff officer or a company commander for some infraction. I was seeing his modus operandi: Put the company commanders and staff under more pressure and they will deliver.

At one meeting he tore into Captain Eiler about a wrecker being parked outside of the Transport Company office. "Wreckers belong down in the mo-tor pool, captain. If I see that wrecker in front of your office again I'll wrap it around your fucking neck." He paused, taking a cigar out of his mouth. "Do you get my drift?"

Captain Eiler took a gulp and nodded. "Yes, sir." I noticed the flush in his face. I also knew that he would be going back to the company office to chew out somebody in keeping with the Marine Corps slogan of "shit rolls downhill."

That night Jack came into the hooch upset. Captain Eiler held a company meeting and chewed out two sergeants over the wrecker issue. "How much more can I take from that hypocritical S.O.B.?!"

"How bad was it?" I asked.

"He made more threats about this reflecting on our fitness reports. He kept slamming his fist on the desk yelling about us being incompetent," said Jack. "And he's still marking cards on everyone in that little file box that he keeps locked up."

Lieutenant Colonel Kinneburgh was absent from another staff meeting, be-ing called up to division G-4. Major Ashworth presided in his absence. It was a benign meeting until Andy Garrison announced that the movie for the troops that night would be *Dr. Strangelove* starring Peter Sellers as Group Captain Lio-nel Mandrake and Sterling Hayden as General Jack Ripper.

Shocked, Major Ashworth leaned forward. "Where are the movie cans?"

"In my office at Psy Ops [Psychological Operations], major. They were dropped off from special services," said Andy.

"Lieutenant Garrison, after this meeting you will exchange those cans with another battalion," said Major Ashworth. "I don't care how you do it but get another movie for tonight."

Andy looked at his watch. "Major, it's after four in the afternoon. Why does the movie have to be exchanged?"

"Because of the content in that piece-of-shit film. Because the director, who is also one of the screenwriters, is a homosexual communist! I won't have our troops seeing his trash!" Major Ashworth looked at his watch. "You better leave now."

"Try the Seventh Engineers, Andy," suggested Captain Hansen in a calm voice. "I'm told that they have a Doris Day movie over there."

Andy stood, nodded to Captain Hansen, picked up his notebook, and left the room.

The exchange worked. Andy came back with *Caprice*, starring Doris Day and Richard Harris. And the troops got to see a lovely Doris Day fashion show that night.

14

Teacher

Chicago, September 29, 1968

Hi Frank,

Got your tape explaining the marginal fitness report you got signed by a major who hardly knew you. It seemed very unfair but I'm sure you will overcome it. We know life is not fair and that often the wrong people end up running things. We have to roll with the punches. As your father once said, "so what if you get knocked down. The real fight is getting back up." Pearls from Spike!

So glad to be working for Head Start. We began by reading all the new guidelines coming from Washington, D.C. We were told that even some of the top administrators in the Chicago School District were caught off guard with the summer program being implemented so fast.

They pushed us through a training program that had our heads spinning. Then we went out in teams in the "back of the yards" neighborhood, knocking on doors of homes where little English is spoken. The parents were very suspicious of us at first, young white school teachers trying to explain how to prepare children for kindergarten. It was exhausting and frustrating. Many of the families have that "fortress mentality," keeping the kids inside the home.

We started late, trying to incorporate six weeks in the summer pre-school to make up for living five years in poverty where the parents are speaking another language. After several tries the parents realized what we were trying to do. And that gave us access to the kids who did come to the designated schools. We stayed with the lesson plans. The first called for them to do crawling exercises. This is to develop motor skills. I don't know who came up with this theory to develop young children but it seemed to work.

During the second week we walked them down to the local fire station. The Chicago firemen were very nice . . . and cute! Why are firemen cuter than policemen? The kids played all over the fire engines. It's nice to see the social skills develop.

My teacher's aide is a real character. She has some wild stories. This is because she's a former hooker, if you can believe that! She told me yesterday that this work is "way too hard." She's thinking of going back "on the street" where the money is better. I hope I don't lose her because she's a good assistant.

We walked the kids down the block and showed them Mayor Daley's house, explaining how the city is run. For some of them it was the first time that they heard the word Mayor. You guys over there are not the only ones who have to win hearts and minds.

Head Start is still in its infancy. There is a lot more work to be done, but I'm sure the kids will be ready to learn when they start school. They love to learn new things. Hard to believe they were so shy at the start.

Mom and I did some day sailing over the weekend, out on Lake Michigan with Joe Trindl. It was a fun sail. However, his boat doesn't have a head. After a couple of beers we had to use a bucket down below. He saw nothing wrong with that. Ugh! It gave me an idea to send you a present.

You got my tape that I've been assigned to Bradwell Elementary to teach 4th grade. Can't wait to have my own class. My lesson plans will follow the Chicago Public School guidelines but of course I'll include art & music to make learning fun. Maybe I'll have them make a tape for you like you had the Vietnamese kids do for me. Wish you were here to teach them history. They'd love you!

And now I can breathe easier because you won't have any more convoy duty. Somebody is watching over you. Stay well.

Love & Kisses, Patty, XO

15

Kilo Mike Alpha

By the first week of October 1968 the Camp Maintenance program was in high gear. Sergeant McEllany traded a bulk amount of paint with some people in the 11th Marine Regiment, the artillery unit across the road. He also came into an SKS semiautomatic World War II Russian rifle that he used to barter for a huge supply of three-quarter-inch exterior plywood from the Seabees down at Deep Water Pier. I never asked how he acquired the rifle knowing that we would never get that much plywood through normal channels. When I mentioned to Lieutenant Colonel Kinneburgh that we managed to "scrounge" plywood from the Seabees he said, "Don't tell me how you did it, just don't leave any tracks."

I drew up a list of items that we could get through Captain Hansen's office. This was balanced by a list of items that we couldn't get but could barter with other units. One of my assets at Camp Maintenance was an old M-38 jeep and a six-by truck that we used for "supply runs." Soon the area outside of my Camp Maintenance office looked like a storage yard. I now had sergeants from the other companies making inquiries about what they could trade for; I was becoming a wholesale businessman. The Camp Maintenance program was moving forward, even sparking competition among the companies.

We had started on a new wing for the troops in the mess hall, which already had a reputation as one of the best in the First Marine Division. The stagework in the camp theater was extended in both directions to accommodate larger rock bands. The previous dressing room behind the stage was to accommodate both male and female performers. A separate dressing room for the female performers was quickly constructed, complete with vanity tables and mirrors.

Sergeant McEllany, through his contacts at the air wing, got several castoff jet-fuel pods to be installed for holding water in the troops' shower area. The pods were cleaned out with soapy saltwater and were set in above the showerheads, reservoir-style. It was a simple jungle expedient that carried instant satisfactory results. While this was happening Sergeant McEllany used his combat engineer contacts to draw up plans for a battalion chapel and a gift shop next to the main gate. We also began work on an extension to the base barber shop along with reinforcing the new communications command bunker. At the end of each day I had to meet with Sergeant McEllany and make a list of what was accomplished. At the end of the week I had to submit a typed report detailing the week's work. I had a free hand in all of this—no interference from either Captain Eiler or Major Ashworth. And I got to see how Colonel Kinneburgh was making the company commanders jump, particularly one company commander.

The month of October also showed Lieutenant Colonel Kinneburgh's power contacts both at division headquarters and Headquarters Marine Corps. On October 6 we had an inspection visit from Brigadier General J. E. Williams, Commanding Officer, 9th Marine Amphibious Brigade. Colonel Kinneburgh wanted me at his side to answer any questions about the Camp Maintenance projects. During the inspection tour General Williams asked Colonel Kinneburgh, "John, how's Ginger?"

"She's fine," answered Colonel Kinneburgh. Yeah, it helps to know people.

On October 14 Brigadier General Ross Dwyer made another appearance. It was more than clear that he was checking on things and would report back to his boss, Major General Carl Youngdale. On October 19, General Dwyer returned for another visit, obviously pleased with his decision to relieve Major Pearson and the way in which the battalion's appearance was improving with new leadership.

Division Special Services had now installed an office directly across the road from our battalion. From this office the USO shows were booked and scheduled to the various units in the division AOR. And on a weekday night a combination band was booked into our refurbished open-air theater. It was an international group, an Australian band that dressed like the Beatles, a Korean singing group that called itself the Fabulous Korean Kittens, and an American chanteuse named Marty Perreau. The emcee was Frankie Perdazzo, a wisecracking young guy from New Jersey who wore a tight shiny suit under a flamboyant pompadour hairdo.

Before the evening meal was being dished up that afternoon it was all over the compound that there was a "heavy duty" USO show that night. As I recall, there were two convoys going out in the morning. The Rough Rider was going to Phu Bai through the Hai Van Pass; the smaller convoy was going down to the 5th Marine Regiment at An Hoa, a hot area southwest of Danang known as "Arizona Territory."

Ninety minutes before the start of the show the troops began drifting into the open-air theater that my crew had refurbished only days before. The USO troupe hadn't even arrived and it looked like a standing-room-only audience.

As the sun settled into the mountains behind us, a miniconvoy of two personnel carriers and a six-by truck rolled into the compound. The personnel carriers brought in the performers with their costumes while the six-by carried the band's props and equipment. As they were unloading next to the stage Major Ashworth approached Frankie and introduced himself. "I'll need to see your rundown sheet for tonight's show."

Frankie pulled his suit bag out of the personnel carrier. He had been asked this question countless times at other units. "Rundown sheet?"

"Yes, your songs for tonight," explained Major Ashworth.

"Uh, I don't handle that, I'm the emcee. You'll have to check with our manager." Frankie pointed toward the stage where the band was setting up. "Up there somewhere." Frankie turned and walked toward the men's dressing room.

Major Ashworth then approached Sergeant Major J. F. Pike, who had recently joined the battalion. "Get a hold of the rundown sheet, the song list. I want to make sure that there are no antiwar songs on it."

Sergeant Major Pike shrugged and guffawed. "Major, if there is a rundown sheet it's probably laced with antiwar songs. The troops love that stuff."

"Irregardless, I don't want them hearing those songs," said Major Ashworth.

The band continued setting up on the stage as the performers prepared themselves in their respective dressing rooms. What Major Ashworth didn't know was that there was no manager. Beyond that, there was no so-called rundown sheet.

Within a half-hour darkness had settled in. The guard had been mounted and set up out on the perimeter in the company sectors. Every bench seat in the theater was taken. Colonel Kinneburgh had issued a verbal battalion order that the front rows were reserved for the troops. If NCOs and officers wanted to see the show they should stand off to the side. This countermanded a previous order that had the two front rows reserved for officers and senior NCOs.

The troops were getting anxious for the show to start. They started a slow clap, which quickly gathered unison and became louder. And then a chant started, "Go! Go! Go! . . . Yeah! Yeah! Yeah!"

Suddenly the lights went down; the stage was black. There was some rustling on the stage and then the lights came up. The band, dressed in Beatles costumes and wigs, was now in position. The drummer even had a resemblance to Ringo Starr. A round of applause came up from the audience. Then came a fanfare.

Frankie Perdazzo came onto the stage and approached the center microphone, taking it off the stand. He turned and signaled the band for another fanfare.

In the back, near the sound and light control boards, Major Ashworth was standing next to Sergeant Major Pike. "Cut off the microphone if this guy makes any antiwar statements," ordered Major Ashworth. Sergeant Major Pike gave a slight nod.

Amid the clapping Frankie smiled and held up a hand. "How ya doin' Gyrenes?" The clapping got louder with hoots and yells from the audience. Frankie held up a hand again. "I'm your emcee, Frankie Perdazzo. Bob Hope says that you Marines have stormed more beaches than Annette Funicello and Frankie Avalon."

The Marines in the front rows began to boo and hiss. Then Frankie added, "Okay, okay! We have one helluva show for you guys."

A Marine in the second row stood and cupped his hands over the mouth. "Get off the stage, wop!"

Frankie glared at the Marine, who also looked Italian. "How about that! One wop calling another wop a wop!" A short pause and then, "A wop bobba loobop, a wop bam bam!"

There was more clapping. Frankie had the audience back again. He smiled. "To start off, we have the Fabulous Korean Kittens!"

The band struck up another fanfare as three Korean women, swathed in tight dresses with kitten ears on their heads, hustled onto the stage while Frankie replaced the microphone. The women also had false whiskers marked on their cheeks. They went into a medley, a stunningly poor imitation of Diana Ross and the Supremes. But the troops loved the medley, yelling off their starving, uncritical heads. The medley set a new dimension to poor imitations, concluding with "Stop in the Name of Love." Each time, when the backup singers sang the title, it came off as "Stop in the Name of Rove!"

When the medley ended the Fabulous Korean Kittens rushed offstage as Frankie appeared again. He then waved the Kittens back for a bow, "The Fabulous Korean Kittens!"

Standing off to the side I noticed several Marines passing half-pint bottles around, keeping them low. Frankie adjusted the microphone and said, "Hey, this next honey is just that, dripping blonde hair like butter."

The same Marine in the second row stood and threw up a hand. "Avanti! Avanti!" Then the Marine raised his right arm and placed his left hand in the crook of the elbow, jacking up the arm. This brought on more yelling from the troops.

Frankie pointed to the Marine. "Paisan, your fly is open!" The Marine suddenly looked at his crotch. "Gotta get everything zipped up before the next act." A drum roll came from behind Frankie. The Marine sat down. "So without further adieu . . . you all know what an adieu is?" He took a pause. "That's what *you* do when she says *don't!*"

The drummer gave several strokes on the snare drum. Groans and moans came from the audience. They wanted the next act.

Frankie asked, "I wanna know something. Does USMC stand for Uncle Sam's Misguided Children?" This line got some mild laughing. Then Frankie went to the punch. "Or is it Uniformed Shit and Mass Confusion?"

The audience jumped to their feet clapping and yelling, throwing "V" signs into the air. Frankie raised a hand, bringing on another drum roll. Then the Marines settled back down. "And now I present Miss Marty Perreau."

Marty came out in a tight-fitting, gold-sequined evening gown. She took the microphone and blew a kiss to the audience. "Hi guys!" The Marines gave off a quick applause. Then Marty said, "We were told that this battalion runs convoys all over the Danang area and through the notorious Hai Van Pass." She paused. "And we were told that you have rolled through a lot of ambushes and firefights. They call you Rough Riders, the Rolling 11th." Another pause as more applause came. "We at the USO can't do anything about the ambushes; we'll leave the convoys to you. What we can give you is a little bit of home . . . and a little bit of what you've been missing. This is for you guys, the troops fighting this war."

Marty then went into her first song. A soft quiet settled in over the Marines as Marty began singing a love ballad. There was no more yelling and clapping. She had quickly captivated every troop in the audience with the spell of her voice. It was remarkable at how the tone in the theater had changed in minutes.

As Marty continued singing Frankie was enjoying a cigarette off to the side of the stage, wiping his forehead with a hand towel. Major Ashworth had worked his way from the back of the theater and approached him. "You're pretty cute with those remarks about the Marine Corps."

Frankie nodded, exhaling. "It's part of our standard repertoire. Gets a lotta laughs, every show."

"Anymore cracks about the Marine Corps and we'll cut off your microphone, understand me?" snapped Major Ashworth.

Frankie smiled. "Uh, they tried that down in Chu Lai." He paused. "It caused a small riot. Had to call in the MPs. That officer got reprimanded. You open for that, major?"

Major Ashworth grimaced, irritated at Frankie's tone. "I'll allow the jokes but no snide cracks about the Corps."

"It's not what you allow, major. It's what I say that entertains your troops. And I'll go on doing it, you dig?" Frankie dropped his cigarette and stomped it out. "In the meantime Kilo Mike Alpha, major." Frankie snapped a small salute, with a finger, and walked toward the dressing room.

Major Ashworth stood there stunned as Marty continued singing. And then Major Ashworth suddenly realized what Frankie had said in phonetic alphabet: "Kiss My Ass!"

The next morning a clerk in the personnel office typed a letter of protest to Special Services. Since Frankie Perdazzo was a civilian contractor to the USO this was Major Ashworth's only option. The letter detailed the encounter between the two, quoting the straight lines and the punchlines. It concluded by recommending that this particular USO troupe be banned from the First Marine Division AOR: You'll never work in this town again!

Major Ashworth signed off on it. The letter was sent to USO in Danang with copies to Special Services and First Marine Division Headquarters. Nothing ever came of it. I always wondered whatever happened to that flashy, smart-assed Italian from New Jersey.

The following week my crew of Vietnamese carpenters was taking a meal break from working on the barbershop. They were enjoying fried rice, bamboo shoots, and tea when a personnel carrier rolled through the main gate. It pulled up in front of Lieutenant Colonel Kinneburgh's headquarters. A captain and a staff sergeant from CID (Criminal Investigative Division) had a quick conference with the colonel. Then the captain and the staff sergeant got back into the personnel carrier and drove to the barber shop. Within minutes "Papasan," the older Vietnamese barber, a tall, lanky man with a Ho Chi Minh–type goatee, was led out in handcuffs and placed into the back of the personnel carrier. We never saw him again.

Later, we found out why. At night Papasan was working with a VC cadre out in the road leading to the valley, marking ambush sites and planting road mines. He had been doing it since the start of the January Tet Offensive.

Major Ashworth was stunned when he found out. "My God, that man used to shave me!"

———

Overall, Papsan was an aberration. It happened to be pure luck that he was discovered as a result of our People to People program. In addition to the Med Cap operations (Medical Civic Action Programs) the People to People program included the building of an orphanage in Khon Son along with various Psy Ops, which came under Lieutenant Andy Garrison's S-5 office.

One of the colorful elements that came from this program was the showing of American cartoons to the villagers, which many had never seen. After showing the first series of cartoons it soon became evident that the unquestioned favorite was the *Roadrunner* series, which began as a supporting show to the Warner Bros. *Bugs Bunny* cartoons. In 1965 Warner Bros. began distributing *Roadrunner* as an independent cartoon character, just in time to parallel the U.S. Marines landing in Vietnam. *Roadrunner* became an instant hit with the villagers because of the repeated sight gags and pratfalls of its nemesis, Wile E. Coyote.

16

Kriegspiel

A week after getting Patty's letter on the Head Start program a package appeared on my bunk one afternoon. I opened it and pulled out a plastic urinal. It had two Velcro tags on the back, at top and bottom. Not only did I not believe what I was holding; I didn't know where to put it. The most obvious place would be at one of the "piss tubes" around the compound. But that was too obvious. *No*, I thought, *the next best place to put this bugger is on the door to the officer's shower.* And let the chips, or in this case the urine, fall where it may.

That night I was working late in the Camp Maintenance office. It was dark when I got back to the hooch. Most of the NCOs and officers were down at the club watching the movie. Within a short period the front of the door to the officer's shower was now decorated with the plastic urinal.

The next morning I started my normal routine, checking and supervising the various Camp Maintenance projects. In the afternoon a staff and company commander's meeting was called for at 1600 (4 P.M.). We were all sitting at the table when Lieutenant Colonel Kinneburgh entered with Major Ashworth, Sergeant Major Pike, and Captain Corliss, who quickly set up a covered easel. The colonel sat down, holding his cigar, and led off by saying that somebody tacked a fake urinal onto the door of the officer's shower. He took the cigar out of his mouth and looked around the room. "When I saw it this morning it looked real. Then I wondered who had the wherewithal to put it there instead of at one of the piss tubes."

I let a few moments go by. Then I said, "Colonel, I'll own up to it."

Captain Eiler, sitting across the table, chimed in with a sneer, "Aw, for Christ's sake, Frank! Still the college boy!"

Colonel Kinneburgh held up a hand. "Let that go. I'm not mad that Lieutenant McAdams tacked up a fake urinal on our shower door." He took a pause. "I want to know which one of us was stupid enough to use it!" He paused again. "That's what I'm pissed about, pardon the pun." There were several muffled laughs and snickers around the table. I looked over at Captain Eiler, who was glaring at me, aware that his criticism had fallen flat. Then Colonel Kinneburgh added, "When we're finished here, Lieutenant McAdams, you'll need to perform a plumbing extraction on the officer's shower door." Another pause. "I'm only glad that it wasn't a fake commode."

I nodded with a smile. Colonel Kinneburgh then went to the agenda. His first item was a surprise and the reason for the easel. "Gents, since we have no convoys tomorrow I'm scheduling a Kriegspiel for tonight. The company commanders are hereby on notice." He turned to Andy Garrison. "Lieutenant Garrison, you'll cancel tonight's movie. We're all going to be on perimeter or in our respective bunkers. It will be as if we're being probed and infiltrated from outside of the perimeter wire."

Sergeant Major Pike had a quizzical look. "Kriegspiel, sir?"

Colonel Kinneburgh nodded. "It's German for war game. It was first used in Prussia in 1812 for training officers in their army. Now, I'll acknowledge that we're in a relatively safe area. But I have no idea what would happen if suddenly we got probed or had to deal with an outright night attack." He took another pause. "Gentlemen, we've got the time and I'm going to find out." He turned and nodded to Captain Corliss, the S-3 operations officer.

Captain Corliss stood, holding a notebook. He walked to the easel and threw back the cover, revealing a map of Khon Son, the road through it, and the rice paddy to our front. He then went through the five-paragraph order for the war game, Operation Trip Wire. The situation was that the 11th Motors compound was being infiltrated and hit from three sides. He gave the grid coordinates for the enemy sightings, to our left front, directly on our front, and along the road going through the village of Khon Son out to Happy Valley, Route 542. Since this was a battalion exercise there would be no friendly attachments.

The mission was next. "We will defend the battalion compound by repulsing any enemy probes and night attacks. We will also deploy two night patrols with the missions to reconnoiter and inform the battalion as to any further enemy movement."

Next was the execution. Captain Corliss continued, "Alpha Company will launch a squad size patrol, ten Marines, consisting of a sergeant patrol leader, radioman with a PRC-25, and a corpsman. The patrol route, check points and coordinates will be issued to the company commander. A second squad sized patrol will originate with Transport Company in the same manner. Bravo and Charlie companies will remain intact along their perimeter sectors."

I watched as the company commanders took notes while Captain Corliss used his pen as a pointer along our perimeter. "Alpha and Transport company commanders will designate their respective patrol leaders who will select the patrol members. Each Marine will carry his M–16 and a bandolier of ammunition. Alpha Company patrol will head out at 1900; Transport Company patrol will depart at 1930."

Captain Corliss took a pause and continued, "Command and Communications. The battalion commander will be present in the command bunker with the sergeant major, psychological operations, camp maintenance, supply and the operations section. The battalion executive officer will take up a position, to monitor radio traffic, directly between the Bravo and Charlie command bunkers."

I sat there listening to the operations order as it unfolded. It now became apparent as to why Colonel Kinneburgh wanted a command bunker built—something his predecessors never considered. Periodically I looked over at the company commanders feverishly taking notes. I noted the concerned look on Captain Eiler's face and thanked the stars in my alignment that I would not have to participate with Transport Company in this exercise.

How was he going to handle this, I wondered.

There was a tense silence in the officer's mess that night. Everyone was concerned about their role in the Kriegspiel. Only hours before we seemed to be passing another quiet day on our combat tours. And now we were to participate in a sudden war game, also in a combat zone. The suddenness of the combat order gave it a feeling of the real thing.

As twilight came I headed toward the command bunker. When I arrived, carrying helmet and flak jacket along with my .45 pistol and a notebook, the furniture was set up: a tactical table covered with maps along with a perimeter diagram of the four company sectors.

Staff Sergeant Robert Langford, the senior communications NCO, had two radios set up on a shelf above a banquet table where several operators sat. I smiled at Lance Corporal Jenny, who nodded back. One radio was set to the assigned battalion frequency. The second was to be used for communications with the two patrols on another frequency.

At 1800 (6 p.m.) the exercise kicked off. Captain Corliss and Lieutenant Colonel Kinneburgh had several scenarios to be sent to Bravo and Charlie companies at different times while the Alpha and Transport patrols were out. The patrol members were at their respective command bunkers getting the combat order and organizing their lines of march.

The Alpha patrol went out first, heading north along the road behind our compound toward the 7th Engineer Battalion. At a marked checkpoint they were to turn east and continue along a dirt path toward the rice paddy. As the patrol leader called in the first two checkpoints Captain Corliss and Colonel Kinneburgh plotted them on the map. Colonel Kinneburgh then turned to Andy Garrison: "Lieutenant Garrison, the village chief is at the front gate with a problem."

Andy then left the command bunker with a PRC-10 handheld radio and headed to the front gate, where a clerk from the operations section was waiting with a scenario. Andy then radioed back what he had learned: The village chief was reporting "movement" on the north side of the creek where it intersects with the village road at Khon Son on Route 542. Andy then relayed the grid coordinates.

As soon as the sighting was reported Captain Corliss contacted the Transport Company command bunker and issued a "fragmentary order," modifying the previous patrol order. The previous order had the Transport Patrol heading southwest along the road to Happy Valley. Down that road was an abandoned pagoda, which was a checkpoint. That direction was now changed, with the patrol to head out northeast along Route 542 in the opposite direction. The patrol was given the call sign "Tango 7." Their first checkpoint would be where the creek intersected with the road. In the meantime Alpha patrol called in another checkpoint.

Major Ashworth, who was down between Bravo and Charlie companies, was now issuing scenarios to those company commanders and reporting in. The Marines at the radio table were taking messages from all four companies, the patrols, and Andy Garrison at the village gate. I drifted back and forth from the radio table to the tactical maps. Things seemed to be going smoothly until a transmission came from Transport 6—Captain Eiler. The Transport patrol had yet to move out; they were still adjusting to the fragmentary order that changed the direction of the patrol.

Lieutenant Colonel Kinneburgh got on the horn to Transport Company. "Transport 6 this is Revolver 6. Get that unit out, post haste. Do you read me, over?"

I heard Captain Eiler's voice, "This is Transport 6, roger and out."

By this time the Alpha patrol had reached its objective point, so it was turning around and heading back. The Transport patrol was still adjusting to the change in direction. Captain Corliss went to the battalion radio this time and requested a situation report from Captain Eiler. Several moments went by as we waited for the answer. Then Captain Eiler came on the net: "This is Transport 6 actual, Tango 7 is departing the Charlie Papa."

Colonel Kinneburgh grabbed the handset from Captain Corliss: "Transport 6, this is Revolver 6, be advised that Tango 7 is fifteen mikes [minutes] behind schedule. Do you roger, over?"

"Roger, Revolver 6, Tango 7 is departing, out."

Colonel Kinneburgh gave the handset back to the operator and turned to Captain Corliss, "Goddamnit, this is exactly what I didn't want. The Alpha patrol is on its way back and the Transport patrol has yet to leave."

We waited in the command bunker for the next hour as Tango 7 patrol called in checkpoints. When Transport patrol arrived at the creek Alpha patrol returned. About an hour later the Transport patrol returned. With both patrols safely back in the compound Colonel Kinneburgh shut down the exercise. He turned to Captain Corliss: "Tell Captain Eiler to report to my hooch as soon as possible." Then Colonel Kinneburgh turned to me: "Lieutenant McAdams, follow me!"

We left the battalion bunker and went to the commander's hooch. It was the first time I was inside the CO's living quarters. I immediately noticed that it was the nicest hooch in the battalion, complete with a wash basin and mirror, a landline phone, and a battalion radio hookup. Colonel Kinneburgh sat at his desk and motioned me to a chair by the door. I expected our discussion to be about the Kriegspiel exercise. Instead, it was about the construction of the battalion chapel. He explained that his request for a Navy chaplain came through. Father Matthew Horvat, a Jesuit priest and a full lieutenant in the Navy Chaplain Corps, had reported earlier in the day.

I explained how the framing was up, with the sides and roof sections next in line. The wooden foundation was on supports that raised it several feet above ground because of a nearby slope that could cause water damage during the monsoons. While discussing this there was a knock on the door. It was Captain Eiler.

Captain Eiler entered and stood a few feet inside the doorway. I was behind him, off his right shoulder, an interesting triangular configuration. Captain Eiler didn't even know that I was sitting only feet from him.

"Okay, right to it," began Colonel Kinneburgh. "What the fuck happened to your patrol?"

"Colonel, we had to adjust after getting the frag order. Initially the patrol was supposed to go out in—"

"I know where the fuck the patrol was supposed to go. Captain Corliss and I drew up this exercise. Your company was issued a frag order, a change in direction because of a supposed enemy sighting. Time was allotted for that, yet the patrol was still late getting off." Colonel Kinneburgh leaned forward. "I want to know why."

"Colonel, we, uh, had to plot the new direction," said Captain Eiler.

"You had time for that," said the colonel. "That's why the Transport patrol was scheduled to leave thirty minutes behind the Alpha patrol." He paused, waiting for an answer. There was none. "Fifteen minutes, fifteen crucial minutes where nothing was happening in your sector."

There was more silence. Several thoughts went through my mind. I thought of my Thuong Duc convoy, with division keeping me waiting for thirty-five minutes in an actual combat situation. And then I thought of Phu Gia Pass, where Captain Eiler was off the radio net for more than ten minutes. I was feeling sorry for the guy as he stood there.

"I have four companies in this battalion. Three of them performed well during this exercise. One of them fell short," explained Colonel Kinneburgh.

"Colonel, it was because of the change in the patrol's direction. I explained that to the patrol leader. He was the one who—"

"You are the Transport Company commander, Captain Eiler," said Colonel Kinneburgh, his voice getting louder. "What your company does or fails to do is the fault of one man." He took a pause. "Am I coming through to you?"

Captain Eiler softly said, "Yes, sir."

"Very well, that's all," said Colonel Kinneburgh.

Captain Eiler nodded, turned, and walked out. Colonel Kinneburgh then looked at me. "Now, then, we were talking about the chapel."

After leaving Lieutenant Colonel Kinneburgh's hooch I went back to my Camp Maintenance office. I checked the agenda for the next day, put my notebook in the desk drawer, and headed back to my hooch. It had been a long day and I was aching for some sleep. At the hooch I was putting my helmet and flak jacket away when Jack Carmetti entered and went to his bunk. He took off his flak jacket and helmet. Then he threw his helmet against the locker. It hit with a loud bang and rolled over on the deck. I looked over at him, "What's with you?"

Jack gave off an angry look. "What do you think?"

"The captain?"

He nodded. "He called a company meeting and reamed everybody. We are all total fuckups and incompetents. And it will reflect when the time comes."

"Who was the patrol leader?" I asked.

"Sergeant Shipley," said Jack. "Good man, but he got his ass royally chewed. It was all his fault, according to our fearless captain." Jack sat on the edge of his bunk staring at the deck. "I bet Eiler is in his cubicle right now, writing on those card files that he keeps on all of us."

"The colonel called him up to his hooch and gave him a butt-chewing. I was sitting next to the door. Eiler didn't even know I was there," I said.

"There was confusion when the patrol's direction got changed," said Jack.

"He was given the grid coordinates," I said. "I was in the command bunker when the frag order went down."

Jack took a deep breath. "Apparently Captain Eiler transposed two digits on the grid coordinates from the first order to the frag order. The correction caused the delay. It was his fault and, true to form, he blamed us."

The next morning I was coming back from the construction on the chapel and found Jack waiting for me in my office. He didn't have to say anything; I could tell the mood from his expression. "Bad morning?" I asked.

He nodded. "It's getting worse at the company office. Even the clerks are afraid to say anything. One of them, along with Sergeant Shipley, has requested a transfer. We ask Eiler a question and he yells at us."

"Captain Corliss is writing the after-action report on the exercise," I said.

"I'm sure we'll hear about that when it comes down." He shook his head.

"Is he still sleeping in his flak jacket?" I asked.

Jack nodded. "From what I hear, yes. And that's not all."

I cringed. "What now?"

"During the exercise Gunnery Sergeant Rayhorn saw a trooper turn and line up Captain Eiler in his sights."

I shook my head. "Oh, shit! What did Sergeant Rayhorn do?"

"He yelled at him. Some of the troops thought it was funny. It happened just before we got the frag order. I like the irony in all of that, a frag order to Captain Eiler," observed Jack. (In the military, and especially during the Vietnam War, the intentional killing of an officer by someone under his command was known as "fragging." The term came from the weapon, an M-26 fragmentation hand grenade with an effective casualty radius of fifteen meters.)

We chatted for about ten more minutes. Then Jack got up and left. I looked at my day's agenda and saw that I had a time gap in the afternoon, between 1400 and 1500 hours. I had avoided this issue for too long. The situation in Transport Company was escalating at frightening speed. I recalled Captain Hansen moving to another hooch. The reports on the Transport Company meetings were getting out of hand—the false grave marker, screaming and yelling at people, fist slamming on the desk and the never-ending excuses for not commanding a convoy. Something had to be done *now*. If someone did get to the captain, particularly inside the compound, there would be an immediate investigation. The standard three questions would be asked: What did you know?; when did you know it?; and what did you do about it? The last question would be the most incriminating. I had endured a lot over the months; to date I had ducked doing anything about it. *Nice shot, McAdams.*

I purposefully took a late lunch, sitting alone at a table in my own thoughts. When I got back to the Camp Maintenance office my Marines were out at different jobsites. The Vietnamese carpenters were cutting plywood panels for the chapel. *Good*, I thought. I got into the old M-38 jeep and headed out to division headquarters. It was time to meet with Major Brent Bradley in the G-4 office.

I got to know Major Bradley after he reported in as the operations officer under Lieutenant Colonel Arnold. He had an easygoing attitude. Things, however bad, never seemed to upset him. The operations clerks gave him the nickname "Major BB" out of affection. With the latest changes in the G-4 section he was the only contact I had there.

I parked the jeep in the visitor's section of the division parking lot. The G-4 offices were in two Quonset huts; the radio room, monitoring the convoys, was in the division headquarters complex. I told one of the clerks who I was and that I needed to see Major Bradley. Within moments Major Bradley appeared and I followed him to a rear cubicle, where he motioned me to a chair. "I hear that they have you on staff now. How do you like it?"

"It's different, I have a lot of leeway with Colonel Kinneburgh," I said.

"He's wasted no time making changes," said Major Bradley. "Your battalion has been inspected a lot lately. With good results, I'm told."

"Yes, sir," I said. "And I've met all the inspectors."

"So what brings you here?" he asked with a smile.

I paused, thinking for a few moments. "Can this meeting be off the record, major?" He nodded. The smile was gone. "It's the situation in Transport Company. It was bad when I transferred out. And it's gotten worse, much worse."

"Captain Eiler?" he asked.

I nodded, remembering the incidents that Sergeant Thomas and Sergeant Rayhorn related to me. "His hair-trigger temper has gone over the line. He snaps at the troops, sneaks around their hooches trying to catch them doing something, listening in on their conversations. Initially there was a price on his head, two thousand MPCs to the guy who got him. That's when he stopped taking convoys." I could see the seriousness in Major Bradley's eyes. I continued,

"Within a short time that price went to five thousand. He's even keeping a secret card file on the sergeants and junior officers."

"How do you know that?" asked Major Bradley.

"The office clerks and the sergeants. It's common knowledge," I explained. "He's sleeping part of the day in his flak jacket with a loaded pistol nearby. He does most of his office work at night."

"Mac, is it possible that this is trooper frustration, young kids blowing off hot air?"

"I wish," I said. "A couple of months back he was checking the line down at the perimeter. He came across a mound of earth with a marker." I paused to get a reaction from Major Bradley. He nodded, listening. "The mound of earth was a false grave. The marker had Captain Eiler's name on it."

More silence. Major Bradley picked up a pen and began doodling on a pad. He seemed deep in thought. "Why didn't you keep this within the battalion? You could have gone to Colonel Kinneburgh."

"I thought of that, major. But Colonel Kinneburgh is new; he's the third battalion commander I've served under," I explained. "I couldn't be sure of his reaction."

"Do you realize that you have violated the chain of command, coming here like this?"

I paused for a moment. "Yes, sir, I gave it a lot of thought. But if I didn't relay this to someone up here I would have a real conscience problem if he went down. Major, if nothing is done they're going to get him, sooner or later."

Major Bradley held up his hand. "Okay, you've made your case." He shook his head. "Now, then, young lieutenant, you get your college-educated butt out of my office." Another pause. "And this meeting never took place."

I nodded, stood up, and walked out of his cubicle. I wondered, *What have I done?*

Driving back to the compound I felt empty. I deliberately went out of the chain of command, met with Major Bradley in confidence, and had nothing to show for it. The only thing I did was get it off my chest to someone who could possibly change something. It felt like a fruitless effort. I gave some thought to the possibility that Major Bradley would call Colonel Kinneburgh and the meeting would suddenly be on the record. Then I would be called on it. And an old Marine Corps expression would kick in: "This will reflect."

The chapel was completed just before Thanksgiving. Even though it was a nondenominational chapel the first service held was a Catholic mass. It was impressive; the Vietnamese carpenters had done good work. Three of them even attended the mass.

It was about a week later when I entered the Headquarters Company office to check the Camp Maintenance mailbox. The chief personnel clerk, Sergeant Ralston, approached me. "Headquarters is getting a new company commander, lieutenant."

I remember not even looking up, glancing at some memos. "Where's he coming from?"

"Your old outfit, Transport Company," said Sergeant Ralston. He shook his head and went back to his desk. Did I hear him correctly?

My surprise was sudden and joyful. Captain Eiler was being transferred to Headquarters Company. Who would know why? Maybe there was a God after all. Later I was told that there was a huge celebration in the Transport Company hooches that night. By contrast the office clerks in Headquarters Company assumed a grin-and-bear-it attitude, preceded by a reputation.

The movie that night was Mel Brooks's hit *The Producers* with Zero Mostel and Gene Wilder, a satirical comedy about two men who set out to produce a Broadway flop about Adolf Hitler, intending to abscond with the funds after the play closes to terrible reviews. Instead the flop becomes a comedy hit. The film was the most talked about one in the I Corps area. The club was packed that night with several officers coming down from division to see the film. Among them was Major Bradley.

Jack and I were at one end of the bar with several of the new lieutenants who were learning the Rough Rider ropes, "snapping in." At the other end of the bar was Major Bradley. I locked eyes with him. He gave me a slight smile, raised a glass, and winked.

I smiled and nodded back. Nothing more was said between us about Captain Eiler. His relief, a new captain, assumed command the next day.

As we got closer to the Christmas season Lieutenant Andy Garrison combined two projects with the villagers in Khon Son. He scheduled a late-afternoon luau with the village elders. That would be followed by the screening of several Warner Bros. *Roadrunner* cartoons, which had become a favorite of the children, showing the futile exploits of Wile E. Coyote trying to capture the cunning and elusive Roadrunner. Wile E. Coyote had a plethora of devices and hardware coming in packages from the ACME Corporation (American Company that Makes Everything). Despite the sophisticated equipment Wile E. Coyote was foiled at every turn. I have often thought of us, in those years, as a U.S. military force with advanced hardware chasing a cunning and elusive enemy. And I'm still surprised that it had parallels to those Warner Bros. cartoon characters.

After the luau the Psy Ops crew set up a portable generator and the projector with the sound system. As soon as the sun went down the cartoon show began. However, when Andy returned that night he had a present for Lieutenant Colonel Kinneburgh—a Vietnamese delicacy in a paper bag. The delicacy was pig's brain. The villagers sawed off the top of a pig's skull and removed the brain. It was a delicacy only with the locals; it looked like chicken liver. Colonel Kinneburgh thanked Andy for the present, adding that he would enjoy the delicacy at a later time. We never saw the paper bag again.

Several days later I was returning to my office from a jobsite. Sergeant McEllany informed me that Colonel Kinneburgh's office just called. "They want to see you at headquarters ASAP, lieutenant."

I didn't think anything of this, a marked change from my previous days of being called to the battalion commander's office. Often I would get calls from Colonel Kinneburgh wanting to see me about the status of some camp project. And I thought this would be the drill. When I walked into the headquarters Major Ashworth looked up from reading a memo. "He's waiting for you, Lieutenant McAdams."

Somehow I detected a "gong" in Major Ashworth's tone. In a few moments I would know why. I reported in to the colonel and immediately noticed my OQR on his desk. Something was definitely in the wind. And it wasn't fitness-report time. I quickly had the thought, *My God, I'm going to be transferred!* Colonel Kinneburgh motioned me to a chair.

"To the point, have you ever heard of Operation Taylor-Common?"

I nodded. "Yes, sir, because of our convoys going down to An Hoa."

"Taylor-Common kicked off earlier this month. General Dwyer is commanding a task force. They had a lieutenant from Force Logistics handling the convoys, coordinating the turnarounds down there." I wondered where this was going. "Well, that lieutenant somehow got himself wounded and was medevaced." *Uh-oh, red flag!* "Since then there's been no convoy coordination. Division wants a lieutenant with convoy experience who has at least three months left on his tour. That lieutenant not only has to have convoy experience but will have been through his share of shit." He paused. "Do you get my drift?"

My mouth went dry. Suddenly I recalled, several times, being told that my convoy days were over. *Tilt!* "Yes, sir, I get your drift."

"Lieutenant, this is a call from division and me. You are to get down there and unfuck that mess so that the convoys go in and out with more efficiency."

"It's almost Christmas, colonel. I still have some projects to finish," I said.

"Sergeant McEllany can handle it. He's trained as an engineer. And he's a good scrounger."

"How much time before I leave?" I asked.

"You go on temporary duty with the task force the day after Christmas."

"How long will I be down there?" I asked.

"For the duration or until that fucking mess is cleaned up, whichever comes first." Another pause. "You'll report to division G-4 in one hour. Lieutenant Colonel Peterson will give you a brief. We're sending you down there with a MRC-109 radio jeep and a driver."

"Who's the driver?" I asked.

"Lance Corporal Jenny. He's supposed to be a good communications man." He nodded to me with a smile. I stood, realizing that my world had just been jolted. All bets were off. "Your orders will be cut tomorrow."

"Yes, sir. Anything else I should know?"

"Yes, I told division that I was sending my best lieutenant. You did a good job at Camp Maintenance. And you got it done faster than I thought." Another smile. "Be safe down there."

I nodded and walked out. Going by Major Ashworth's desk I saw him look up. "So, you're going back on the road," he remarked.

"Yes, sir, temporary duty on Operation Taylor-Common," I said.

"They only serve powdered milk down there. And the lieutenant you're replacing got medevaced. Are you aware of that?" My stomach turned seeing that he had a slight smile.

"Yes, sir, I am."

"How much time do you have left in-country, Lieutenant McAdams?"

"About three and one-half months," I replied.

"You're aware of course that they get hit down there almost every night."

"Yes, sir, I've heard that," I said.

Another smile. "Well, keep your head down."

I turned and walked out. As I headed back to my soon-to-be-vacated office I recalled how many convoys Major Ashworth had been on: none. He was the investigating officer on the Thuong Duc convoy. He initiated a nonpunitive letter of censure and recommended that I be taken off the road. And now, after a short time in a staff job that I was beginning to like, I was not just going back on the road; I was going to *the Arizona Territory* while he smiled.

Semper Fi, Mac.

When I arrived back at the Camp Maintenance office Sergeant McEllany was waiting with some of the crew. They were standing in front of the office as I approached. I looked at them for a moment trying to decide how to tell them what was going down. Sergeant McEllany held up a hand. "We heard the scuttlebutt, lieutenant. You're on orders to the Arizona."

"That saves me from explaining anything," I said.

"How come they picked you? We thought you'd be with us until you rotated stateside," said Sergeant McEllany.

"That's what I thought. The lieutenant I'm replacing was medevaced." A silence came over the group as I looked at Sergeant McEllany. "I have to get up at division for a brief. I'll meet with you when I get back. It's going to be your desk from now on."

About twenty minutes later I pulled the M-38 jeep into a slot in the division parking lot. The last time I had been up here was to see Major Bradley about Captain Eiler. Getting out of the jeep I noticed a CH-46 helicopter lifting off from the 1st Force Recon helipad. Another insert going out. At the door to the G-4 office I met Lieutenant Robinson coming out. He nodded to me. "Hey McAdams. Going back on the road, I hear."

"You heard right," I said.

Walking off he quipped, "Don't blow up any trucks down there."

"I will . . . if they keep me waiting. Bet your ass on that!" Robinson stopped and turned around with a surprised look as I walked into the G-4 office.

I only had to wait a few minutes before I was shown to Lieutenant Colonel Peterson's cubicle. He was a stocky man with a receding hairline and glasses. He looked like a typical staff officer, efficient and intellectual, good at his job. He motioned me to a chair next to his desk. "I've already spoken to Colonel Kinneburgh, so you know why you're here." I nodded. "You were picked for this because of convoy experience with enough time left in-country."

"Yes, sir, that's what I've been told." I paused. "I began this day knowing that I would have no convoy duty, doing my job as a staff officer."

Lieutenant Colonel Peterson smiled and pointed to a framed quote hanging nearby. The quote was in Bold Gothic: IN THE BEGINNING WAS THE WORD . . . AND THE WORD WAS CHANGED!

"Lieutenant McAdams, you're being assigned to this because of a logistical nightmare that is a total cluster. You heard about the other lieutenant?" I nodded. "He was just getting things organized when he got hit."

"Yes, sir, I know," I said.

"Okay, you're here to learn what you're walking into. You better take some notes," suggested Colonel Peterson. He stood and walked to a nearby wall map as I took out my notebook and began writing.

Lieutenant Colonel Peterson began explaining that VC and NVA forces were using various regions, called base areas, for training and support facilities. The previous base areas were taken out with artillery bombardment and infantry operations. Since then intelligence discovered a new one, Base Area

112, located southwest of An Hoa. Base Area 112 was perfectly positioned to threaten either Danang or Tam Ky. MACV (Military Assistance Command, Vietnam) in Saigon suggested that an operation be conducted to clean out this area. The planning began in late November.

On December 4 III MAF (Third Marine Amphibious Force, Danang) activated a temporary command, giving it the codename Task Force Yankee. General Creighton Abrams (the commander of all U.S. forces in Vietnam, known as COMUS MACV) came up from Saigon and was briefed as to the operations plan. At the conclusion of that brief General Abrams said, "It sounds fine. Go!"

Lieutenant Colonel Peterson explained that Brigadier General Ross Dwyer was appointed Commanding General of Task Force Yankee. "This consists of three battalions from Colonel James Ord's 5th Marine Regiment which is already based at An Hoa. Other units include artillery batteries from the 11th Marines plus the 1st ARVN Ranger Group and one brigade of the Army Americal Division. Task Force Yankee has set up fire bases on selected hills in the area to support infantry sweeps along the Song Thu Bon River, both sides of Liberty Bridge, Goi Noi Island and the notorious Arizona Territory. The fire bases have the code names of Pike, Spear, Lance, and Mace."

There was so much information here that I had to take notes in quick shorthand. He continued, "Liberty Bridge, at Phu Loc 6, was blown by enemy forces. Since then convoys, under the control of the Force Logistics Command (FLC) at Red Beach have to be ferried across, four to five vehicles at a time. This is a time consuming and tedious process. And it may get worse because of the coming monsoon season. After the convoys get ferried across the river they stage on the Phu Loc side. Then they head down Liberty Road, the seven-mile stretch to the An Hoa combat base. Your primary mission will be to coordinate those convoys going and coming along Liberty Road. That road is the main supply route for Task Force Yankee."

Lieutenant Colonel Peterson returned to his desk. He handed me an envelope. In the envelope were two three-by-five cards. I smiled, thinking of the three-by-five cards that Captain Eiler used for negative records on us lieutenants and NCOs. The first card had two radio frequencies written on it; the second had my assigned radio call sign: Rush Act Yankee.

"What's Liberty Road, that seven-mile stretch, like?" I asked.

He turned and looked at the wall map. "As you can see it winds around and cuts through several rice-paddy areas. 1st Battalion, Fifth Marines, provides security at Phu Loc and the road. But that doesn't solve everything."

"Snipers?" I wondered.

Lieutenant Colonel Peterson nodded. "They harass the convoys. And there's a constant problem with booby traps and road mines."

"What is the convoy turnaround time like?" I asked.

"In one word, shitty. We get a convoy down there and sometimes it takes one to three days to get it back. In the meantime another convoy comes in. And that's where the clusterfuck is." He grimaced, shaking his head. "Part of this is a communication problem between your battalion and Force Logistics, acting like jealous schoolboys."

I closed my notebook then glanced at the three-by-five cards. The enormity of the situation was registering. Outside of Hoa Vang and Cam Le Bridge this was going to be my toughest assignment. And there was a good chance that I would be a casualty. I looked up at the wall map. "Is there anything else I should know?"

"Yes, you should know about the hospital," said Colonel Peterson. He got up and approached the map again, pointing to a spot between two twists in the seven-mile stretch. "Right about here is a hospital staffed by German medical personnel, nine doctors and seven nurses." He gave off another grimace. "They not only treat allied troops from Taylor-Common but also wounded NVA soldiers."

I looked at the map, stunned. "They treat enemy soldiers, right there?"

He nodded returning to his desk. "They can do it because they're neutral." I stood, realizing that my briefing had concluded. He shook my hand. "Good luck, lieutenant. Get it done."

Driving back to 11th Motors I thought about the irony of the previous four hours. Division G-4, which had kept me waiting for thirty-five minutes out in Thuong Duc Valley, a situation that caused a letter of censure along with a marginal fitness report, was now asking me to clean up a convoy mess. *Asking me?* I was under orders.

Further, my risk of going out of the chain of command to get Captain Eiler transferred had paid off. He was out of harm's way while I was now going in— going in to replace somebody who had been medevaced. It made me think of my epiphany at Camp Hansen.

When I returned to the Camp Maintenance office I met with Sergeant McEllany and summarized the current projects. Then I cleaned out my desk and turned it over to him.

The first thing I did back in the hooch was to get a letter off to Patty. And then I wrote to my parents. I was upbeat in both, downplaying the new assignment. Why worry anyone stateside at this point?

Father Matthew Horvat celebrated Christmas Eve mass with me as the server. It was the first time I had served mass since high school. I sensed that Father Horvat was deeply troubled with choosing the right words for his sermon. He explained that next year at this time we should all be "someplace safe," that this holiday season was anything but merry. He concluded by wishing us a "blessed Christmas." Christmas Day was quiet and uneventful.

The day after Christmas Lance Corporal Jenny and I began preparing the MRC-109 jeep that would take us down to the An Hoa combat base. That night I held a convoy briefing in the conference room. The Rough Rider convoys were still going north to Phu Bai through the Hai Van Pass. Anything going southwest to An Hoa was defined as a Task Convoy.

When I concluded my briefing I realized that it was the first one where Captain Eiler was not in the back taking notes. Afterward I dropped in at the Staff/Officers club for a departing beer. Several times I had to answer questions like, "You've done your time, why did they pick you?"

My only response was, "Ask them, I'm under orders."

After I left the club I walked by the Transport Company office, reflecting on my time there. I stood in the dark knowing that those troubles were behind me now. One chapter had finished while another was beginning.

I walked around the company office, hearing music coming from the open-air theater. The last reel of *The Sound of Music* was playing, and appropriately the number I heard going by the theater was "So Long, Farewell." I kept walking. *Where would I be tomorrow?*

17

The Seven-Mile Stretch

The next morning I took a hardy breakfast at the mess hall, went to Lieutenant Colonel Kinneburgh's office, and read the overnight G-2 intelligence messages. I saw where there was a lot of enemy movement in the Arizona. *Good, right where we're going.* After drawing my shotgun and bandolier from the armory I met Lance Corporal Jenny at the MRC-109 jeep and we drove down to the motor pool to assemble with the Task Convoy. Appropriately it was a chilly, overcast morning. I checked in with Defend and we left the battalion compound, going by First Marine Division Headquarters, around Freedom Hill to Route 540. Going south on Route 540 we made a quick stop at Hill 65 and picked up some more vehicles. We waited at Hill 65 for the engineers to sweep the next leg of Route 540, going south to Liberty Bridge. Shortly, we got a green light. We were cleared to Liberty Bridge and the Arizona Territory.

Prior to Operation Taylor-Common kicking off Liberty Bridge was blown up by an NVA unit. While a new bridge with pilings was under construction by the Seabees a field expedient was set up by the 1st Bridge Company. This was a primitive pontoon-type ferry that could carry only four to five vehicles, a tedious procedure. A normal convoy could take up to five hours for a total crossing. On the other side, Phu Loc 6, the convoy would stage until fully formed. And then with a tank escort, the final leg down Liberty Road, the seven-mile stretch would begin. It would end at the An Hoa combat base.

The seven-mile, southerly stretch started out with two turns, the first to the right and the second to the left, as we continued, passing rice paddies on both sides. I studied the terrain and a ridgeline to the left. The tree lines gave perfect cover for a sniper or a mortar crew. We then made a wide sweep, crossing a set of railroad tracks, and continued to An Hoa. I kept an eye out for the

German hospital that Lieutenant Colonel Peterson mentioned. From the road I couldn't see anything that looked like a hospital.

Before heading into the An Hoa combat base we passed a wide field that was being used to stage the outgoing convoys. Across the road from the staging area I noticed several hooches. And I also saw the sign:

GRAVES REGISTRATION, a grim reminder of reality.

Most of the hooches were medium-sized GP (General Purpose) tents with thick plywood floors. There were several permanent-type structures with corrugated tin roofs. At the far end was the airfield—one long runway that could handle a C-123 cargo plane. This area was known as the LSA, or Landing Support Activity. I also noticed that we were in a basin-like area. This meant poor drainage during heavy rains and monsoons.

I reported to the 5th Marine Regiment S-4 officer, Major Lynn Behymer (pronounced BEE-hymer), a Harvard graduate with salt-and-pepper hair, who gave me a quick rundown of the logistical mess, outlining three main problems: (1) No control at the staging area; (2) no control inside the cantonment; and (3) vehicles being used by unauthorized personnel.

"What about convoy commanders and security?" I asked.

Major Behymer laughed. "If there are tanks around they'll escort the trucks to Liberty Bridge. As to convoy commanders, what commanders? One day it's Force Logistics the next it's 11th Motors." He shrugged. "And there's no communication between the two. They're like schoolboys fighting. As for the drivers they don't even know who their daddy is." Major Behymer added that I would be assigned an MP for traffic control.

I made some quick notes, recalling what Lieutenant Colonel Kinneburgh told me: "unfuck that mess." Major Behymer gave off a sympathetic smile. "Get settled, and tomorrow you can start taking this heavy cross off my back."

When I left the S-4 office my head was reeling. I hadn't even unpacked my gear and I had no idea where to start cleaning this up. I sat in the jeep looking at my notes. Lance Corporal Jenny looked at me. "Lieutenant, are you okay?"

I shook my head. "No, I'm not okay."

Later, I settled into a hooch with two other lieutenants on the northwestern edge of the compound. The two lieutenants were Chuck Hughes, a University of Maryland graduate and a former infantry platoon commander, now an assistant operations officer. The other was John Connolly, from Philadelphia, Major Behymer's assistant. They were helpful in getting me oriented. The hooch consisted of canvas flaps on the sides, a wooden floor, and a corrugated roof. The furniture was basic military, several cots and a writing desk, similar to 11th

Motors. Just outside of the hooch was a slit trench. Beyond the slit trench was the perimeter wire covering our sector. John accompanied me to the mess hall late that afternoon. After we sat down he pointed to another table. Sitting there was a heavyset Anglo woman. "She's one of the nurses from the German hospital."

"They take their meals here?" I asked.

John nodded. "They're polite but keep their distance. Still, it's nice to see a western woman."

When I got back to the hooch I dashed off a letter to Patty telling her that I arrived intact. Then I looked at my briefing notes from Lieutenant Colonel Peterson and Major Behymer. I knew that people would be watching my moves within the coming days. Who's this new lieutenant who will be handling the convoys?

It had been a long day and I had no trouble sleeping . . . until we got hit with a rocket and mortar attack around 2 A.M. The first rounds hit off in the distance. Then more came in closer. By this time we were in the slit trenches with helmets, flak jackets, and weapons. Several more rounds came closer to our wire. And then somewhere a machine gun and some small-arms fire responded. This went on sporadically for the next half-hour. I decided to stretch out on the bottom of the slit trench for some sleep. Within a few minutes I had nodded off.

I was half-asleep when I felt something on my leg. I thought it was some dirt that had toppled in. Then I felt something moving up my right leg. It wasn't dirt; it was moving up my calf. By this time I knew what it was: a Goddamn rat looking for something to munch on. I slowly maneuvered my right hand next to my thigh. The rat then moved closer and started crawling over my hand and up my right arm. *Oh my God, if this guy takes a bite. . . .*

Within a quick second I flung my right arm up in the air, flinging the guy out of the slit trench. Then I was up, with my .45 pistol out. In the moonlight I could see him getting his bearings. I took aim and squeezed off three quick rounds. All I saw was the bugger's backside scrambling out toward the wire and the enemy. Here I was, with an expert pistol rating, and I couldn't even hit a rat in the bright moonlight.

Somebody down the line yelled, "Hey, cease fire! Cease fire!" He had no idea what I was firing at. The rest of the night was quiet.

I had my first MRE the next morning. Back then they were called Long Range Patrol Rations (LURPs). They were a cut above the old C-rations, precooked to be mixed with hot water. And suddenly you had chicken à la king, beef stew, or pasta and meatballs. These were so stocked with calories that one only had to eat two daily—morning and evening. At this point the LURPs served Lance Corporal Jenny and I well. With the present situation we didn't have the time to hit the mess hall down at the LSA.

At the S-4 office I was notified that a Force Logistics convoy would be crossing the river to stage at Phu Loc 6. Lance Corporal Jenny met me at the radio jeep with our assigned MP, Corporal Roland Robertson, a stocky young black man. Then we headed to the staging area.

The trucks from my arrival convoy were already there for the return trip. I now saw what Major Behymer meant by no control. The trucks were parked haphazardly. Many of the drivers were standing around, some without flak jackets, others without helmets. They looked liked the proverbial Raggedy Assed Rangers.

I pulled up, got out of the jeep, and signaled for an assembly. Then I told them to get to their vehicles and return wearing helmets and flak jackets. Within a few minutes they were back and I explained that we would be heading up the seven-mile stretch to Phu Loc 6 in convoy. A quick glance told me that there were no trucks with .50-caliber ring mounts. But there were two trucks that had M-60 machine-gun teams. They would be the security element. Corporal Robertson would be my traffic cop, placing each truck in the convoy line and keeping count. I explained what the vehicle spacing would be and to be aware of snipers along that stretch. This got their attention.

Lance Corporal Jenny checked in with Defend to see where the Force Logistics convoy was. We got a situation report from the engineers, through Regimental S-4. They were almost done with the daily road sweep.

When the road sweep was complete I gave the signal to start up. I told the lead driver to keep his speed at ten miles per hour until we had a convoy line. As the trucks moved out Corporal Robertson directed the gun trucks one-third and two-thirds in line. When we moved out of the staging area I noticed several officers and NCOs watching us. I knew the word would get back to Major Behymer before my return. Soon enough there was some control.

Down the road I had Lance Corporal Jenny pull alongside the pace truck to keep the speed constant. Then we pulled to a stop where I could check the truck intervals. I remember giving the drivers a thumbs-up as they passed me. One truck was flying a City of Chicago flag. I gave that driver a big thumbs-up, with a laugh to Major Ashworth back when he ordered me to take down my Irish shamrock flag. Then I got back in the convoy line.

As we moved around a bend at the railroad tracks I heard a "snap" overhead. Jenny and I exchanged looks. "Sniper," he said. I nodded and we kept going, but I made a mental note of where this happened.

The rest of the way was uneventful. When we arrived at Phu Loc 6 the convoy halted and I went into the compound to check on the ferry operation. The Force Logistics convoy had yet to arrive. I was told that the ferry operations would begin taking this convoy across. I then grabbed a senior NCO and informed him that he was now the convoy commander on the other side, along Route 540 to Hill 65, and to keep the speed down along with the proper intervals.

I stood on the hill watching the slow and tedious process as the first set of trucks crossed on the ferry. This was going to be at least several hours. For the first morning on the job I had turned a gaggle of trucks into a convoy. The only incident along the way was a sniper—a harbinger of things to come.

It was hours later when the Force Logistics convoy was fully staged on the Phu Loc side. I met the convoy commander, First Lieutenant Caldwell, and explained who I was, that I would coordinate his convoy into An Hoa, and that he would have a tank escort at pace and trail down the seven-mile stretch. Lieutenant Caldwell listened to me with a stoic expression. When I finished he said, "We're Force Logistics. We don't have anything to do with First Marine Division."

"You will now," I replied, adding, "This convoy is supporting Task Force Yankee and Operation Taylor-Common."

He stared at me for a moment. Then he said, "We'll get in line. And once we do stay out of our way. I'm tired of taking care of trucks from 11th Motors."

I recalled Lieutenant Colonel Peterson and Major Behymer telling me about the schoolyard fighting. With all the disorganization I now had an additional fight on my hands. I wasn't going to get into it with Lieutenant Caldwell in front of the troops. In a calm voice I said, "We'll work this out . . . one way or another."

Lance Corporal Jenny positioned the jeep behind the lead tank and we headed south on the seven-mile stretch. On the way the sniper made his presence known again at about the same point in the road. The round went overhead and plunked into some paddy water—Maggie's drawers. In Marine Corps jargon that meant a missed shot.

When we arrived at the staging area I had Corporal Robertson keep the trucks in line. And then I checked with the drivers to make sure they knew where to drop off their cargo as Lieutenant Caldwell sat in his jeep watching me. If a driver didn't know where to go I would link him up with one who did. The perishables went to the mess hall; the tanker trucks went to either bulk fuel or down to the LSA if they were carrying JP-4 (aviation gas); the ammo trucks were next, followed by engineer cargo. This took some time but

Corporal Robertson and I got it done. While this was taking place I had Lance Corporal Jenny call in to S-4 requesting a meeting with Major Behymer and Lieutenant Caldwell. We were informed to "come right in."

I then approached Lieutenant Caldwell and said, "Major Behymer wants to see both of us in the S-4 office." I paused and added, "Right now." He gave me a grim nod.

Minutes later we were sitting in front of Major Behymer's desk like the angry young officers that we were. Major Behymer began by explaining that he was in contact with First Marine Division G-4 and Force Logistics Headquarters at Red Beach. "Each headquarters feels that this communications breach must end." He paused. "That means from now on the convoys from Force Logistics and 11th Motors will be coordinated by Lieutenant McAdams once the trucks arrive on the Phu Loc side."

Lieutenant Caldwell asked, "Who will be the convoy commander, major?"

"The designated one," replied Major Behymer. "But the coordination will be the responsibility of Lieutenant McAdams, who is attached to my section and Task Force Yankee for the duration." Lieutenant Caldwell sat there with a brooding look. This was grating him, but there was nothing that he could do. Major Behymer then asked, "Do either of you have anything to add?"

Caldwell and I shook our heads at the same time. "I hope this changes things," I added.

Major Behymer said, "These convoys, whether from 11th Motors or Force Logistics, are to accomplish one thing—and only one thing—support Task Force Yankee and Operation Taylor-Common."

Lieutenant Caldwell and I walked out together. In front of the S-4 office I said, "You need to check with Lieutenant Chuck Hughes in operations." I pointed to the sandbagged operations bunker.

"For what?" he asked.

"Your convoy is down here for the night. The gun trucks need to be set in at strategic places on the perimeter."

Caldwell gave me a reluctant nod. Then he walked off to the operations bunker. I knew he felt that I was impinging on his convoy control. I also knew we'd never be friends. But I hoped that we could work together.

Within two days of that meeting the convoy operations showed improvement. In the morning I would coordinate the return convoy, making sure all cargo was off-loaded at its proper point. After the road sweep I would accompany the convoy down the seven-mile stretch, with or without a tank escort. Again, at the bend crossing the railroad tracks, we would take another shot from our sniper friend. He was obviously using our whip antenna as an aiming point. As usual the round would crack overhead or hit off to the side. I remember Lance Corporal Jenny saying, "Lieutenant, that guy couldn't hit a barn if he was inside of it."

"Tell you what," I said. "Next time we bet as to which side the round hits, over our heads or in front of us."

Lance Corporal Jenny smiled, "You're on."

New Year's Eve was quiet until after the eleven o'clock hour when we heard small-arms fire. This was followed by a steady shower of flares turning night into day. It was all friendly fire as we welcomed the new year. Chuck Hughes, John Connolly, and I stood near the perimeter wire, watching as one of the most historic years in the twentieth century ended.

The next day I was informed that the Division Motor Transport officer wanted a memo from me summarizing the state of Motor Transport operations at the An-Hoa Combat Base from December 27, 1968 to January 5, 1969. I began writing an outline knowing that everyone on the First Marine Division G-4 staff would see it. I looked at this memo not as an entrance exam or a midterm but as a final.

Back at 11th Motors, during this time, Captain Eiler's character traits surfaced in his new command. It was an especially dark night when he began moving in between two of the troops' hooches in Headquarters Company. He was holding an unlit flashlight. Then he saw several troops walking toward a four- holer outhouse. It looked suspicious to him—a possible pot party about to take place. He waited several minutes then approached the four-holer, holding the flashlight. He opened the screen door and entered.

And he was quickly jumped from the rafters.

Captain Eiler went down, dropping the flashlight. The flashlight was then picked up by someone and repeatedly used as a blackjack. Two more troops then entered the four-holer as the beating continued with severe blows to the head and face along with several kicks to the ribs. And then the troops scurried off into the night shadows. One of them even took the flashlight.

Several minutes later Captain Eiler grabbed his soft cover and struggled to his feet. Then he made his way, bloody and bowed, back to his hooch.

The irony was that this occurred in Headquarters Company, not Transport Company.

Despite the ill feeling from FLC the convoy coordination at An Hoa continued with improvement. Although the convoys alternated between 11th Motors and Force Logistics I made sure that the truckloads and drivers were treated equally.

Each day I made additional notes to organize in my memo to the division motor transport officer. This would be the only way my efforts would be known at division headquarters. Beyond that the staff needed to know that the communication breakdown was being corrected. I was also getting to know the other convoy commanders from Force Logistics. These lieutenants didn't carry the same attitude that Lieutenant Caldwell had.

Each morning I had Corporal Robertson prepare a list of outgoing vehicles. When the day's convoy came in the convoy commander would have a manifest of cargo. The trucks would pull into the staging area and be grouped according to their destinations. And then they would head to their unloading points. The .50-caliber gun trucks would be assigned to strategic points on our side of the perimeter. Before my arrival this security aspect hadn't been employed.

I was astounded at this. But it symbolized the communication breakdown. And now it was corrected.

As things were falling into place the basin got hit with a torrential downpour, a vanguard of the coming monsoons. The staging area turned into a sea of brown mud. As the rain continued the seven-mile stretch was closed. It was a respite for me; I used the downtime to complete my memo to division. The rain also affected the NVA. The rocket and mortar attacks abruptly stopped.

It was hammered into me as a history major at Loyola University that the best writing is in rewriting—constant editing and rewording. With enough changes I sat down in Major Behymer's office and began transferring my notes to a single-spaced typed memo. Two days and three drafts later I had a completed draft with two carbon copies. I gave Major Behymer the first copy and I kept the second. With the original I got in the jeep with Lance Corporal Jenny and went down to the LSA. The memo went out in a Huey helicopter with the afternoon guard mail.

As the monsoons continued that week a curtain of inactivity settled in at the An Hoa Combat Base. No convoys in or out. And, at times, flight operations were halted.

A Force Logistics convoy was stuck in the compound for the duration. The convoy commander was Lieutenant Kurt Sanderson, a tall, sandy-haired guy who played safety for a small eastern college. I checked with Chief Warrant Officer Bruce down at the LSA and got some Red Cross kits for the drivers and gunners. It looked like another day or two before the road would be open.

Late one afternoon Sanderson came into the hooch with a couple of six-packs. And before long we found ourselves in a literary trivia game. To this day I can't remember exactly who came up with the idea or who set up the rules.

The four of us sat in a circle: me, John Connolly, Chuck Hughes, and

Sanderson, a diverse quartet. The rules were simple. One would recite the opening line from a famous classic. If someone recognized it within thirty seconds he got two points. If it took under a minute he got one point. If nobody got the title the guy who quoted it got five points.

We started slow and built on it. Sanderson gave the first line: "Call me Ishmael." We all got it—*Moby Dick*. Two points all.

Next came Hughes: "Whether I shall turn out to be the hero of my own life, or whether that station will be held by anybody else, these pages must show." We all got that—*David Copperfield*. Again, two points all.

Connolly was in deep thought for a moment. His eyes squinted. Then he said, "If you really want to know about it, the first thing you'll probably want to know. . . . " He stopped and looked at us. Silence around the circle, intense thinking. The minute was up. Connolly softly said, "*The Catcher in the Rye.*" Five points for Connolly.

All eyes turned to me. I already had my line prepared. "In my younger and more vulnerable years my father gave me some advice. . . . " Silence at first. I was sure that I had them.

Then Hughes blurted out, "*The Great Gatsby!*" Two points for Hughes.

It went back to Sanderson. He grinned and said, "Last night I dreamt that I was back at Manderly."

We all got it: *Rebecca*. Two points around.

Hughes came up with another one. "When he was thirteen my brother Jem got his arm badly broken at the elbow." More silence for several moments.

Connolly began jabbing his index finger in the air in frustration. "Jem . . . Jem!" Then he held up a hand, *To Kill a Mockingbird!* One point for Connolly.

It came back to me. I had another line ready. "It was love at first sight." They all stared at me.

Then Sanderson said, "*Romeo and Juliet.*"

I shook my head; Sanderson was docked two points.

Hughes gave off a smile and said, "*Catch-22!*" Two more points for Hughes.

We went on for the next hour, getting more competitive and eclectic. And we started on the second six-pack. We tapped into Hemingway, Orwell, Faulkner, Carson McCullers, James Joyce, and Stephen Crane.

And the rain continued. In the end, that afternoon, I came up last, jumping in with too many quick answers while Chuck Hughes won. Connolly and Sanderson finished in the muddling middle.

Jenny and I were up early the next morning. The word came down that the road had been opened. Convoy traffic was to resume. But we had time to get a hot breakfast at the mess hall down at the flight line. At the next table sat a doctor and nurse from the German hospital. I wondered who their patients might be on this day. When we arrived at the staging area Corporal Robertson was waiting next to a .50-caliber gun truck as an escort. I remember looking up at the gunner on the ring mount wondering if this would keep the sorry sniper from taking a potshot. In my mind I had formed a picture of him: a dedicated teenager from a nearby hamlet working with a World War II Russian SKS semi-automatic rifle and a crooked sight.

We headed out with Lieutenant Sanderson's convoy after getting cleared by the engineers. I called in to Task Force Yankee operations that we were departing for the blue line (Phu Loc 6). We went slow because of the soggy condition of the road. The engineers had used a grader to eliminate some of the mud, but it was still slow going. I told Jenny that the sniper would hit off to the right. He shook his head. We slowed down at the railroad track bend and then we heard it. *Crack!* The round went overhead somewhere. Jenny looked at me, "Off to the left. That's two bits you owe me, lieutenant." I nodded, making a vow to do something. That bugger was getting on my nerves.

As usual it took several hours for the incoming convoy to be ferried across the river four trucks at a time. The convoy commander from 11th Motors was Lieutenant Jim Smith, one of the newer guys. He complained that everyone back at the battalion was preparing for an inspection visit from General Leonard F. Chapman, CMC. Lieutenant Colonel Kinneburgh no doubt was anxious to have his former boss see how he had changed the battalion.

While we were waiting I went into the Phu Loc operations bunker and requested a tank escort for the return trip. I figured this might make the sniper think twice about taking another shot. My request was cleared and an M–48 tank was on the way. The coordination was working. Ask and you shall receive.

By the time the convoy was staged on my side two platoons of infantry, going into An Hoa, managed to hitchhike on the front trucks. There was an overflow, so those troops scrambled aboard the rear end of the tank. Jim Smith gave me a thumbs-up. I called into Task Force Yankee that Rush Act Yankee was departing the blue line with a complete wagon train. We headed south on the seven-mile stretch.

As we came around the second wide bend some Marines from Alpha Company, who were manning the roadside security, signaled for the tank to stop. After talking with the tank commander a Marine approached my jeep, which was between the tank and the convoy pace truck. I asked, "What's the problem?"

"We have a KIA lieutenant," said a sergeant. "He needs to get Graves Registration."

I got out and looked over at the closest tree line. "Was it a sniper?"

The sergeant shook his head. "No, he tripped a grenade-can booby trap near the tree line." I knew the booby trap well. It was a time-tested jungle trick. They would take one of our grenades, pull the pin, and stuff it into a C-ration can, spoon intact. Then they would tack the can, right-side up, to a tree or a branch and run a tripwire across a nearby path. When the wire was tripped the can would turn upside-down, depositing the armed grenade on the ground with an eight-second fuse, simple and deadly.

The tank and the first trucks were jammed with people. I looked at the sergeant and said, "Put him in the back of my jeep. Is he wearing dog tags?"

The sergeant nodded, turned and signaled to his men. The young Marine was brought to my jeep wrapped in a poncho liner. He had no helmet or flak jacket, just jungle trousers and a green T-shirt. He was set into the backseat. One would have mistaken him for being asleep.

For some reason the sniper held his fire on the return trip. I'm sure it wasn't out of respect for the dead. Just seeing a tank come rumbling down that road, with a convoy trailing, would give any shooter second thoughts.

At the staging area Jim Smith coordinated with Corporal Robertson on offloading the cargo. And then Jenny and I exchanged dreaded looks. Graves Registrations was across the road.

The closest we could get with the radio jeep was about thirty yards because of the mud. If we went any farther the jeep was sure to get stuck. Jenny pulled up to a stop. We said nothing for a few moments. Then I said, "You stay with the radio. I'll take him in."

Jenny helped me get the body out of the backseat. At first I thought of doing a fireman's carry. But one look at the mud field told me that there was too much of a chance for him to slip off or for me to stumble. Instead, I decided on a cradle carry. I took off my flak jacket. Then the body was adjusted in my arms. He was about my size and weight. I shifted my weight and began the slog through the thick mud field, which looked like a chocolate milkshake lagoon.

Each step was unsteady, with my feet sinking into the mud. I would pull up a foot followed by a deep sucking sound. Then I would put that foot back into the mud, trying to keep my balance. When my feet went in they would sink beyond my boot level, halfway up the calf.

I kept looking at the Graves Registration hooch, which didn't seem to be getting any closer. I kept thinking that I was carrying a young Marine who was alive earlier this morning and that his family would be receiving the tragic news within forty-eight hours. This made me realize that I didn't even know his name or hometown.

I was feeling his weight all the more. And it wasn't just his weight. With my feet sinking into the mud and coming back up for another step my calf and thigh muscles were tiring. I kept slogging forward, keeping my eyes on the door at Graves Registration. *Can't drop him,* I kept saying to myself. I envisioned what he would look like covered with brown mud.

No, I said to myself, *he's not going to be muddied. He's not going to be muddied!*

The irony of this suddenly hit me. Here I was, struggling physically with all sorts of thoughts running through my head, and he couldn't feel a thing, not even knowing who was carrying him or where we were going. I remember saying out loud, "Don't worry, we're almost there." As my body shifted, trying to pull a foot out of that thick sucking mud, his head moved as if to nod approval at my comment.

When we arrived at the base of the hooch steps I gave an exhale, went up the steps, maneuvered the screen door open with a muddy boot, and entered. Then I set him on the floor and rested for several moments. The screen door suddenly opened. I turned and was looking at a Navy corpsman. I remember him as a heavyset guy working a toothpick between his teeth. He shook his head, "Hey man, this is our office." He pointed to his right. "The morgue's next door."

For an instant I wanted to punch him in the face. He didn't see the bars on my collar. At that point I didn't care. I just wanted this Marine settled.

I bent down and picked him up. We went back out and over to the next hooch, the morgue. Inside there was a line of stretchers on a wooden floor. On the last stretcher was a body. My Marine would have company. I set him on the closest stretcher and eased his head down at the end. When I pulled my hand away I saw that it was matted with blood and brain matter. That's where he was hit with the grenade shrapnel.

Then I noticed that his eyes were half-opened, staring at the ceiling. Often, the eyes don't shut all the way during the death process. With my clean hand I reached over and gently shut his eyes. Then I looked at his dog tags. I stared at the name for several moments, committing it to memory. My mind drifted back to that moment on the *Ticonderoga* when I closed the eyes of Disbursing Clerk Marineau, who had shot himself.

I stood and looked at him for a final moment, a young Marine felled by a crude booby trap. His war was over, without any mud, a Marine I never met. At the jeep I pulled out my notebook and entered the Marine's name and service number.

When we arrived back at the staging area Corporal Robertson had dispatched most of the trucks to their unloading points. Jenny and I followed several of the trucks down to the LSA, where I needed to talk to Chief Warrant Officer Bruce. Off to my right were several sergeants sitting on lawn chairs, enjoying the break in the weather. Right in the middle of my conversation with CWO Bruce the airfield began to get hit. Whizzing and whining sounds came overhead and slammed into the tarmac. And then came the mortars, getting closer, WHAM! WHAM! WHAM! They were out there, beyond the wire along the river, raining that stuff in on us.

Everyone took off heading for the nearby bunkers. One of the sergeants, a stocky overweight man, couldn't free himself from his lawn chair. He wrestled with it for several moments. Then he gave up and took off for the bunker with the lawn chair still attached to his butt. I had a difficult time running behind him, laughing as the rounds continued coming in.

Inside the bunker, as the pounding continued, two sergeants tried to pull the lawn chair off the hunkers of the other sergeant. I even reached over to give them a hand. Another round landed nearby, shaking the ground. And with that the lawn chair popped loose. Then the attack suddenly stopped. The sergeant, now out of the lawn chair, was obviously embarrassed. He kicked the chair with his foot, looked around the bunker, and softly said, "I thank you gents and my ass thanks you!"

The next day we staged Lieutenant Smith's convoy and moved out after getting the green light from the engineers at the road sweep. The only event on the way up to Phu Loc 6 was the sniper. And I was wrong again as to which side he would hit on. Jenny quickly reminded me that I owed him a half-dollar. What I did notice was that the sniper's aim was getting better. Maybe he got a rifle with a better sight.

As we were waiting for the Force Logistics convoy to be ferried across from the other side I got into a conversation with some of the tankers. They were talking about the Super Bowl upset. With the mention of upset I asked, "You mean the Jets won?"

One of the tankers was laughing. "Damn straight, lieutenant. The Jets came in eighteen-point underdogs. Baltimore and Johnny Unitas couldn't do anything. Joe Namath even predicted, the day before, that the Jets would take it."

I shook my head. *Unbelievable!* "You're sure about that?"

The tanker smiled. "Baltimore got a touchdown at the end. But it was too late. Jets took them, 16–7." He paused, sipping on a canteen cup of coffee. "My brother-in-law had five hundred bucks on the Colts. I bet he's kicking himself right now."

Another tanker said, "Lieutenant, this is the year of the underdog."

I remember smiling at him. "Yeah, maybe it is."

The return convoy was uneventful. Even the sniper was silent from his perch. However, I still had a plan to do something about him . . . or her. One could never be sure.

After we got the convoy settled and dispatched to the unloading points I reported in to Major Behymer. The first thing he said was that division got my three-page memo. I looked at him, "And?"

Major Behymer smiled. "They liked it, showed improvement. Good job." Then he picked up the landline phone and put a call through to division. He held up a hand for me to stand by. And then he began speaking. I had no idea to whom he was talking. Then he put a hand over the speaker end. "Uh, Major Robb at G–4 would like to talk to you."

Interesting. Major Charles Robb was a former White House aide and Lyndon Johnson's son-in-law. He began his tour in country as the commander of India Company, Third Battalion, 7th Marine Regiment. Now that he got his gold oak leaves he was in the G–4 office supervising the logistics on Operation Taylor-Common. I took the phone from Major Behymer. "Lieutenant McAdams."

"This is Major Robb at G–4. I saw your memo," said the voice on the other end. "What I'm concerned about is the convoy turnaround time. You should be able to get a convoy in and back in one day."

"Right now, major, that's not possible. There's always a logjam at the river. And they shut it down at night," I explained.

"Oh, no, lieutenant. Someone's pulling the wool over your eyes. That ferry is operating all night long," replied Major Robb.

Like learning about the Jets upset in the Super Bowl, I couldn't believe what I was hearing. "Major, the ferry is shut down at night because of enemy activity on both sides of the river."

"Are you sure about that?" asked Major Robb.

"Positively, major, I've been down here since December 27. And I'm on that road every day." I paused, thinking quickly. "If you came down here you'd see what I mean."

Silence on the other end for several moments. "Okay, Lieutenant McAdams, I'll take you up on that. Put the major back on the line." I nodded and handed the phone back to Major Behymer.

They chatted for several moments. Then Major Behymer hung up and looked at me. "You just talked LBJ's son-in-law into taking a convoy down here." He shook his head. "He thinks the ferry operation goes all night long."

That night we all ended up in the slit trenches as a result of another rocket and mortar attack. Most of us knew the calendar, that the Lunar holiday was approaching, and that these irritating night attacks could be a preview of Tet '69.

The next morning Jenny and I stopped along the seven-mile stretch at the Charlie Company base camp. I asked the company commander about snipers in the tree line on the right side of the road. "Which sniper?" he asked. "There are about five or six of them doing their thing out there."

"This one has a perch near or behind the German hospital," I said. We went to a map table and I showed him the approximate location.

The captain nodded. "Yeah, we know about that guy. He's been moving around, usually fires one round and takes off. That's why we've never been able to get him."

I made a motion with my right hand. "What about a patrol going parallel to the road and coming up behind him?"

"That might work," he answered. "But you'd have to be sure that he's out there. He knows your convoy schedule. That's why he takes potshots."

My mind was already planning something. I thanked the captain, went back out, and got into the jeep. We headed out to catch up with the Force Logistics convoy. And right near a bend a round hit just behind us on the right side of the road. Jenny looked at me. "That's seventy-five cents now, lieutenant."

The ferry procedure at Phu Loc 6 was just as long and tedious as before. But this time Major Robb, from G–4, was able to see it firsthand and even talk with some of the people at the CP on the hill. I was also surprised to see that Jack Carmetti was the convoy commander with Jim Smith at trail. Jack explained that as soon as division headquarters announced that Major Robb would be an observer on the convoy "certain people took notice." It was the first time that Major Ashworth and Captain Eiler showed up at the staging area. Had Major Robb not been an observer there wouldn't have been any concern.

The convoy had a tank escort down the seven-mile stretch. And again, the sniper obviously felt that discretion was the better part of his valor. No shot fired. While the trucks pulled into the staging area, with Corporal Robertson directing traffic, I approached Major Robb, who was climbing down from the bed of a six-by truck. I saluted and introduced myself, adding, "We chatted on the phone. Glad you could make it down."

He nodded and smiled, looking around the area. "I see what you mean now. You've got quite a resupply assignment."

"Yes, sir," I said. "It was a real cluster when I got here. And it took a while to get things smoothed out."

He cast a look around the staging area. "This operation is one of the biggest that the division has put together. That's why they installed a task force with General Dwyer commanding, to reinforce the fire bases."

"My only drawbacks right now are the seven-mile stretch out there and the nightly rocket and mortar attacks," I added.

"I can see that," he replied. "Which way is the airstrip?"

I pointed in a northerly direction. "Down that road."

He shook my hand. "If you need anything from division let us know. Keep up the good work."

Major Robb quickly hitched a ride to the airstrip. As I watched him leave I felt that it was a win-win situation. He saw, firsthand, how we were coordinating the convoys. And he got a realistic view of the primitive ferry procedure at the river and that it was indeed shut down at night. My suggestion that he take a convoy down here and see for himself was said in an offhand manner. He took me up on it and it paid off.

That night Jack explained that he would be dropping off at Phu Loc 6 to coordinate the ferry crossings. Jim Smith would take the convoy back to Danang. And, right on schedule, we hit the slit trenches later. Our convoys had a schedule and so did the rocket and mortar attacks.

The next morning we took the convoy back to Phu Loc 6, where Jack got off to assume his new duties. On the way up the sniper fired again, this time from a different position but in the same locale, near the German hospital. The convoy continued to Danang with Lieutenant Jim Smith commanding. There was no incoming convoy coming down from Danang. So on the way back I had Jenny pull off the road and drive up the side road to the hospital complex. It was a group of four to five buildings with several vehicles parked nearby, two of them Range Rover ambulances. The center building had a red cross painted on the roof.

I walked to the edge of the hospital grounds and studied the terrain and a nearby tree line. He's out there in that tree line somewhere, I figured. And he'll most likely be waiting for another convoy or my jeep to come down the road. But on this day there would be no convoy. I now had an afternoon along with a plan.

When we arrived back at An Hoa I made a map recon in the jeep. Then I went into the operations bunker to request a patrol order. The regimental commander, Colonel James Ord, was there with Major Behymer and Lieutenant Chuck Hughes. Another man was there, a grizzled "old Corps" gunnery sergeant, an unlit cigar sticking out of his mouth. I explained to Major Behymer that I needed a ten-man patrol with a PRC–25 to head out of An Hoa in a southerly route, going parallel to Liberty Road, the seven-mile stretch. We would then turn northeast, using the road as a guide to where I suspected was the latest sniper perch. We would come up behind him. The objective was not only to take him out but bring him in.

The gunnery sergeant was the operations NCO, a hardened Korean War veteran. Colonel Ord simply smiled, nodded, and headed off to a staff meeting.

I pressed my case in front of Major Behymer, Lieutenant Hughes, and the gunny. I wanted to get a patrol out there before the afternoon shadows set into the tree line. The gunny and I went to a nearby wall map and I pointed out the approximate location of the sniper perch. He listened attentively, nodding at certain points. Then I summarized my argument and waited for his response. The gunny took the unlit cigar out of his mouth and gave me a wondering look. "Lieutenant McAdams, are you presently reading a good book?"

I was stunned by the question. *What did a book have to do with a sniper harassing our convoys? Maybe the gunny had gone around the bend,* I thought. I replied, "It so happens that I am reading a good book." The book was James Jones's *Some Came Running.*

The gunny said, "Then I suggest that you go back to your hooch and continue reading that good book."

I looked over at Major Behymer. He was silent, waiting for the gunny's rationale. I appealed my case. "That little bugger is out there taking potshots at the convoys. It's gone on for too long."

"Has he *hit* anything?" asked the gunny.

I paused. "Well, no, not yet."

The gunny nodded. "Let's say you take your patrol out to that tree line. And let's say you get your little bugger. And you bring him in." He paused and added, "Walking or in a poncho liner. But let's say that you get him." I nodded, waiting for the punch line. "Do you know what that will do?"

"Yes," I replied. "It will stop that sniper from shooting at us."

The gunny shook his head. "It will force them to replace that little bugger." Another pause, "With someone who no doubt will be a better shot."

Tilt.

The gunny smiled, putting the cigar back in his mouth. "Lieutenant, go read your book."

I spent the rest of the afternoon with James Jones.

Later, in Major Behymer's office, I picked up a copy of *Pacific Stars & Stripes.* The lead story was about Richard Nixon's inauguration as the thirty-seventh president of the United States. I also noticed a sidebar about the coming strategic changes in Vietnam.

The next day the convoy schedule resumed. It was taking longer to get the trucks across the river because the convoys had increased in size as Operation Taylor-Common continued. After a convoy got settled I would grab a package of LURPs and a section of C-4 plastic explosive. I didn't want to take the time to hike to the mess hall for the evening meal. Instead, I would dine al fresco in the hooch. This meant heating up a canteen cup of fresh water on an improvised stove. The stove consisted of a small C-ration container. With my combat knife I cut a small piece of C-4 and placed it in the container-stove. Then I lit it, causing an instant, high, crackling heat. In no time the burning C-4 had the water at a hot temperature. I then poured the water into a LURP pouch of Chicken à la King. I swirled the hot water around for several moments and then cracked a beer. My jungle entrée was now ready. This would allow me time to work on writing letters. I was always careful not to stamp out the C-4 because it would do what it was designed for—explode. A little water would extinguish the stove.

On this night I wanted to get the first letter off to my mother-in-law, Joan Rafferty. Before Patty and I left for Staging Battalion at Camp Pendleton I wrote a series of instructions, steps to be carried out in case I was killed, insurance, burial, and so on. I sealed the instructions in an envelope and asked Joan to keep it. If I returned she was to discard the envelope. When I went to the staff job, at Camp Maintenance, I naturally assumed that my combat time had ended. So now I had to explain that I was back in harm's way for the duration of this operation. And I realized that each morning, heading down that seven-mile stretch of Liberty Road, could be my last. Or I could catch a load of shrapnel during a rocket and mortar attack. I'm not at 11th Motors; I'm in the Arizona, where "one never do know."

I remember being about halfway through the letter when I heard loud noises coming from the First Ranger Group hooch next door. At first I didn't think anything of it. Then the voices became shouting. I wondered, *What the hell is going on?* Then came more shouting. Something definitely was going on next door.

Getting up from the writing table I grabbed my pistol belt and strapped it on. I went out the rear door of the hooch, facing the perimeter wire. The yelling was still going on. Before entering the First Ranger hooch I quickly lifted up a canvas flap. For an instant I thought of Captain Eiler back at Transport Company.

Peering into the hooch I saw a young, bareheaded Marine holding an M-16 on eight U.S. Army officers and South Vietnamese Rangers. He had them lined up against the screen door at the far end. The young Marine was waving the

M–16 back and forth, ranting about something. Each of the Army officers and South Vietnamese Rangers had their hands up, total fear etched on their faces.

I didn't need a wall to fall on me to realize the deadly situation. And I knew that I had seconds to figure out something or people were going to be wounded or killed. Two options raced through my mind: get some assistance from whomever; or take the initiative. I looked around, realizing I was alone in dark shadows—absolutely nobody around. I drew my .45.

With stealth, I opened the backdoor to the hooch, holding the pistol in my right hand. The young Marine didn't hear me enter. He was still ranting about something, pointing the rifle at an Army officer. Quickly, I moved up behind him. As I got closer he heard my boots thudding on the wooden floor.

He started to turn, facing me.

I was close enough to dart my left arm over his shoulder, grabbing the rifle stock and forcing it upward. Then I brought up my pistol and placed it behind his right ear. "Let it go!" I commanded.

The young Marine released his grip on the M–16 and sank onto a nearby cot. Then he put his face in his hands and began bawling like a baby.

The Army officer rushed forward and grabbed the rifle, saying, "Oh, thank God!" He pulled the magazine from the well and ejected a round from the chamber. Then he looked at the selector. "Christ, he had it on full automatic!" The troops often referred to full automatic as "rock and roll."

The young Marine was now holding his face in his hands, swaying back and forth on the cot, babbling something about losing a buddy. It was obvious that he was on something, possibly several things. When I placed my .45 in the holster I realized that it was empty. In the rush of things I had forgotten to insert a magazine. *Just as well,* I thought. It made me think of the convoy ambush where I forgot to load the shotgun.

Whatever deadly potential this incident had was now passed. Several of the officers shook my hand, greatly relieved. I turned and looked at the young Marine. Earlier in the day he was probably a proud warrior. Now he was a sagging mess. With one quick burst he could have taken out everyone. And if he survived, he would be facing a life sentence at the Portsmouth Naval Prison. Or worse.

I identified myself and shook hands with the Army officer. Then I returned to my hooch, cracked a beer, and attempted to finish the letter to Joan. I decided to finish it some other time because my hand was shaking. I realized, once again, how close I came.

In the morning I would be going back on the road. It was almost the end of January 1969. I had been down here for about a month. *What more was going to happen? My God, I almost got killed tonight—by one of our own.* I imagined what Patty would have thought, standing at a graveside, in widow's weeds, after taps had just been played for her "brave" husband who had been killed by a fellow Marine. War isn't just hell; it's the dark side of humanity.

Two days later Lieutenant Chuck Hughes came into the hooch during an afternoon break. He wanted to know my social security number. "What do you need my social security for?" I asked.

"You're being written up for an award," he said.

I gave Chuck my number. After he left I thought of Hoa Vang and Cam Le Bridge. I did so many things during that fight, including three ammo runs under fire. And I got nothing for it. Here, in a matter of minutes, I disarmed a young kid who had gone around the bend and I get written up. *Semper Fi!*

Several days later I learned the backstory that led to the night of January 22. The young Marine was on a patrol in the Arizona when his unit came under fire. He was third in line. The point man and the man behind him were the first to fall, both KIA. After returning to An Hoa he apparently got high on something. And when he saw the South Vietnamese Rangers enter the First Army Group hooch he decided on some retaliation. I never saw him again.

18

Tet '69

By the first week of February 1969 I felt that the convoy coordination had shown a 75 percent improvement; there was nowhere to go but up. Materiel was rolling in on a steady convoy basis. Retrograde, spent artillery shells, was going back to Danang as scheduled. And Operation Taylor-Common continued. When Lieutenant Caldwell came in on a Force Logistics convoy we kept our distance. I wasn't going to concern myself with his attitude, which hadn't changed.

Lieutenant Jack Carmetti notified me that the ferry would be closed for repairs during the upcoming weekend. That gave me a window of downtime. And I could use it to get back to 11th Motors for a hot shower and a good meal.

I asked Jenny if he was interested in flying back to the battalion for a respite. Jenny said that he'd rather stay in An Hoa and catch up on sleep. So the next morning I packed a bag and strapped on my .45, leaving the shotgun behind. At flight operations, down at the LSA, I didn't have to wait long. I hitched a ride on a Huey, telling the crew chief that my drop-off was the 11th Marine Regiment, the artillery battalion across the road from 11th Motors. On the way we had to pick up an officer at a nearby fire base. Going into the LZ (landing zone) we took some enemy fire. Then the door gunner opened up with several bursts from his M-60. And that silenced whoever was firing at us. From the fire base we headed up to Danang. And once again I saw what a beautiful country Vietnam is—thick green foliage and thin rivers winding east to the Bay of Danang.

What will become of this country?, I wondered again.

The Huey put down at the 11th Marines helipad. A thumbs-up to the crew chief and they were off again, heading north toward the Hai Van Pass. I changed from helmet to soft cover and headed across the road, through the main gate of 11th Motors. It was here where I realized that my clothes had that faded-dusty jungle look. I didn't look like a Motor Transport guy; I was with the infantry at a combat base in the Arizona, out on the road every day.

As I headed to my old hooch Major Ashworth came out of his office. He was surprised to see me. I saluted him, "Afternoon, major."

"Lieutenant McAdams, what are you doing back here?"

"They shut down ferry operations for two days. I hitched a ride on a Huey to get a hot shower and a decent meal," I explained.

He gave me a close look, him with boots shined by a hooch maid and neatly pressed utilities. "I hope you brought a clean uniform. We're having visitors from Third MAF for the evening meal." Third MAF was the Third Marine Amphibious Force, the main headquarters of all Marine forces in Vietnam. The visit was no doubt the result of one of Lieutenant Colonel Kinneburgh's high-level invitations.

I shook my head. "Major, all I have is a change of skivvies. I'm flying back in the morning."

"Still, make sure you get cleaned up," said Major Ashworth. Mother Superior turned and walked off.

I watched as he headed down to the motor pool. I thought of the Marine from Alpha Company who I carried in through a mud field. And for a quick second, I saw the faces of the eight Army officers and South Vietnamese Rangers facing a crazed Marine holding an M–16 on full automatic.

A month down at An Hoa and all he cares about is my appearance because the battalion has visitors. He didn't even inquire about the operation or what had been accomplished down there. I was halfway tempted to invite him down to see the operation firsthand, like Major Robb. I didn't because I knew what his answer would be.

Despite being gone for five weeks my cot was still open. I quickly undressed, wrapped a towel around my waist, and headed to the showers. It was a treat to stand under a hot showerhead for a change. I lathered up some soap and gave myself a close shave.

At the mess hall I dropped in on Staff Sergeant Hans Thunberg, the chief cook, who I worked with while the mess hall was being upgraded. Staff Sergeant Thunberg complained that Major Ashworth was all over him for two days to have chocolate ripple ice cream for the Third MAF people. The mess crew was frying steaks, to order, for them. I took an early meal with Andy Garrison in an attempt to keep out of the way of the VIPs. Andy explained that he was now the battalion defense counsel and had to prepare for an upcoming special court-martial. The charge was possession of marijuana.

It was a kick to be back at the Staff/Officers club that night, hearing what was going on in the battalion, about the convoys north to Phu Bai and Hue City. Several people asked me about the operation at An Hoa, how long it would be going on. It was the NCOs, the senior sergeants, who wanted to know more about Operation Taylor-Common, the ferry operations, and the Arizona. I connected with Staff Sergeant Thomas, Gunnery Sergeant Rayhorn, and Top Duncan.

And then I heard about Captain Eiler's beating in the four-holer. Everyone seemed to think that the unnamed culprits were from Transport Company despite the fact that the mugging occurred in the Headquarters Company area. I was also told that Captain Eiler stayed away from the Staff/Officers club until his facial wounds began healing. I was relieved that the beating didn't result in his death. Still, there was some residue that made me feel sorry for the man. Because of his character traits he had to fear not only the war but also the men he was commanding.

There was a movie that night but I can't recall the title. I settled in the hooch and got a good sleep. In the morning I took an early breakfast and then paid a courtesy call on Lieutenant Colonel Kinneburgh. He had seen a copy of my memo and related how Major Robb and the division G-4 office were coming around to appreciating the resupply convoys from our battalion and Force Logistics. As I left his office I passed Major Ashworth's desk. He was working on some paperwork and didn't even look up as I left.

At Headquarters Company I had to sign two forms. One of them was a confirmation of participating in Operation Taylor-Common. The other was my qualification for the Combat Action Ribbon. I had never heard of this ribbon. One of the clerks told me that it was a newly approved ribbon to parallel the Army's Combat Infantryman's Badge (CIB). While I was signing the forms Captain Eiler walked in. The first thing I noticed were the scrapes and bruises on his face. He nodded to me and went to his cubicle. *What a strange war this is*, I thought.

At the 11th Marines helipad I noticed two civilian types wearing bush hats and safari jackets. They were also packing .38 revolvers in shoulder holsters. I knew right away who they were—"spooks," CIA field agents. I approached them and smiled, "Where are you guys headed?" They turned and looked at me. One had a stoic expression; the other smiled. Nothing more from Laurel and Hardy. I nodded and went to another part of the helipad. And the three of us waited in jungle silence for a helicopter. War is strange and tragic, but it also has its ironic moments. Here we are, on the same side, and they won't talk to me.

At 11th Motors the drug problem was escalating. And another Transport Company Marine, Lance Corporal Dan Crawford, was apprehended by the duty NCO one night outside of his hooch smoking a joint. Crawford quickly stubbed the joint out with his foot. However, a second joint was found in his utility jacket pocket. He was brought up on office hours with the recommendation for a special court-martial.

When Lieutenant Andy Garrison received the court file as defense counsel, he took note of the appointed board. This consisted of five officers: Major Ashworth, president; and members: Captain Corliss, Captain Eiler, and two lieutenants. Andy was given a two-week preparation time.

After meeting Lance Corporal Crawford, Andy came away with a favorable impression: a nice kid who made a mistake and was willing to accept punishment. However, the mood against drugs had intensified both in the battalion and at First Marine Division Headquarters. With Major Ashworth sitting as president of the court and Captain Eiler at his side, it was more than evident that Lance Corporal Crawford was going to be made an example of. A maximum sentence from a special court-martial for this offense could carry six months in the brig, six months loss of two-thirds base pay, and a bad-conduct discharge (BCD). In Marine Corps jargon it was termed "six, six, and a kick."

With the current headquarters tempo in the battalion Andy knew that the board would be going for the maximum sentence. His challenge was to prevent Lance Corporal Crawford from receiving "bad paper," a BCD.

Crawford realized his mistake and was willing to accept brig time, a bust, and loss of pay. And he was fully aware that a BCD would cause him to lose most of his VA benefits and possibly follow him for the rest of his life.

Major Ashworth and Captain Eiler both felt that Lance Corporal Davis previously got a light sentence, for the same offense, which was upheld in review. Davis, however, had possession, whereas Crawford was using. Still, both officers felt that it constituted the same offense.

Andy began outlining his defense. Because of the facts he decided upon pleading guilty and then work on a strong extenuation and mitigation. His strategy was twofold: use Father Matthew Horvat, the battalion chaplain, as a character witness; and get Major Ashworth and Captain Eiler off the board. The former appeared easy enough; the latter was a thorny challenge.

Lance Corporal Crawford was advised to make several visits to the chaplain's office so that Father Horvat could become more acquainted with the accused. While this was taking place Andy pulled the OQRs on each court member. After perusing the records his saw an opening. Three of the five court members were Catholic. Major Ashworth and Captain Eiler were not Catholic. His defense strategy was taking shape.

When the court convened Andy had his proverbial ducks in line. First Lieutenant Jim Smith, the trial counsel, swore in the members of the court and the defense. Andy then pulled a startling one-two punch. He challenged Captain Eiler for cause. His argument was that Captain Eiler, the commander of the accused, had prior knowledge. Captain Eiler was caught off-guard. He turned to Major Ashworth for a ruling. Since it was a challenge for cause Major Ashworth had to allow it. Captain Eiler grabbed his soft cover, gave Andy a glare, and left the courtroom.

Next was the preemptory challenge for the defense. Andy stood at the defense table and named the president of the court: Major Ashworth. A surprised silence came over the room. Captain Corliss was just as surprised as Major Ashworth. With Ashworth gone Captain Corliss, as next in seniority, would be president.

The shock wore off in a few moments. It was obvious that Major Ashworth and Captain Eiler had no idea these challenges were coming. The board was now reduced to three. And the three, about to hear Father Horvat's character testimony, were all Catholic.

Captain Corliss took over as president after Major Ashworth left in a huff. It was noted for the record that the board was reconstituted. The plea of the accused was next: guilty. After that the court went to extenuation and mitigation.

The tribunal listened as Father Horvat gave his character testimony. Lance Corporal Crawford came off as a good Marine who made a mistake. He added, "Because of his character and record Lance Corporal Crawford has the potential to serve the remainder of his tour and be a credit to the Corps. He is also willing to serve his punishment for this mistake."

It took the court members fifteen minutes to agree on a sentence. Lieutenant Andy Garrison and Lance Corporal Crawford stood at the defense table as the sentence was read: to be sentenced to thirty days in the Danang brig; to be reduced to private (E–1), and to forfeit two-thirds of base pay for three months.

Crawford turned to Andy and smiled; there would be no BCD.

Later that afternoon.Major Ashworth called Andy into his office. "I didn't appreciate your courtroom trickery, lieutenant. It was an underhanded stunt."

Andy shook his head. "My defense was legal and above-board, major. I was granted a challenge for cause and a preemptory challenge. And I took advantage of both to give the best possible defense."

Major Ashworth sneered. "We'll have to see how the convening authority reviews this. That young man deserved a BCD."

"Not according to the court's decision," replied Andy.

Two weeks later the convening authority upheld the sentence. Major Ashworth and Captain Eiler had no choice but to accept the ruling.

———

When I returned to An Hoa, Lance Corporal Jenny and I went back on the road. Jack Carmetti was now coordinating the ferry operations at Phu Loc 6 while I handled the coordination once the convoys got across. Naturally there was increased radio traffic between him (Hansworth) and me (Rush Act Yankee). During these days I saw more improvements in the operation. Jack had stepped in and hit the ground running.

Each morning the 7th Engineers would sweep from Son Thu Bon River down the seven-mile stretch to An Hoa. About halfway they would meet with an engineer team sweeping the road coming up from An Hoa. While this was taking place the 1st Bridge Company would be preparing the ferry for the day's crossings. The ferry would take local traffic across while waiting for the Danang convoy to arrive. When the convoy arrived it had priority. A normal convoy crossing took at least four to five hours, with the one coming down alternating with the convoy going back. While this had become the daily routine at Phu Loc 6 the Seabees were building a replacement one-lane precast concrete bridge with pilings. Upon completion a convoy crossing would take fifteen to twenty minutes.

We had heard that there was a buildup of intelligence information with Tet approaching. And this year the holiday was to come later in the calendar. And it did. Not with a bang but with several bangs on the early morning of February 23.

The NVA kicked off the '69 Tet Offensive with several coordinated attacks in and around Danang. At the First Marine Division Headquarters they hit the reverse slope of Hill 327 with rockets and mortars followed by a sapper attack resulting in many casualties.

Tet began for An Hoa shortly after 1:30 A.M. with a likewise rocket and mortar attack. The initial attack concentrated on the airstrip and the northeast corner of the perimeter, exactly to the opposite of where my hooch was. The observation tower down near the LSA was also a target and soon was ablaze while the occupants put up a valiant but mortal fight.

I ended up in a slit trench with John Connolly, Chuck Hughes, and a number of others rousted out of sleep. We slept in our skivvies with our utilities under our cots for a quick grab. Still, we found ourselves getting dressed in the slit trenches as the bombardment continued. I remember tightening my belt, lacing my boots, and putting on the flak jacket. Then I remembered that I forgot my helmet. I was always forgetting something in the rush of things.

Suddenly I remembered the MRC–109 radio jeep. It was parked in front of the S-4 office. The thought of it being in such a vulnerable place, in a cluster of hooches, made me consider a quick run to get it to a safer area. When the rockets and mortars took a pause I was up and out of the slit trench, doing a forty-yard bareheaded dash to the jeep. As I approached the jeep I felt that the pause was for some distant NVA mortar crew to reposition and reload.

I got to the jeep, jumped in, and started it. I saw the sandbagged operations bunker and quickly figured *no—too obvious a target*. What I did was drive to an open area and park it. The NVA mortar teams used certain targets. I figured that they would never pump rockets and mortars into an empty field. So I parked the jeep right in the center of an open area. I turned off the engine, got out, and began the sprint back to the slit trench. As I started running the rockets and mortars resumed hitting around the perimeter. When I got closer to the slit trench I heard a whizzing sound pass my left ear thumping into a mound of sand near the edge of the slit trench. I stopped and looked at what had landed. It was a white-hot, jagged piece of shrapnel, most likely from a 122-millimeter rocket. More rounds were coming in so I jumped into the slit trench, still bareheaded.

The attack went on for most of the night. And again, we slept in the slit trench. Periodically I would rouse myself and look out at the perimeter wire. Someone was firing a rifle. And then someone else would also fire. I lowered myself back down for a few more z's. Again, I thanked the Divine Providence in giving me a gene for quick recon naps.

The morning sun gifted us with an all-clear siren. The first thing I did was return to the mound of sand and find the jagged piece of shrapnel that came so close to taking off the left temporal region of my head. It made me think of the first enemy dead body I saw, that Chinese adviser to the NVA unit that had made an attempt on a bridge security team near Phu Bai. I could have looked like that, one-third of my head missing. I bent down, picked up the piece of shrapnel, and brought it back to the hooch. (As I write this that four-inch, jagged piece of shrapnel rests on a marble base on my desk, a daily reminder of the fortunes of war, of how close I came.)

I went back to the open area and retrieved the MRC–109 radio jeep, sitting there in the morning sunshine without a scratch. I got in and drove back to the S–4 office. Then I opened the screen door and entered. It was eerie; nobody was there. I stood next to the doorframe looking at an office in shambles. It looked as if a team of marauders stormed through. Desks were canted to one side; typewriters were dumped on the wooden floor; papers, memos, and reports were strewn all over. One of the typewriters was the machine on which I had typed the final draft of my Motor Transport memo. As I stood there I smelled the acrid stench of gunpowder. Then I realized it was a scent of leftover TNT blowing through the area. I bent down and picked up a picture frame.

The picture was a reproduction of a celebrated cartoon, in Bill Mauldinesque. It showed a tough, grizzled infantry sergeant, a three-day growth of beard, with helmet and flak jacket, .45 strapped on his hip, holding an M-16 rifle. The caption stated, "YEA, THOUGH I WALK THROUGH THE VALLEY OF THE SHADOW OF DEATH I WILL FEAR NO EVIL . . . BECAUSE I'M THE TOUGHEST MOTHERFUCKER IN THE VALLEY."

As I held the picture frame in my hand I noticed that the glass was cracked. I remember staring at the vertical crack for several moments. Then I placed it on a nearby desk. I always regretted not taking that picture frame with me. I felt it was a metaphor of the war. Actually, I already had my personal metaphor—the jagged piece of shrapnel.

By the end of the day we learned that major targets from Saigon up to Danang and farther north at Quang Tri came under coordinated attacks. In those places the enemy was quickly beaten off. At An Hoa during the initial rocket and mortar attack the enemy was able to cut the outer perimeter wire and toss explosive satchel charges into one of the ammo berms. As the ammo began to explode it tossed shrapnel and fire into the other storage berms. After some sporadic fighting the enemy broke contact and fled northeast across the river. Approximately seventeen to twenty dead enemy soldiers were left hanging in the perimeter wire. Major Behymer's office was notified that approximately 15,000 artillery rounds along with 40,000 gallons of fuel were destroyed. I was told that the convoys and numerous supply drops from C-123 cargo planes would have to make up the difference. And we needed to start immediately. At the same time we knew that the nightly rocket and mortar attacks would continue. I was glad that I had taken the time to fly back to 11th Motors for a respite. It would be a while before this let up.

The next two weeks were focused on getting the artillery and fuel supplies back to the previous levels. The mornings were spent getting the overnight convoy prepared, including retrograde. After the road sweep the outgoing convoy would head up the seven-mile stretch and stage for the river crossing. Then I had to coordinate the incoming convoy from Danang. These were bigger convoys because of the artillery and fuel demands. The sniper kept to his routine, constantly cranking off a round at us as we were either going up or coming back. And I kept losing quarters to Jenny. When the convoy arrived in An Hoa I would meet with the convoy commander about the drop-off points and the places to position the .50-caliber gun trucks for the night. Each night the gun trucks were placed at a different strategic point. When there was a break in the routine I would head to the hooch for a quick recon nap, knowing that the night would be interrupted with a rocket and mortar attack. Jenny would do the same. And, on schedule, we usually ended up in the slit trenches until the break of dawn.

With the artillery and fuel levels reaching where they were before the Tet bombardments began the convoy resupply was working on its own, better than ever. I began to see the results of my effect on the resupply for Operation Taylor-Common. It made me think of Lieutenant Colonel Kinneburgh's graphic prompt to "unfuck that mess."

Just after the middle of March, Defend in DCC called Rush Act Yankee. I was in the staging area when it came over the radio. I keyed the microphone and identified myself, "Defend, this is Rush Act Yankee, over."

"Rush Act, we request that you call this station on lima-lima, over." It was a voice I had never heard over the radio net. Lima-lima meant a landline phone. It was a red flag; something was brewing higher up.

When Jenny pulled up in front of the S–4 office I told him to wait for me. I went inside and told Major Behymer that I had to call division on the landline phone. He nodded and pointed toward the phone. I quickly got through to DCC. And then I was informed that Lance Corporal Jenny and I would be returning to 11th Motors on the outgoing convoy the next day, March 19. I was surprised by the suddenness of it. My time with the 5th Marines, Task Force Yankee, and An Hoa was ending. I was also told that the convoy turnaround time could now stand on its own. I will always remember the phrase: "You won't be replaced, there's no need."

I exited the S–4 office. Standing there next to the door was Brigadier General Ross Dwyer, commanding general of Task Force Yankee. I snapped off a quick salute. He nodded and returned the salute with a reply: "Lieutenant, how are you?"

"Fine, sir," I said. As I watched him walk to the operations bunker I thought of that day down at Cam Le Bridge when I first saw him. Then I recalled the staff meeting at 11th Motors and the difficult decision to relieve Major Pearson, replacing him with Lieutenant Colonel Kinneburgh. And now the head guy down here had just said hello to me on my next-to-last day on Operation Taylor-Common. Ross Dwyer, a Stanford graduate, was commissioned a second lieutenant in 1942. He personified so many multidecorated Marine Corps officers who came out of "civilian" colleges and rose to flag rank without attending a service academy. I always felt that that is what set the Marine Corps apart from the other services: There never was or ever has been an exclusive "Marine Corps Officers Military Academy." Ross Dwyer retired as a major general in 1974. He passed away at age eighty-two in October 2001.

I stood next to Jenny, who was still sitting in the driver's seat of the jeep. I smiled at him. "What is it, lieutenant?" he asked.

"We're done here," I said.

"Good, I can get some sleep," said Jenny.

I shook my head. "I don't mean that we're done for today. We're done, period. We're going back to 11th Motors with tomorrow's convoy."

Jenny turned and stared through the windshield. He shook his head and smiled. He didn't have to say anything. There was a look of relief written all over his face. Mission accomplished.

The night was uneventful. In the morning I got my gear ready and headed to the mess hall, which had been in a state of repairs since the first Tet attack. After a full breakfast I headed back to S-4 for a farewell to Major Behymer. John Connolly said that he was in the operations bunker.

Major Behymer was sitting in the bunker with the gunnery sergeant who had talked me out of taking a patrol to get the hapless sniper. Sitting next to him was Colonel James Ord, commander of the 5th Marine Regiment. I nodded to the three men. Then I looked at Major Behymer. "I'll be heading back with the morning convoy, major."

Colonel Ord took off his glasses and smiled at me. "Who are they replacing you with, lieutenant?"

I shook my head. "Nobody, sir, they tell me my job is done."

Colonel Ord motioned with his glasses to Major Behymer. "Lynn, write something up on Lieutenant McAdams. He's done a hell of a job."

Major Behymer smiled and picked up a pen. "When did you get down here?" I explained that I arrived December 27, 1968. He made some notes, stood, and shook my hand. "Good luck, Frank."

We waited for the engineers to finish the road sweep. I said goodbye to Corporal Robertson, adding that he could return to his unit. I made a note to write up a letter of commendation for him, how he was able to sort things out in the staging area.

As the convoy headed out Jenny pulled our jeep in line behind the convoy commander. Before we approached the bend at the railroad tracks I predicted that the sniper would ding something off to our right. After we turned at the bend we heard a crack go overhead and land in some paddy water off to our left. "That's three dollars you owe me, lieutenant," said Jenny.

At Phu Loc 6 the incoming convoy from Danang had already arrived. As the slow and tedious ferrying process began I went up on the hill to the CP. Jack Carmetti was there with several MPs. He introduced me and we sat on the side of a sandbagged bunker. I had about two weeks left in-country. And I knew that this could be the last time Jack and I would be together because he got orders to Camp Lejeune. We opened two cans of beer and reflected on our time in 11th Motors and now on Operation Taylor-Common. Somehow we got on the subject of Captain Eiler and how he was transferred to Headquarters Company, where he received a beating. I asked, "Do you think it was Transport Company or Headquarters that got to him?"

Jack shook his head. "Doesn't make any difference. The man is damn lucky that he's still alive."

I remember looking down at the river, watching that primitive ferry transporting several trucks across. "Whatever will become of this country?"

"We'll continue until a pullout date. Then all hell will break loose. After the dust settles we'll become allies." He gave off a wry smile. "And maybe we'll build a few resort hotels on the bay." I took a long look at the river down below. Then I turned to Jack. "I guess it was about growing up and finding out something about ourselves."

After we arrived back at 11th Motors I heard what happened during Tet '69. Like most of the compounds in the area they took some rocket and mortar rounds. Alpha and Bravo Companies were probed, the enemy trying to cut through the wire. But they were beaten back. Bravo Company got credited with several kills.

I settled into the old hooch and then reported to Lieutenant Colonel Kinneburgh, who wanted me to start on an AAR. "I understand you gave Colonel Ord a rough time down there." I remember giving him a quizzical look as he smiled. He was playing with me. "You did good. Let's let it go at that."

On the way out I went by Major Ashworth's desk. "Oh, Lieutenant McAdams?" I stopped and looked at him. "Make sure you get your after-action report in on time."

I nodded to him and walked out. I never knew exactly what he did at that desk. And he had absolutely no idea what we did down at An Hoa.

The next week was spent outlining my AAR and the letter of commendation for Corporal Robertson. I also wrote up Lance Corporal Jenny for a Bronze Star. In reality I wanted him to get a Navy Commendation Medal with a "Combat V." So I recommended a Bronze Star knowing that someone up the chain would knock it down one. So it goes in the Corps. I had no idea what Major Behymer had written for me. The paperwork would have to catch up. My stateside orders were to the 13th Motor Transport Battalion at Camp Pendleton, California. Four weeks of leave would allow me time in Chicago to reunite with Patty and take our time driving to the West Coast. When I turned in the shotgun to the battalion armory I realized something: Despite all the convoys I was on with that weapon I never fired it.

My rotation day finally arrived. It was early evening when I signed out at Headquarters Company carrying an officer's Val Pack (a gray, multicompartment suitcase with leather handle) and a sea bag. I collected the orders to Camp Pendleton and my OQR. One of the clerks told me that my paperwork from the 5th Marines arrived. For a moment I didn't know what he was talking about. Then he added, "You're being written up for two awards, lieutenant."

I didn't even ask what medals the recommendations were for. Operation Taylor-Common would continue, along with the war. The convoys and the patrols would be going out in the morning. *Had anything changed since I reported in as a green second lieutenant? What difference did I make?* In a way I balanced my own book, indirectly killing eight enemy soldiers that day at Hoa Vang. Then I saved the lives of eight South Vietnamese Rangers and Army officers; it was one step back and one forward. I thought it was ironic that I blew up a truck yet saved a jeep. I got nothing for saving the jeep, but I did receive a letter of censure for the truck. *Semper Fi.*

With my orders and OQR I walked out of the office. It was dark as I picked up my Val Pack and slung the sea bag over a shoulder. There was a jeep waiting for me in the motor pool. About ten yards from the company office I heard a voice behind me. "Hey, Frank!"

Standing to my rear, in the night shadows, was Captain Eiler. I could barely make out his face in the dark. I quickly thought of the things that came about because of him: the wrong-foot speech in front of the company, the ambush at Phu Gia Pass, the price on his head, the hair-trigger temper, sneaking around the troops' hooches at night, his reaction toward Bobby Kennedy, the false grave marker, and my marginal fitness report. I looked at him for a final moment. And then he said, "Good luck." I realized that that was the best he could do.

I responded with one word, "Thanks." There was no salute. Then I adjusted my sea bag and headed down to the motor pool and a waiting jeep.

I stayed in a transit barracks that night. The next morning I boarded a Continental 707 for Kadena Air Force Base on Okinawa. As we settled into our seats I recalled my arrival day, being greeted with the Death March from a bugle. And now we all waited anxiously as the jet lumbered on its taxi run. Then we headed down the runway to takeoff. A cheer went up inside the cabin. The lieutenant next to me raised a hand. I looked over at him. He had tears running down both cheeks. I didn't have tears—only memories. I turned and looked out the window. Below, a convoy was staging at Red Beach, preparing for the run to Phu Bai through the Hai Van Pass.

I realized that the Divine Providence was giving me a second life. The challenge was to do something with it.

I thought of a quatrain that Patty had sent me: *Remember the time, Will I ever forget, The South China Sea, And the people I met.*

19

Homecoming

After several days of processing on Okinawa my name finally appeared on a draft—the list of Marines slated to fly out in the morning. I spent the last night with some Marine officers in the club at Camp Hansen. Upon leaving I passed the corkboard. There was a current list of SEA SERVICE DEATHS posted. I gave it a cursory glance, not recognizing anyone.

Outside I noticed that the flags were at half-staff. Later I found out why. Former President Dwight Eisenhower passed away at Walter Reed Army Hospital. It was March 28, 1969.

The flight across the Pacific was long. I remember passing the hours sleeping and reading. We made a fuel stop in Honolulu, where I phoned Patty to confirm my arrival time in Chicago. Walking back to the plane I thought of our parting in the last hours of R&R. The last leg of the Pacific flight seemed to drag endlessly. We finally landed at George Air Force Base near Victorville, California. From there four of us shared the taxi fare to Los Angeles International Airport, where we caught our flights to HOR—our home of record.

At O'Hare International Airport I walked off the plane in my Class A uniform with ribbons and badges. Patty and her mother were there along with my mother. One of the first things I said to Joan, my mother-in-law, was to get rid of the instruction letter that I gave her thirteen months prior. She nodded with a wide smile. On the way to baggage claim I noticed several people, in faded, tie-dyed clothes and long hair, giving my uniform ugly looks. I thought nothing of it; I had survived a combat situation.

My parents had separated again. This time my mother had taken an apartment with my younger brother Brian in suburban Oak Park. Coincidently, on the other side, Patty and her mother had moved into a newly constructed high-rise apartment building on South Shore Drive. It was the same address as the house where I spent my high-school years—6700.

I remember spending the next two weeks greeting family members. My

244

father treated me to a lunch at the Sherman Hotel downtown with some of his law associates. The conversation was mild. When the discussion turned to the war someone at the table quickly moved it to another subject. I got the drift, as Lieutenant Colonel Kinneburgh often suggested. Naturally these men were glad that I had survived. However, it was evident that they did not want to discuss the war. After the lunch my father remarked, "We're seeing the difference with our wars. I came back a hero. You simply came back." He was prophesying what I, and thousands of returning Vietnam veterans, were about to encounter.

Patty and Joan scheduled a homecoming gathering with relatives and friends from high school and college in the high-rise's party room on the top floor. It was now strange and ironic to be living at the same address where I grew up, our house replaced with a highrise. When people asked me what I did in Vietnam I simply replied, "I ran truck convoys, didn't walk to the war."

Then someone would ask, "Did you see much action?"

I would nod and respond, "My share and then some." It went no further.

However, I did tell a humorous anecdote or two. My father used to do this with his World War II stories. He stayed away from the serious and tragic stuff. Now I was doing the same thing.

A college acquaintance took me aside. "I want you to know that I wanted to go. But I failed the physical." I nodded and he added, "Asthma." There was a pregnant pause. Then he said, "I still feel bad about it."

"Don't," I said. I walked off, thinking of the hawkish student at Loyola who took the handball off-ramp. He supported President Johnson and didn't care for the politics of the dovish students. And he hid behind a fake physical exam, enough said.

During those days I spent a lot of time reading and looking out of the apartment window that gave a commanding view of Lake Michigan, south to Rainbow Beach and north to Jackson Park Harbor. I kept wondering who would be commanding the next convoy through the Hai Van Pass or south to An Hoa. I was glad to have this time to adjust.

The afternoon before Patty and I were to leave for California I broke away for a walk through the Jackson Park Golf Course. In the winter, as a young boy, I used to sled down the hill in front of the Comfort Station. In the fall my friends and I used to play touch football on one of the adjoining fairways. It was early spring as I walked toward the little bridge that went across the lagoon. In my recurring nightmare this is where the four VC soldiers, AK-47s at high port, used to chase me. And now there was only a struggling soul peacefully practicing his chip shots.

I nodded to myself, taking a final look. Then I turned and walked off.

20

Camp Pendleton

I will always remember the drive west to California as a soothing respite—a vacation through the heartland and then diverting to the southern route through New Mexico and Arizona. We drove maybe five or six hours a day, calling ahead, using a tour guide for a good hotel-motel en route. Then we would look for a good restaurant. Part of me wanted it to never end. Previously we had the looming prospect of a war. And that prospect was still present—but only if I opted to stay in the Marine Corps. If I signed on to that I would be returning to Vietnam, as a captain, within eighteen months.

I already knew that I wasn't going to "re-up." I had pushed fate far enough. There was a new world out there. And our generation was changing so fast that the older generation resented it. The White House was reducing the troop level. But at the same time contingency plans were under way to intensify the war. These plans would lead to B-52 bombing raids over Hanoi, as well as the incursion into Cambodia. Instead of coming together the generation gap was widening.

The values of the World War II generation were being challenged from all sides. Hollywood reflected that challenge in film: *Midnight Cowboy*, about the underside of Manhattan seen by a sickly con man and a naïve male hustler; *Easy Rider*, a surprisingly popular, low-budget road picture about two dropouts who ride across the country on motorcycles; *They Shoot Horses, Don't They?*, a dark look at a Depression-era dance marathon; *Bob & Carol & Ted & Alice*, a contemporary glimpse at the rationale of wife-swapping; *The Prime of Miss Jean Brodie*, about a Scottish school teacher at a private girls academy who imparts erroneous information to her impressionable students; and *Butch Cassidy and the Sundance Kid*, a chronicle of two real-life turn-of-the-century outlaws who were constantly challenged by a changing world that leads to their demise. American films have always reflected the tempo of the times.

The world of rock music was drastically changing young people's attitudes. I saw it with the USO show troupes that came through our battalion. The emcee with The Fabulous Korean Kittens, Frankie Perdazzo, personified that. Patty had seen the change firsthand in the year I was gone. Now I was hearing it from her as I was going to what the Marine Corps referred to as a "stateside billet." With it came a different set of problems.

We had to camp out in a motel in Oceanside for about ten days. It was a difficult time, taking meals outside, constantly looking for the right apartment, and not knowing when this would end. We finally found a two-story townhouse near the high school. This was fortunate because I could use the track around the football stadium for morning runs.

While Patty set up housekeeping I reported in to my new command, Transport Company, 13th Motor Transport Battalion, Fifth Marine Division. The company commander was Captain Bill Keller. His XO was First Lieutenant George McConnell, a mustang. Another recent officer reporting in was First Lieutenant Steve Crittenden. It was through Steve that I heard about Jack Carmetti and what happened at Phu Loc 6 several hours after I left.

Around 3:30 A.M. on March 19 an NVA force managed to infiltrate the compound and blow the generator. The enemy began using flamethrowers and throwing satchel charges all over. Jack ran out of the back of his tent and went to the aid station to assist with the wounded and dying. After a Huey landed and took off with casualties Jack and Sergeant Major William Fales headed out to check on several MPs who assisted at the river crossing. Running down the finger from the hill the group confronted ten NVA soldiers. One was about to light up the area with a flamethrower. Jack and Sergeant Major Fales opened fire. Someone hit the flamethrower tank and it exploded, sending flames all over. At each bunker they found several more NVA soldiers and quickly dispatched them each time. By this time a "Spooky" C-47 (a heavily armed transport prop plane) came on station and began laying down an incredible fire around the perimeter. The fight began to subside on the hill, but the nearby artillery battery was still blasting away.

When first light came a large patrol from the 1st Battalion, 5th Marines, went out to check the area. Later it was determined that the NVA unit was part of a reinforced battalion with the mission to overrun and destroy Phu Loc 6.

After the enemy withdrew that morning the Seabees, who were building the bridge replacement, dug a large trench on the An Hoa side. In the trench went the bodies of seventy-two NVA soldiers. For their actions that night Jack and Sergeant Major Fales were awarded the Silver Star. It was later reported that from the action on the other side of Phu Loc 6 Hospitalman Second Class

David Robert Ray, a Navy corpsmen with Delta Battery, 11th Marine Regiment, was posthumously awarded the Medal of Honor.

About two weeks after reporting to 13th Motors I was notified that an awards formation was scheduled for the coming Friday afternoon. I was also informed that I was the subject of the awards formation. My recommended awards from the 5th Marine Regiment had come through.

The formation was initially scheduled for the grinder—the drill field. However, a sudden rainstorm forced it inside the headquarters. I remember feeling awkward, standing in front of a detachment of Marines who barely knew me. The battalion CO, Major Tom Collins, read the citations for a Navy–Marine Corps Medal and the Navy Commendation Medal (with "Combat V"). The Navy–Marine Corps Medal was for disarming the Marine at An Hoa, saving the lives of eight Army and South Vietnamese Rangers. The Navy Commendation Medal was for my overall performance on Operation Taylor-Common, exposing myself to hostile fire on the seven-mile stretch. For whatever reason there were no medals presented at that time, only the signed citations. I received the medals later.

Afterward George McConnell told me that I had something in common with President John Kennedy. "What's that?" I asked.

"He was awarded the Navy–Marine Corps Medal for saving the lives of his PT boat crew in the Solomon Islands." George smiled. "You're in good company."

After the awards formation, for some reason, I thought of the young Marine who I carried in through the mud field. I had his name and hometown filed away. I looked it up. His home of record was in southern Los Angeles County. A quick check with Los Angeles information, and I had the home phone number. I waited for Patty to take a shopping trip. Then I went to the phone. I stared at it for several moments. My hand shook as I picked up the receiver. Slowly I dialed the number. I remember taking a deep breath with a dry mouth. After the second ring I heard a "Hello?" It was a man's voice.

I asked if this was the home of the Marine. Then I gave the casualty date. The man replied that it was. "I'm his father."

"I want you to know that I carried your son in that day."

"Oh, you did," he replied. "Well, the Marine Corps didn't tell us much other than he was killed doing road security in a place called An Hoa."

"That's right," I said. "I was doing convoy coordination on that road." I paused and took another breath. "I should tell you that he didn't suffer. Death was instantaneous. It was from a booby trap."

"He was given a military funeral." A pause. "We're a Marine Corps family.

I was in the Pacific in World War II. My father was with the 5th Marine Regiment at Belleau Wood in World War I."

"If you'd prefer I'd be glad to make a call to your home some day," I said.

"No, you don't need to," said the man. "We prefer to let it go. We do go to the cemetery at times." He took another pause. "Thanks, Marine, for bringing him in."

The conversation ended. I hung up the phone and sat down, deep in thought. When Patty returned I was still sitting in the chair staring into space. She took one look at me. "Are you all right?"

"I will be in a while." I stood and gave her a hug. Then I went upstairs and stretched out on the bed, staring at the ceiling, realizing again how fortunate I was. My eyes began to water.

My time at 13th Motors was short. One morning I was informed that my name was on a transfer draft, along with other recently returned first lieutenants, to the 1st Battalion of the 2nd Infantry Training Regiment at the San Onofre Area.

At the battalion headquarters I met the commanding officer, Lieutenant Colonel Thomas Kennedy, a broad-shouldered man with blond hair. My new assignment was XO of Delta Company. Colonel Kennedy added that as soon as I snapped into the routine I would be the next company commander. There weren't enough captains to go around. This was a real plum—a company commander as a first lieutenant. With it would come new challenges and decisions.

Delta Company was situated within walking distance of the battalion headquarters. The troops were housed in a series of Quonset huts leading up to a latrine on a hill. The headquarters hut had a company emblem out in front. Underneath it stated "Delta Devil Dogs" around a caricature of a fighting bulldog. The company commander was First Lieutenant Douglas Kruse, who did his combat tour as an infantry platoon commander with the Third Marine Division around Quang Tri. He summarized the training schedule and introduced me to the office staff and sergeant instructors.

Every four weeks the training companies would pick up four platoons of young Marines, graduates of recruit training at San Diego. They would be billeted in the nearby Quonset huts. The next day the infantry training would begin. This started with an orientation in an open-air theater where the company staff would be introduced. They would then be issued M–14 rifles, which would be followed by care and cleaning instructions. The next morning training would begin, covering such military subjects as Marine Corps history, squad and platoon tactics, patrolling, and setting a defensive perimeter. Classes would be held in each subject with field exercises to follow. There was also a familiarization class with the M–60 machine gun. On Fridays a forced march with full field packs would take place, going up one of the nearby rugged hills. At the conclusion of the four weeks the Marines would get orders either to the Fleet Marine Force in Vietnam or to specialty schools. They would graduate on a Friday morning. The staff would then take the noon meal in the mess hall. Afterward a new company would be bused in from San Diego and the cycle would begin again.

Doug also warned me about the battalion XO, Major Brant Holloway, a tall, dark-haired man. "There are company commander meetings every Friday to check reports and training. Major Holloway is especially hard on new lieutenants coming in as company commanders."

"Why is that?" I asked.

"Because Major Holloway is one of the few field-grade officers in the Marine Corps who has never served in Vietnam. He knows that he needs a combat tour to be considered for lieutenant colonel," explained Doug. "He's particularly jealous of first lieutenants coming back with a heavy chest." He paused and added, "I happen to know that he's checked your OQR."

"I don't get it," I said.

"Just give him a wide berth," cautioned Doug. "The least little thing can set him off."

For the next two weeks I observed the training schedule of Delta Company. I stayed in the back during classroom sessions. And I got to know the office staff. The company headquarters was run by First Sergeant Allen Masters, a tall, lanky, soft-spoken man. He had two office clerks doing the typing and filing. Gunnery Sergeant Charles Roundtree, a genial, stocky black man with fifteen years of experience, floated from office to the field. There were four sergeant instructors, each assigned to one of the platoons. By the end of the second week each of the sergeants would nominate a platoon guide. These would be the student leaders for the rest of the training cycle. The sergeants would also nominate a company guide. Final decisions would be approved by the company commander.

At the end of this training cycle graduation took place in the open-air theater. After graduation the troops received orders to their next duty stations. That afternoon I assumed command of Delta Company during a short staff formation where the change-of-command order was read. Afterward Doug signed over the property inventory, cleared out his desk, and headed to his new position in the battalion personnel office. I was now commanding officer, Delta Company, 1st Battalion, 2nd Infantry Training Regiment. My XO was a mustang, Warrant Officer Tom Farrington, a slim aficionado of tennis who was in the final months of a twenty-four-year Marine Corps career. At the company commanders meeting that afternoon I was introduced to the other commanders. After the meeting Major Holloway approached me with a warning: "Do not deviate from the training schedule. Get your reports in on time, supervise your company staff, and we'll get along."

At the orientation for the new company I introduced the Delta Company office staff and the sergeant instructors. Then I gave a quick summary of the importance of their training in the coming four weeks. I remember summing it up: "You are here to learn basic infantry tactics and methods. These will give you the tools to survive and come home. Pay attention in every class, learn everything you can. And, God willing, you'll come back." I walked off the stage satisfied, even thinking back to Captain Eiler's "wrong-foot" speech in Vietnam where he used the word *I* five times.

What I didn't know was that Major Holloway was in the rear of the assembly. As the company was forming to march back to the Quonset huts Major Holloway motioned me off to the side. "Lieutenant McAdams, as an experienced officer you should know the mission of the Marine Corps in combat." I nodded. "That mission is to close with and destroy the enemy."

"Yes, sir, I recall that phrase from OCS," I said.

"You are not to use the word *survive* in your orientation address. That's not why we're here. You're to explain to these young Marines that they are to close with and destroy the enemy. Are we clear on that?"

I took a deep breath, looking at the single National Defense Service ribbon on his chest. In the Marine Corps it was referred to as the "Shirley Highway Medal." The Shirley Highway is the thirty-five-mile stretch of I-95 between Quantico, Virginia, and Washington, D.C. "Yes, sir," I replied. "I'll tailor my remarks accordingly." As he walked off I wondered why I was always having philosophical disagreements with certain captains and majors.

After I felt settled in as a company commander I purchased a Honda off-road motorcycle. That weekend Patty and I took a daytrip down to La Jolla Cove and enjoyed a picnic lunch. The motorcycle helped us feel like we were dating again back at Loyola University. I was feeling at ease now. As a company commander I had a working staff that efficiently carried out a set training schedule. Or so I thought.

My first leadership test surfaced that week. From the classes and field exercises the four sergeant instructors kept close eyes on the young Marines, looking for leadership traits. During a meeting in my office, on their recommendations, five names came up. These were the selectees for the platoon and company-guide positions. One young Marine stood out, PFC Victorian. He was the honor man of his platoon at the Recruit Depot in San Diego. His proficiency and conduct marks were in the outstanding category. He also had an associate of arts degree from Los Angeles City College. This was an easy decision. PFC Victorian, an impressive, younger black man, would be the company guide, whereas the other four would be assigned to platoons. That afternoon I signed off on a company memo making the appointments. The announcements were made at the evening formation just before mess call.

That night Patty and I enjoyed a peaceful dinner. Then we tuned into *Rowan & Martin's Laugh-In*. The popular TV program was a series of quick comedy sketches that had a Vaudeville foundation. My favorite character was Dan Rowan's portrayal of General Buck Wright, a buffoonish four-star clown. I thought it was a healthy turn on the military mentality. Rowan knew the military well, having been a fighter pilot with the Fifth Air Force in the Western Pacific during World War II.

When I came into the office the next morning First Sergeant Masters greeted me with a grim look. "Skipper, we have a problem." Translation: *I* have a problem. I gestured for him to meet me in the office. He followed me in and closed the door. I sat down, prepared for anything. First Sergeant Masters explained that one of the platoons was from a county in Alabama. They were recruited en masse at the county seat and stayed together through recruit training. I patiently listened as Masters unfolded the scenario. There was an ad-hoc committee of three from this county platoon requesting to meet with me. I slowly nodded and added, "Because PFC Victorian is black."

I could tell that First Sergeant Masters was angry and felt unsettled by bringing the situation to me. At this point I knew that my staff was waiting to see how the company commander would handle it. I looked at my watch. We had about twenty minutes before the morning formation. "Bring them in now," I said.

Within five minutes First Sergeant Masters returned. In front of him marched three young white Marines. Masters handed me their enlisted record books (ERB). I motioned for First Sergeant Masters to remain; I wanted a witness. The three Marines stood at attention in front of my desk. I put them at parade rest and began looking at their record books. I went to their proficiency and conduct marks from recruit training. Then I scanned their formal education backgrounds. PFC Victorian was head and shoulders above them. None had any college courses; one was a high-school dropout. "Who's the spokesman here?" I asked.

The Marine in the center said, "I am, sir." He stated his name.

"And what is your request?" I asked.

"Well, sir, it's the company guide, PFC Victorian," said the Marine.

"Has he done something wrong?" I asked.

"No, sir. It's just that, well, sir, we're from Alabama and. . . . " His voice trailed off. I nodded, gesturing for him to continue. "Well, sir, we don't want to take orders from . . . a guy like him."

I nodded again and exchanged looks with First Sergeant Masters. "A guy like him is a Marine who was honor man in his recruit platoon. He already has the stripe of a PFC plus an associate degree from Los Angeles City College." I paused. "How many of you have taken college courses?" Silence from the three. I continued, "PFC Victorian has already demonstrated superior leadership traits and is more than qualified to be the company guide."

"With due respect, sir, the county platoon would like to see a white guy as the company guide." I could sense that this was getting very uncomfortable for the three Marines. I had to blunt this now, or I would lose it—and my staff—as a company commander.

I exchanged another look with First Sergeant Masters. "Okay, here's what I'm proposing." I pointed to the phone on my desk. "In a few moments I'm going to call the battalion commander, Lieutenant Colonel Kennedy. I'm going to request office time with him on this matter. And you three are going to come with me, to stand tall in his office with the battalion sergeant major." I then picked up the phone. "And you can state your request to the colonel."

The Marine in the center quickly looked at the other two. They both shook their heads in frantic motions as I began to dial. "Uh, sir, uh. . . . " I sat there holding the phone. "The committee, sir . . . would like to withdraw the request."

I replaced the phone in the cradle. "Very well." Then I looked at my watch. "The matter is closed." I looked over at the first sergeant. "It's time for the formation."

First Sergeant Masters nodded with a smile. He called the three to attention and marched them out of the office. The day's training was about to begin and I breathed a deep sigh. After the company marched out of the area I ordered First Sergeant Masters to break up the Alabama county platoon. "Change their bunk assignments, checkerboard style. I don't want any hut to be all white or all black." Before the evening formation the new bunk assignments were carried out.

In the late spring I registered with North Point Associates, a recruiting firm in San Diego that specialized in placing outgoing military officers with companies in the Southern California area. I thought it would be a good way to test my transition to civilian life. Here I met Ray Miller, a pleasant man in his early forties, who was one of the "personnel administrators." I remember filling out a detailed personnel profile. Ray explained that the interviews would be conducted in their offices and that the interviewees should be in "appropriate business attire."

My first interview was with a large insurance company searching for candidates for their executive training program. The two interviewers seemed nice enough. But I felt that the program they described was too structured for me, someone coming out of the Marines. After the interview I thanked Ray for setting it up but declined. He had an enthusiastic attitude and said, "We'll click somewhere. There's a communications company looking for people with writing skills. You interested?"

I was definitely interested. This was a newly formed communications outfit setting up closed-circuit TV programs for large corporations across the United States and in Canada. This had potential. And my feature writing for *The Loyola News* would be an asset. Ray set up an interview for the following Monday afternoon.

That weekend a racial incident erupted in nearby Fox Company. When I heard the details I became thankful for the Delta ad-hoc committee. The Fox Company commander had neglected to integrate his platoons. Racial feelings boiled over, causing several fistfights. The area OOD was forced to call out the guard to quell the disturbance and separate the groups. Several injured Marines were treated at sickbay.

That Monday afternoon Lieutenant Colonel Kennedy called an emergency company commanders meeting. Attending the meeting would be two investigators from the Naval Investigative Service (NIS, forerunner of NCIS). The Class A uniform, ribbons, and badges, was called for all company commanders. Warrant Officer Farrington would supervise the Delta Company training schedule while I was at the meeting. We had also heard that the Fox Company commander was relieved of command that morning, replaced with his XO.

I brought a business suit, white shirt, and tie with me that morning, knowing that the meeting could drag on. I hung them in a locker in my office. The meeting began with Lieutenant Colonel Kennedy making a statement about the challenges of leadership in today's Marine Corps, that what occurred in Fox Company would never have happened had the commander issued a directive to "break up the platoon huts in checkerboard style." I was still feeling relief as he said this. "We're lucky that all we got out of this incident was some broken noses and a few bruised faces. Had it not been broken up when it was. . . . " His voice trailed off. "Gents, we were fortunate this time. We're here this afternoon to make sure that there isn't a next time."

Colonel Kennedy then had the lead NIS agent give an overview of the racial situation not only at Camp Pendleton but also in Oceanside and San Diego. The antiwar movement was growing along with planned demonstrations at President Nixon's Western White House in San Clemente. He also explained that NIS was investigating the recent theft in the mainside armory where more than a dozen M-16 rifles were stolen.

Periodically I kept glancing at my watch, knowing that this was too important of a meeting to duck out on. I stayed to the end, sacrificing my time to change clothes for the interview. When the meeting ended I raced back to Delta Company and told Warrant Officer Farrington to take the evening formation. I would check in with him later.

The traffic down the I-5 to San Diego that afternoon was tight in spots. Still, I was able to get a parking space in front of the office building within five minutes of the interview time. I grabbed a quick look at my reflection in the car window, adjusted my overseas cap, and headed to the lobby. When I approached Ray's desk I noticed a surprised look. "Frank, you're supposed to be in a business suit."

"Couldn't be helped," I replied. "I had a long meeting."

He breathed a frustrated sigh and pointed toward a nearby door. "Well, go in and give it your best shot." I didn't like his troubled look.

Two men were waiting in the interview room. Both appeared to be in their mid-thirties, sharply dressed. I introduced myself and explained that I had an unexpected meeting at Camp Pendleton and rushed down the freeway. They both nodded and introduced themselves.

We sat down at the table. The first interviewer studied my profile while the second opened a notebook, pen at the ready. I knew the drill: The first interviewer would be asking the questions while the second took notes. It made me think of the "good cop/bad cop" syndrome.

The first interviewer began by explaining what his company did, how it was a new startup with a lot of potential, and that they were expanding into Canada. I noticed the second interviewer staring at my chest, the ribbons and badges. The first interviewer noted on the profile of my writing for *The Loyola News* and asked if I had any samples. I said yes but not with me. "Did you do any writing in the Marine Corps?"

I nodded. "After each engagement, or ambush, we would have to write afteraction reports." I remember taking a pause and smiling. "Yes, I did a lot of writing. And I still am."

The second interviewer pointed to my ribbons with his pen. "What are those top ribbons for?"

I felt uneasy. "Uh, they're for some things that happened in Vietnam. Somebody saw me do something and I got written up."

With wide eyes the second interviewer asked, "Did you ever kill anyone over there?"

I was caught totally off-guard. Then I said, "I was in some pretty hairy situations. And I'm very lucky."

"What's your position at Camp Pendleton?" asked the first interviewer.

"I'm a company commander in an infantry training battalion," I replied.

"How many in your company?" he asked.

"About 265 young Marines," I said. "It takes a lot of management." I added the last statement hoping that it would have a positive effect.

"If you become part of our team you'll be working with top-notch people," said the first interviewer. Then he added, "It won't be like leading a ragged bunch of high-school dropouts against a machine-gun emplacement."

I felt my stomach drop at the arrogance of his statement. For a flashing moment I wanted to come across the table and whack him in the face. I doubled my right fist, digging my fingernails into the palm, calling for every bit of restraint. "The Marines I served with were brave and dedicated." I paused and added, "I even carried one of them in."

The first interviewer gave off an indifferent shrug. "That happens in every war." There was a silence in the room. Then he added, "Nobody's going to care what you did over there. They're going be looking at how you can contribute to the company."

I stood, breathing a disgusting sigh. I remember glaring at both of them. Then I said, "Gentlemen, I don't want to take up any more of your time."

I walked out. In the outer office I approached Ray's desk. "Sorry, Ray, that company's not for me."

Ray stood, a surprised look on his face. "What happened?"

"It didn't go well," I said.

"Hold on." Ray turned and went into the interview room. About a minute later he emerged. "Frank, you have to learn how to interview. They were testing you. Didn't you see that?"

"If that's how they test then I want nothing to do with them."

Ray shook his head. "Frank, you're in Rome. Do as the Romans."

Ray sat down and looked at his appointment book. There was one more company he wanted to schedule me for. I told him to give me a few days to think about it. All I wanted to do was get out of that building and get home to Patty.

In the corridor I went to the elevator and pushed the down button. I remember waiting for several minutes, wondering when the doors would open. Suddenly Ray came around the corner with the two interviewers, going for a coffee break. When they saw me standing at the elevator the first interviewer stopped and pulled them back around the corner. I continued waiting for the elevator, realizing that these three grown men did not want to ride down with me. I felt like peeking around the corner and giving them a wave. But the elevator doors opened.

An older woman was inside with a frustrated look. The lobby button had already been pushed. The woman looked at me and said, "I'm trying to get to the restaurant on the top floor. Sometimes you have to go down before you can go up." I smiled. Naturally she had no idea of the importance of her pithy comment.

On the drive back to Oceanside I got a sense of what was waiting for me "on the outside." It would be more ugly stares like the ones I saw at O'Hare Airport upon arriving from Vietnam. It was here, driving from the civilian world back to the military, that I made a resolve to meet this syndrome and overcome it, even if it took years. How right I was.

21

A Moonlit Barbecue

The Delta training schedule continued. That Friday I pulled my field pack out of the locker, adjusted it, strapped on my .45 pistol belt, and met the company formation. I gave them a "left-face" and nodded to PFC Victorian, who was carrying the company guidon flag. Victorian took his position in front of the first platoon, behind me. I called "For . . . ward!" The platoon guides repeated, "For . . . ward!" I took a breath and let out, "March!" I thought back to that first forced march in the Philippines as a Navy corpsman at the tail end of the column.

Once more the troops headed out of the fort. Again, there was no John Ford chorus. It was four platoons of young Marines completing a training week, heading up to "Old Smoky," which gave a sweeping view of the Pacific Ocean. We would enjoy C-rations on the crest of the mountain. Then I would lead them back to the company area where they would dress for their first liberty weekend.

The second week of July Lieutenant Colonel Kennedy issued an invitation to the company commanders for a Sunday barbecue at his house on the main side of the base. It was a social occasion, but it was also to gather around the television in the living room to observe the Apollo 11 moon landing. Neal Armstrong, a civilian astronaut, was chosen to be the first human to walk on the moon's surface. The other two on the Apollo 11 team were Colonel Buzz Aldrin and Lieutenant Colonel Michael Collins. The capsule went into lunar orbit July 16 and would land late Sunday afternoon Pacific Daylight Time.

In the Marine Corps when a company commander receives an invitation to the battalion commander's residence it is expected to be accepted. Regrets should be sent only in the event of a family death. Patty and I not only accepted the invitation—we looked forward to it. She would be meeting some of the people I had been talking about at dinner.

The barbecue anticipation was marred on Friday when the major networks announced that Senator Edward M. Kennedy was involved in a tragic car accident on Chappaquiddick Island, part of Martha's Vineyard in Massachusetts. Mary Jo Kopechne, a twenty-eight-year-old Kennedy office worker, drowned. By Saturday morning network news crews were camped out at Martha's Vineyard and the Kennedy compound in Hyannis Port. Throughout Saturday and early Sunday there were conflicting news reports as to what transpired. Some pundits were already speculating how this tragedy would affect Senator Kennedy's White House potential. I thought back thirteen months when we heard that Bobby Kennedy had been shot in a Los Angeles hotel. It also brought back memories of Captain Eiler and his reaction to Bobby Kennedy's death. I wondered, *When will the tragedies end for that family?*

The barbecue was scheduled to begin at 6 P.M. It would give everyone time for a social hour out on the back lawn. The time of the moon landing was scheduled for 8 P.M.

Patty and I dressed in casual clothes. Because it was a pleasant summer afternoon we decided to ride to the barbecue on the motorcycle. I had a base sticker on the left-forward strut of the bike. At the main gate we were waved through with a salute. By the time I parked the motorcycle in front of Colonel Kennedy's house the party was under way. Mrs. Sue Kennedy met us at the door and introduced us to several civilian guests, one of whom was on vacation from Boston. I can't recall his name, so I'll call him Mr. Boston.

After settling in with a round of drinks I remember standing in the living room watching Walter Cronkite at the CBS anchor desk describing how Neil Armstrong would emerge from the *Eagle,* the lunar module, and descend on a ladder to take mankind's first step on the moon. Seventeen months earlier the same Walter Cronkite gave his historic editorial on Vietnam that spelled the beginning of the end for the Johnson administration. The turbulent years of '68 and '69 had come full circle. Behind me, Mr. Boston was commenting on Senator Kennedy's plight and the contradictory news reports coming from Martha's Vineyard and Hyannis Port. "I'm not a bit surprised to see that happen," he said. "I'm only surprised that it didn't happen earlier."

"What do you mean?" someone asked.

"Those Kennedy men, they like their women whether they're secretaries or movie actresses. And they learned it from the old man. The apples didn't fall far from the tree." I remember him nodding and taking a drink.

I turned and walked out to the backyard. I remember looking at the gathering, young Marine officers like myself, company commanders who had survived a Vietnam combat tour. Here we were in the last year of the 1960s with two important events, one tragic and the other memorable and historic, happening during the same weekend. The evening shadows began approaching.

Just before 8 P.M. someone came into the backyard and announced, "He's almost there!"

We refreshed our drinks and went into the living room. I remember someone next to me saying, "My God, this is one of the greatest things!"

There on the screen, live, was a human being descending the ladder of the *Eagle.* Total silence in the room. And then we heard Armstrong's voice: "That's one small step for [a] man, one giant leap for mankind." It sounded a bit garbled but it came through.

The next minute was filled with claps and whoops. And then someone yelled "Ooh-rah!"

We stayed afterward talking about how the space program began, first being shocked with the Soviets launching the Sputnik satellite in the fall of 1957. Then came the sudden rush to improve high-school science programs, followed by the election of John F. Kennedy to the White House. In 1962 at Houston, Texas, President Kennedy predicted that the United States would place a man on the moon by the end of the decade. Many observers, domestic and foreign, scoffed at this prediction. And now we had just seen it live on network television.

It was a clear night when Patty and I got on the motorcycle. We adjusted our helmets and I turned on the headlight. Soon we were on Vandegrift Boulevard heading toward the main gate. Patty moved close to my ear and said, "Take a moment and look up there."

I recall looking skyward at a clear, round moon. The decade of the 1960s had five months left. But for us it was over on this night, on this weekend.

And we would move on to other challenges.

Afterword

It's been said that a timeframe is needed between the decision to write a memoir and the actual writing. For these pages that timeframe covered forty-three years.

There's a quote attributed to Ernest Hemingway when he spoke to a group of college students. Hemingway reportedly said, "If you're serious about writing write about your generation."

Before I left Vietnam I began outlining a novel about a young lieutenant who goes to Vietnam with high ideals and hopes. In the end he pays the ultimate price, a nod to Eric Maria Remarque. It ran to six or seven longhand pages. I wanted to get some thoughts down before I rotated stateside.

After leaving active duty in the Marine Corps I began a six-and-a-half-year journalism career on two Southern California newspapers. During this time I returned to the longhand pages, which became a novella, about 175 manuscript pages. It carried the title *Stagecoach Charlie*—the radio call sign of the protagonist.

The only people who saw the manuscript were my wife Patty and several New York literary agents. After the fifth rejection I set the manuscript aside.

My time as a journalist was timely and fortunate. As a staff writer for the *Anaheim Bulletin* I covered antiwar demonstrations on several college campuses and at the Western White House in San Clemente. I had interviews with California governor Ronald Reagan; former Republican presidential candidate George Romney; the civil rights activist Angela Davis; author Joseph Heller; former Notre Dame football coach Frank Leahy; former JFK White House historian Arthur Schlesinger Jr.; former Marine and antiwar activist Ron Kovic; and the political humorist Art Buchwald. There was also the two-horse parlay of John Wayne and Jane Fonda. When the Jane Fonda story appeared I got my first and only death threat. It was just hot air; I didn't have time to ask if he was a Vietnam vet.

I was also assigned to two Western White House press conferences during the Watergate era. It was educational to see a constitutional crisis playing out as a president was brought down with Shakespearean drama—a king thrown from his horse.

261

During this time I was fortunate enough to win two journalism awards, one a reflective op-ed piece on the resignation of Vice President Spiro Agnew amid charges of taking illegal campaign contributions when he was governor of Maryland.

Afterward I looked around the newsroom and asked myself, "Is this where I want to be in ten years?" I felt that nothing could compare to the lifetime drama of Watergate. And I always felt that Watergate, with its White House bombshells and lies, was the ultimate political experience of my generation. It was a back-and-forth and dramatic test for the United States Constitution. But now it was time to move on.

After leaving journalism I sold several freelance magazine pieces. Then I applied to the Graduate Screenwriting Program at UCLA. My eligibility for the GI Bill covered tuition and books. The first year on campus saw me as a "closet vet." I didn't want anyone to know of my time in the Navy or seeing combat as a Marine lieutenant in Vietnam.

Then I won first place in the Samuel Goldwyn Screenwriting Competition for *California Rain*, a murder mystery about an investigative reporter who uncovers a dark secret about a powerful Southern California family on the eve of an election where something from the past resurrects itself. My journalism experience helped for deep background. The story literally "jumped at my typewriter."

In my second year of graduate school I got an assistantship. And I had to make a decision on my thesis screenplay. *Stagecoach Charlie* was still on a shelf in a cardboard box. I pulled the novella manuscript out, gave it a quick read, and decided to use it as an outline for my thesis screenplay. I changed the title to *Stagecoach Bravo*; the second word carried a better metaphor.

I spent that Hollywood summer in rewrite city, again reliving the Vietnam experience. That fall I went in front of the thesis board and got approval. The screenplay won first place in the Samuel Goldwyn Competition that spring of 1979. I was also informed that I was only the second person to win first-place awards back-to-back since the competition was established in 1955.

Reality quickly set in. I was no longer a "closet vet." A few people thanked me for my service. Then about a week after the award was announced I was standing in the back of a full elevator in Melnitz Hall at UCLA. Someone up front asked, "Who won the Sam Goldwyn award this year?"

Another student replied, "A grad student. It was a Vietnam screenplay."

The first student said, "Christ, not that shit again!"

I said nothing, surprised at my restraint. It's probably why I still remember it.

I had one anchor in Patty. My other anchor was the start of a teaching career on several college campuses along with working freelance as a story analyst for four Hollywood production companies. I continued with meetings at major studios and production companies that showed initial interest in *Stagecoach Bravo*. Carl Foreman, a noted producer and screenwriter (*High Noon, The Bridge on the River Kwai, The Victors, Young Winston*) made several valiant, but futile, attempts to set up *Stagecoach*. He believed in the story. Although nothing happened at that time I thanked him for his loyalty and persistence. I was also part of the standing-room-only congregation at his Mt. Sinai memorial several years later.

Eventually *Stagecoach Bravo* was optioned twice, the latter by Columbia Pictures Television for a two-part miniseries. Soon that optioned expired. I'm still thankful for having a master of fine arts degree as I continued teaching. And I never stopped writing.

Fast-forward to May 2011. By now I had three book publications to my name. I had also written two manuscript reviews for Michael Briggs, editor-in-chief of the University Press of Kansas. After the second review Michael asked if I would consider writing a Vietnam memoir. My response was a quick "No!" Vietnam was behind me.

The next day I was rearranging several file boxes and came across some letters and memos from Vietnam. I opened a long-closed photo album, which brought me back to 11th Motors and An Hoa. The next morning I e-mailed Michael a message stating that I had changed my mind and wanted to pursue the idea of writing a memoir. His response was enthusiastic and very much welcomed: "Send me a proposal and an outline." I had accepted the challenge of going back to the Vietnam experience once again.

The passing of forty-plus years since my service for the U.S. Navy and Marine Corps evokes many memories, especially the countless experiences engaging with many different people—military, civilian, friends, colleagues, family. Michael Briggs, like Carl Foreman—two men from different generations and worlds apart—thought that the story was worth telling. In sum, writing projects never die. They go to the shelf and come back, like the rain in California.

—FJM
Dana Point, California